APOCALYPSE ROULETTE

APOCALYPSE ROULETTE

The Lethal World of Derivatives

RICHARD THOMSON

MACMILLAN

First published 1998 by Macmillan

an imprint of Macmillan Publishers Ltd
25 Eccleston Place, London, SW1W 9NF
and Basingstoke

Associated companies throughout the world

ISBN 0 333 66457 4

1 3 5 7 9 8 6 4 2

A CIP catalogue record for this book is available from
the British Library

Typeset by SetSystems Ltd, Saffron Walden, Essex
Printed and bound in Great Britain by
Mackays of Chatham plc, Chatham, Kent

Contents

Introduction

The more there is of mine, the less there is of yours.
Alice in Wonderland

In April 1993 I wrote an article for the *Independent on Sunday* newspaper about the huge and unquantified risk building up in the global financial system through the use of a new species of financial instrument known generically as derivatives. As part of an imaginary scenario of the problems this might cause, I predicted that in October 1995 a US securities house would lose twice its own capital on a huge unauthorized bet in the derivatives market by a rogue trader whose bosses didn't understand what he was doing.

As it turned out, of course, I was wrong by seven months and the bank was British, not American. Barings went bust in February 1995 when its capital was wiped out roughly twice over by a massive bet in the derivatives markets. The cause: unauthorized trading by a rogue trader whose managers didn't understand what he was doing.

I can't claim any great prescience in making this prediction, and I have to admit that I did not quite foresee the full extent of the dishonesty, incompetence, stupidity and greed that brought about Barings' demise. By the mid-1990s I wasn't the only person who had noticed that there was an accident waiting to happen. Many banks, not just Barings, had begun to treat the financial markets as a glorified casino. Like men with a bad addiction, international bankers had become mesmerized by the short term deal in their scramble for higher profits and bigger bonuses. They were risking their own capital in an unprecedented fashion and the profits became more important than relationships with clients. Bank managements were in thrall to the cult of the dealer. Many industrial corporations and investment companies – perhaps your own pension fund – had taken to placing multi-million pound bets on which way currencies, shares or bonds would move next.

Despite the warning of Barings, nothing much has changed since then in the behaviour of the banks or other big international investors. Stupendous dealing losses have become commonplace. Less than a year after Barings, Daiwa Bank announced a $1 billion loss and few months later Sumitomo Corporation, one of the largest, most respectable trading companies in the world revealed that it had thrown away $1.7 billion in the copper market.

On the heels of Barings' bankruptcy almost every large bank in Europe, the US and Japan claimed that the same disaster could never have happened to them. Many were talking nonsense. There were, and still are, banks whose internal controls were hardly better than Barings. Take, for example, the £90 million black hole uncovered by National Westminster Bank in the spring of 1997 on its options trading. The bank admitted that the loss, accumulated by a single rogue trader over a two-year period, was the result of inadequate management controls – the very thing the Barings collapse was supposed to have taught the banking industry to improve. The loss triggered a plunge in NatWest's share price and caused the resignation of the head of its investment banking subsidiary. It threw into question NatWest's entire policy of becoming one of the world's pre-eminent investment banks. It even prompted speculation that the clearing bank itself would be forced into a merger or a takeover.

But not all such blunders become public knowledge. As everyone knows, banking is to some extent a confidence trick – banks only last as long as their depositors believe that their deposits are safe – so bankers see it as a duty to reassure the public even if that means occasionally misleading them. It is normally not until a bank is in the direst trouble that the public ever gets to hear about it.

So even after the harsh lesson of Barings, the worries about derivatives persist. Outwardly, the message is always the same: 'trust us, we're bankers'. Privately, the more thoughtful derivatives operators remain deeply concerned that Barings was merely a taste, a precursor, a warning of something far worse to come. Just because the financial system did not crack in 1995 does not mean that a somewhat bigger shock could not create the ultimate financial nightmare – what the central bankers call systemic risk – because if we can be sure of anything about the financial system it is that something will eventually go wrong. It always does. It is not a question of if, but when. In the early 1980s it was lending to Latin America; a few years later it was lending on property. The next problem is likely to do with derivatives.

This book is an attempt to explain why that is so. Its subject is a financial revolution that has taken place so fast that even the experts are still trying to catch up with it. Regulatory and legal systems have been left so far behind that the new world of derivatives is a kind of financial Wild West with few rules or codes of behaviour. With this revolution came a tidal wave of speculation: never before has it been so easy for investors of all types to bet the ranch on some hunch about the markets. And it has left governments without the ability to control, or even understand, the financial markets as the speculative assault on sterling in 1992 and repeated attacks on other currencies since then has shown.

But derivatives do not exist independently of the people who use them, so this book is also about the men and women who handle the money, control it, win it and lose it; about who they are, how they behave and why they do what they do. Because as Nick Leeson – the rogue trader who reduced Barings to a heap of rubble – graphically showed, what they do and how they do it makes all the difference.

They are a pretty diverse group but what they share in common is a love of risk and cash. Leeson was not a freak but a fairly typical specimen of their breed who simply overstepped the mark – simply, because in his world that is a frighteningly easy thing to do. His bosses, who allowed him to do so in the pursuit of profits that would swell their own pay cheques, were also pretty representative of their kind, if somewhat more incompetent and greedy than the average.

The modern banking system is no longer controlled by staid men in pinstripes from Oxford or Harvard. Instead it is at the mercy of twenty-eight-year-old dealers who sit down each day with untold funds at a seat in the biggest casino in the world.

Financial derivatives have grown, more or less from a standing start in the early 1970s, to a $64 trillion (that's $64,000,000,000,000) industry by 1996. How do you imagine a number that big? You could say that if you laid all those dollar bills end to end they would stretch from here to the sun sixty-six times, or to the moon 25,900 times; or that it is roughly sixty times the size of the British economy, or about six times the size of the US and Japanese economies combined; or that it is many times bigger than every stock and bond market in the world added together.

One thing is clear: derivatives have transformed the financial system. It has never been so easy to move money from country to country and market to market, nor to move it so quickly, nor to take on so much risk in the blink of an eye. In this new age of finance the rewards and the dangers of making money out of money are many times what they were only a few years ago. Derivatives have fundamentally altered the way the markets, and therefore the institutions and individuals who operate in them, work.

And they are here to stay. In the space of less than twenty years they have become integral, basic, to the whole elaborate structure of international finance. Every time there is a derivatives-related disaster, such as the collapse of Barings bank, it is followed by calls to limit or do away with derivatives themselves. But this is as quixotic an idea as abolishing the motor car. It just can't be done.

A financial derivative is an instrument based on or 'derived' from underlying assets such as shares, bonds, commodities or currencies. In general, it is an obligation to buy or sell the underlying asset at an agreed price and time in the future. Since it usually takes only a small down payment (the margin or premium) to purchase such an obligation, any movement in the value of the underlying asset above or below the agreed price can produce immense profits or losses relative to the original down payment.

The number of instruments invented in the last few years which fit this definition is vast, and their use has become so pervasive that some professionals no longer regard the simplest derivatives, such as 'plain vanilla' futures and options contracts, as derivatives at all. Nevertheless, that's what they are and I include them in my definition just as much as the inverse floaters, sticky jumps Zs, exploding options, zero cost collars and the rest of the bizarrely named menagerie of exotic derivatives that bankers have lately conjured into existence. They all qualify.

Derivatives were invented to limit, or hedge, risk. In a world of international trade, constantly changing exchange rates, unpredictable interest rates and fluctuating commodity prices, the risks have never looked more threatening. Derivatives enable a company to fix the cost of its foreign exchange or raw materials in advance, or borrow money at a cheaper rate. They make the future a more predictable place.

This is good for business – indeed, it's good for everyone. Financial derivatives provide us with cheaper petrol prices, lower mortgage rates, better pensions. If you have a mortgage where the interest rate is capped so that it will not rise above a certain level, for example, you own an interest rate call option. A derivative.

Derivatives are not bad in themselves. Used properly and wisely, they are an undoubted benefit. It is when they are used improperly and unwisely that they become the financial equivalent of high explosive. Think of a derivative as a loaded gun. You can use it in self-defence or for murder. Unfortunately, the temptations to use it for the latter purpose are immense.

This worries many people who work in the finance industry and those whose job is to regulate and police it. What concerns them is the growing fragility of the financial system they have helped to create. Derivatives have built interconnections between markets that never existed a few years ago; they have woven international finance into a single fantastically tight and complex tapestry, yet the fabric seems thinner than ever.

'Derivatives are like nuclear power,' says one former central banker who has had to grapple with the reality of bank collapses and the threat of systemic financial failure. 'As long as everything is working well, the benefits are tremendous: clean, cheap electricity that helps everyone lead more comfortable and prosperous lives. But when things go wrong, they may go horribly, unimaginably wrong: you get Chernobyl or worse. Derivatives have the potential to create an unprecedented financial disaster.'

It could happen. If it does, it will almost certainly be in a way that no one has foreseen. It may be triggered by an extraordinary event that nobody in their wildest dreams had imagined. But more probably it will involve nothing more remarkable than the sort of problems that regularly crop up in the markets, only this time the particular combination of events will be so unusual, so unexpected, the result will be lethal. In times of crisis the financial system reacts in unpredictable ways. The more suddenly the crisis strikes, the worse the trauma is likely to be. Investors, caught off-guard and protecting their own individual interests, will react in all the wrong ways; governments and financial regulators will be confused and paralysed, perhaps making mistakes that worsen the situation; the crisis will spread like lightening across countries and markets, faster than anyone can control until suddenly a local problem has become a global disaster . . .

CHAPTER 1

APOCALYPSE

Let me see: four times five is twelve, and four times six is thirteen, and four times seven is – oh dear!

Alice in Wonderland

The reasons why Jack Horner went home in the middle of the afternoon, when he knew his wife and children would be out, and used his precious Holland & Holland shotgun to blow his brains across the bedroom ceiling were explained in a two-page letter locked in the top drawer of his desk at work.

By the time Horner wrote it his mental state was becoming increasingly unbalanced, yet the letter was nevertheless clear and precise. He didn't try to deflect any blame from himself or pretend he hadn't known what he was doing. He knew, or was almost certain, that he had bankrupted one of Britain's largest banks. What he could not know before he died, however, was that he had also triggered the international financial meltdown that the world's central bankers had for years envisioned in their worst nightmares.

Horner, like many young dealers in the City, had been a young man in a hurry. He was sharp, conscientious, a little more aggressive than most but his bosses appreciated that which was why he had the job of head of futures trading at one of the biggest banks on the planet. He was hungry, he wanted to make money and move up in the world, and at the age of thirty-two Horner had felt he was getting there. He loved his wife, doted on his children and was popular at work. He played squash, jogged and could hold his drink. Each morning at around 6.30 a.m. he left his comfortable four-bedroomed house in Kent, climbed into his BMW and drove the half hour into the City where he settled in to earn his $200,000 a year salary. Although not particularly high by City standards, it was stratospheric compared with what his friends outside finance earned. Horner felt lucky.

He worked for the securities arm of Castle Bank, Britain's biggest financial institution. Like the other high street banks, Castle's traditional business was lending to companies and individuals in the United Kingdom, and, to a lesser extent, abroad. But over the last ten years it had joined the rest of the world's big banks in trading on the money markets as a way of boosting its otherwise rather lacklustre profits. It was the latest fashion in finance and, like bankers everywhere, Castle did not like to get left out. For three years now it had made what its directors and shareholders could only smugly acknowledge as spectacular profits from its dealing activities. They were not very sure why they were good at it since not a single director and none of the shareholders had ever sat before a dealing screen in his life. But the evidence seemed indisputable.

Castle had therefore bought Makinson & Partners, a smallish merchant bank with a stock broking arm and a derivatives trading operation. It was the derivatives Castle really wanted because it saw the derivatives markets as a potential gold mine.

But from the start, integrating Makinson & Partners into its securities operation proved to be a management nightmare. The investment bankers simply resigned if they thought they weren't getting a good deal out of the takeover. It seemed impossible to keep them happy or pay them enough. There was a management chaos right down the line. The boss of Horner's derivatives area, a chinless Etonian, had already been sacked but no replacement had been found, leaving Horner in unfettered control of the futures trading. The head of the back office, where deals were settled and money paid out or received, had not been in work for weeks because of serious illness, leaving Horner in charge of futures settlements too – a situation which everyone recognized was only acceptable because it was purely temporary.

The confusion had led to a sharp fall in income following the takeover which was embarrassing for Castle's top management. Experienced dealers soon felt heavy pressure from the chief executive's office to make as much money in the financial markets as they could before the year end to bolster the group's results. If that meant taking bigger risks, the management would understand. None of this, of course, was committed to paper.

Despite his extra responsibilities, Horner feared for his job as outsiders from Makinson & Partners seemed to get the best promotions. He was desperate not to lose his position; the problem was how to make sure he didn't. Answer: make so much money for the bank that it would not want to get rid of him. How could he make so much money? Take bigger risks. Given his temporary position of unquestioned power in the department, Horner found he could do this with little interference.

Which is where the explanation in his letter began. Horner understood that the usual limits on the size of his dealing were being waived for the time being. He looked around the markets and decided that the volatile emerging markets were where he could make the most money. In particular, he targeted the futures and options markets of São Paolo, Brazil – which were the third largest in the world – and Hong Kong. With the markets so far apart he hoped to spread his risks somewhat.

And then Horner began dealing. He loved the derivatives markets and his eyes would go moist when he thought of the sheer beauty of it, the way he could buy control of, say, $10 billion in stock market exposure or currencies or bonds with a mere $100 million. This was a zero sum game, meaning that when he won – which he usually did – someone else lost an equal amount. It was gloriously simple: life in the jungle, survival of the fittest. Nowhere else could you place such colossal bets. It was the most fun he'd ever had in his life.

By early June, Horner had bought equity futures and options in the new massive São Paolo exchange worth $8 billion and currency futures worth $3.5 billion. In Hong Kong his Hang Seng futures positions were worth another $5 billion. Thanks to the system of margin payments on futures, this cost only $500 million. For good measure he invested a further $500 million in hedge funds investing in these markets. (His total position was more than George Soros had used to kill the British pound in 1992.) But although share prices in São Paolo and Hong Kong both went up, as he had bet they would, neither market was as volatile as Horner had hoped, so he doubled his positions to increase his profits.

Whenever anyone asked what he was doing, Horner told them vaguely that he was arbitraging markets in Latin America and the Far East, implying that his exposures were very short term and fully hedged. Very little risk, in other words. In fact his risk was huge but with the markets going his way his profits were correspondingly large which kept inquisitive managers at bay.

By August his paper profits were in the hundreds of millions of pounds. Then came 1 September. All around the world, people were still on holiday, trading on markets everywhere was thin and slow which meant that it didn't take much to send them hurtling upwards or downwards far faster than they would normally have done. Most of the derivatives traders who worked for Horner were away while he held the fort and watched his profits grow.

But he woke up that Monday morning to find that an unexpected change of leadership in Beijing over the weekend had led to a crackdown on Hong Kong's free trade status within China. A lurch backwards to neanderthal communism looked as though it would kill Hong Kong's economy. Inevitably, the market had nose-dived. By the time Horner reached his dealing screen, his positions were in loss by $800 million and the Hong Kong futures exchange was demanding millions in extra margin payments.

Then came the second blow. At 12.30 p.m., just as the São Paolo market was opening, Brazil announced that it was defaulting on a small amount – $500 million – of government debt to foreign banks. The Brazilian government was directionless, torn by internal feuding and rampant corruption, with no president because the former incumbent had just been thrown out under charges of embezzling billions. The central bank was run by his brother-in-law, a former medical doctor. No one in the Brazilian government seemed to have any idea of the mayhem a debt default might cause.

Remembering the loan debacle of the early 1980s, the Brazilian markets panicked as every foreign investor scrambled to get his money out and the locals lost confidence too. Because liquidity in futures and options markets is so much greater than in the underlying stock markets on which they are based, these markets fell sooner and faster. It was simply easier to dump your equities there than in the cash market, but the falling futures markets dragged the cash markets down with it. By 5.00 p.m. British time, Horner's positions had lost $1.5 billion with a further $1 billion in extra margin calls. He stifled questions in the back office by implying that if the money was not paid out as he required, settlements clerks would find themselves without jobs in the round of sackings that everyone anticipated.

As everyone went home, Horner stayed at his desk to await the Hong Kong market opening. He was haggard and had hardly eaten all day. He had tried to trade out of his positions but when he found how big a loss he would have to realize he decided to hang on. The market would surely turn up again.

Some time during the night the Far Eastern exchanges started to open. Dog tired, Horner stared at his screens and worked the phones. The business of dealing began to seem unreal and the numbers ceased to mean anything to him as he fought with the markets. Normally, he'd have cut his losses and run, like any professional dealer. But this time it had happened too fast and it was too big. His only option, as he saw it, was to fight back. The market would rise, it always did, so he would help it. He piled in and started to buy.

By about 4.00 a.m. Hong Kong had stabilized as the market paused for breath. Horner, by then, had increased his original position by 40 per cent. Now he bought more, but within forty-five minutes the futures and options markets began falling again. At 6.00 a.m. he received a phone call from an official of the Hong Kong exchange about the massive size of his trading and he reasurred him that most of it was for clients rather than on Castle's own account. Castle's own risk was relatively small, he said. The official believed him because the bank's name, after all, was blue chip.

At 6.30 a.m., exhausted, he took a nap on the floor behind a desk in an unused office but was back at his screens by 7.15 a.m. trying to figure out what to do. He was more than $2 billion underwater and his job – his whole life, it seemed – was going up in smoke. Now it was double or bust. He'd heard of dealers being in this position but had never thought it would happen to him. He needed more funds to cover his growing margin calls. Calling Castle's treasury department, he warned them that a complex trading strategy he had in place would demand unusually large amounts of money over the next twenty-four hours. Intimidated by the complexity of his explanation, the clerks agreed to co-operate but asked for written confirmation from Horner's superiors. Horner said they had been sacked – which the clerks entirely understood – but that he would fax a memo himself. He put the phone down before they could object.

When São Paolo opened later that day, Horner was shot down in flames. He bought and bought to support the market but futures and options prices collapsed in the grip of a full-scale market rout. Although Castle did not yet know it, it had lost a total of $6 billion in the space of forty-eight hours. It was the end. Deprived of sleep and dosed on caffeine, cocaine, aspirins and any other kind of drug or stimulant he could glean from around the dealing room, he had lost touch with reality. He wrote a letter explaining what had happened and insisting that he had done nothing – or nearly nothing – dishonest or fraudulent. Placing the letter in his top drawer, he drove home and shot himself.

Which is where the financial apocalypse really began.

TUESDAY   That evening, Castle's chief executive sat grey faced in his office with Horner's letter in his trembling hands, wondering what to do. He had already screamed at the head of the securities division who now sat mute and slumped in a chair across the room. At that moment, a task force of internal auditors were combing through the records to sort out Horner's exact positions. Despite his letter it was still unclear what all his positions were or what the losses might be. It was, however, already clear that most of the bank's capital had gone.

The chief executive picked up the phone, dialled the Bank of England and explained briefly to the head of banking supervision what had happened. There was a stunned silence before the Bank official told him to come to Threadneedle Street immediately. They agreed that for the time being the news must not be allowed to filter out.

But it did. Rumours swirled around Hong Kong and São Paolo

about Castle's massive positions. People had started to put two and two together and the fact that their answer came to five made no difference. Initial estimates on the market put Castle's loss at between $3 billion and $10 billion. When the bank consistently denied it had serious problems, the rumour mill settled on the higher figure as the likely total. Within hours of Horner's suicide, the story that one of the world's biggest banks was in deep trouble was running in every financial market of the world.

The market's reaction to the rumours was two-fold. First, every single bank that had ever lent money to Castle on the interbank money market reconsidered whether it ever would again; and the same banks began to look around for others who might have taken a similar hit and should therefore also be avoided.

At 9.00 p.m., the chief executive and chairman of Castle met the head of banking supervision at his office in the Bank of England building in Threadneedle Street. The Bank's Governor had already been called back from her holiday home in Scotland but would not be in London for several hours. The supervisory department meanwhile phoned the heads of all the British banks, summoning them to a meeting at 8.00 a.m. on Wednesday morning.

WEDNESDAY Overnight, São Paolo had not yet received $2 billion in extra margin payments from Castle to cover its mounting losses. Phone call after phone call from exchange officials were stonewalled at Castle where treasury executives realized that they faced a liquidity crisis if they paid up. Without the money the Brazilian exchange faced liquidity problems of its own. If anyone in the market defaulted, it was responsible for making sure the bill was paid but it could hardly cope with a loss of this size and the Brazilian government's guarantee was no good because the markets no longer trusted Brazil's creditworthiness. So the exchange started selling off Castle's positions to cover its obligations. This both crystallized the loss for Castle and drove the market further down, forcing the exchange to sell yet more of Castle's positions.

London was wet and overcast as the British bankers met that morning at the Bank of England. They gathered in the same committee room where some of them had grim memories of failing to rescue Barings in 1995. The high street banks and merchant banks were all represented. They were told of the situation and asked by the Governor, who had at last arrived, not to cut off their credit lines to Castle. She did not need to explain, of course, that banks depended for their short term funding on the interbank market, and if they could not raise money they would suffer a liquidity problem and possible eventual bankruptcy.

During the meeting the heads of the merchant banks slipped out of the room one by one to answer telephone calls from their offices. They returned looking as if they had been kicked in the solar plexus. The markets had already concluded that if Castle was in trouble, the next most likely British institutions to go would be the merchant banks (memories of Barings were still strong). Deposits were flooding out of these banks which could not find anyone to borrow money from on the interbank market. They therefore had no option but to refuse to keep their credit lines open to Castle because they simply had no money to lend.

Dashing through London by chauffeur-driven Rolls-Royce immediately after the meeting, the Governor of the Bank of England arrived at the Treasury in Whitehall at 11.40 a.m. She and the Chancellor considered making a blanket statement that the UK government would not allow a high street bank to go bust, but decided this might only intensify the panic by confirming just how bad the situation had become. Instead they simply announced a 1 percentage point cut in interest rates to help banks borrow money.

It made little difference. The world banking community had decided to shun all British banks. The Treasury, misjudging the gravity of the situation, made £1 billion available to Castle to cover its losses, but that was hopelessly inadequate. Castle itself was not sure how large its losses were but São Paolo was now clamouring for $3.5 billion.

Castle could not find the cash so the Brazilian exchange was forced into another manoeuvre: it doubled the margin requirement of everyone else with open positions in its markets. Apart from Castle, the biggest players were US banks who now found they had to stump up twice as much margin to cover their positions. Having heard the Castle rumours, they suspected that the São Paolo exchange intended to use their money to plug the hole in its own finances left by the British losses. Unwilling to countenance such a move, two leading commercial banks and four of the largest US investment banks refused point blank to pay any more margin at all. Meanwhile, a whole range of other players, from private investors to small banks to investment funds could not pay either because they had been bankrupted by the extra margin demands on top of the money they had already lost in the market fall. By the end of trading on Wednesday, the exchange was bankrupt.

A few hours later, as the far eastern markets opened, the chaos that struck São Paolo was, in all essentials, mirrored in Hong Kong. The Chinese authorities did nothing. No one knew whether they had taken a political decision to let Hong Kong collapse or whether they simply did not know what had hit them. Either way, the local government in Hong Kong did not have the money to prop up its futures exchange which was now teetering on the brink of extinction. The speed at which assets were sold on the futures market had dragged underlying share prices down further and faster than they would have moved on their own.

THURSDAY By the morning of the fourth day the local problems in Brazil and Hong Kong had become an international crisis. A domino effect of defaults began, and by then everything was happening at once in a hundred places and a thousand institutions.

The panic over Brazil had already spread to every other emerging market in which western institutions had invested. The futures markets of Mexico, Argentina, the Philippines, Singapore, Malaysia and Thailand, which were one of the commonest routes for overseas investors to put money into these countries, collapsed as foreigners sold at any price. By the end of trading in the Far East, the Malaysian, Singapore and Thai exchanges were, like São Paolo, insolvent and many people suspected the Osaka exchange was too.

What was worse for the global financial system, however, was that the virus was already spreading to the world's major markets, just as it did during the Mexico crisis of 1995. In the confusion caused by the collapse of São Paolo, none of the market participants could get their money out. They included banks, hedge funds and ordinary investment funds which needed cash to meet obligations in other markets. To raise the money they began an emergency liquidation of assets in the Chicago futures and options exchanges,

the London International Financial Futures Exchange, and the
Matif in Paris. Prices dropped sharply, dragging down the underlying stock markets in the US, Britain and France.

In the first hour of trading the Dow Jones Industrial Average
dropped 350 points, triggering the 'circuit breaker' on the New
York Stock Exchange which temporarily stopped trading. This was
a rule designed to calm the markets down when they were in
turmoil, but this time it had the opposite effect. Closing the stock
market also brought equity futures trading to a grinding halt. As in
London, the futures had been leading the way down, but futures
traders became desperate when they realized that the underlying
cash market was about to close. Anxious to get out of their positions
at a reasonable price while the market was still open, they sold
everything they could. There was chaos in the futures market
as it spun out of control until the stock market abruptly shut
at 10.55 a.m.

The pause gave the futures brokers time to demand extra margin
payments from clients whose holdings were showing a loss. This
caused havoc because many players simply didn't have the money
available and could not get it by selling part of their holdings, even
at any price, because the market was shut. The New York stock
market reopened at 12.40 p.m. but the futures market was already
anticipating a fall of another 150 points on the Dow, forcing it to
close again within fifteen minutes.

Shaken by these events, the financial authorities around the
world scrambled to analyse what was going wrong, but made a
fundamental mistake. Mostly men and women who had grown up
in a world before derivatives, the central bankers and politicians
believed that a crash could not happen unless there were good
underlying economic reasons for one. Since, at the moment, the
world economy seemed relatively healthy they could not believe
the markets really *were* crashing. They failed to understand that
these days, the markets could take on a life of their own, moved
simply by the power of financial speculation. Thanks to derivatives,
money moved around the world with a speed and complexity that
no one could comprehend or prevent. It was all happening too fast
to do much about.

The authorities also made another mistake. The banking supervisors in the US, Germany and Japan at first assumed that Castle's insolvency was a purely British problem. The Federal Reserve Board and the Bundesbank promised to help Britain support the UK banks. But the problems of the British banks had punched a hole through the middle of the complex web of financial obligations between every international bank. The bureaucrats realized too late that the crisis affected them all.

While they conferred by phone, the British bond market began a swift collapse, again led by heavy futures selling. The bank crisis meant economic problems and trouble for the government, so a sell-off of gilts (UK government stock) began during the afternoon. The Treasury was dismayed to see that the cut in UK interest rates had done nothing to support bonds. It was also no help to sterling which began a precipitous fall.

When the American markets opened, US Treasury bonds also fell sharply. At this point, politicians and senior bankers began to recognize that they were facing a full-scale crash and that it was already, almost certainly, out of control.

FRIDAY Their worst fears were confirmed. As the world turned and one market opened as another shut, a tidal wave of selling swept around the globe. Dealing rooms had to be manned twenty-four hours a day as investors and speculators struggled to control their losses. The stockmarket fall that began in the US on Thursday was passed on to Tokyo the next morning, then to London several hours later, then back to New York. Then the bankruptcies began on an unprecedented scale.

At the centre of the maelstrom were the hedge funds, many with hugely leveraged positions in the futures and options markets which rapidly lost money. They also had massive borrowings from the banks to finance their speculation. As the banks grew more frightened they refused to lend the funds more money, which meant the funds could not meet the margin calls on the derivatives exchanges. Their only option was to reduce their holdings by selling assets, a move which drove the markets down still further. US retirement funds, many of which were also highly leveraged, found themselves in the same position. All investment funds also began to face another problem. Always the last to know when

anything is going on in the financial markets, the general public
was at last beginning to realize the gravity of the crisis. When they
did so, they wanted their money out of stocks and bonds; they
wanted banknotes to stick under the mattress until the crisis had
gone – or better still, gold. To raise enough cash to meet the
redemptions, funds had to sell yet more assets. The markets
plunged again.

Moreover, something totally unexpected had started to happen.
Many investors had been trying to hedge against the falling value
of their shares and commodities by using the futures and options
markets. But the unprecedented volatility of prices made options
prohibitively expensive – so expensive in fact that the market
effectively ceased to work. Liquidity dried up in what everyone
used to think were the most liquid markets in the world. Hedging
became impossible. The protection that investors always assumed
would be there in the event of falling markets turned out to be an
illusion. They were completely exposed to the full force of the
market collapse.

The bloodletting in the stock and bonds markets now became
intense. By the end of the day the New York, London and Tokyo
stock markets had fallen more than 30 per cent since Monday.

Before this, however, the banking crisis worsened. During the
morning, a senior member of the Bundesbank told a television
station that the Germans and Americans were preparing to rescue
the British banking system. The comment persuaded dealers that
the situation was worse than they had thought, causing a new wave
of panic to sweep through the City. Furious British politicians
immediately accused the Germans of deliberately trying to undermine their banks and demanded an apology, but it was too late.
UK bank shares were virtually worthless and the credit rating
agencies were issuing dire warnings of worse to come. Relations
between the Bank of England and the Bundesbank became so
strained they virtually ceased to co-operate.

That afternoon, the Fed followed London by announcing a
1 percentage point cut in interest rates. (The Germans reluctantly
followed with a $\frac{1}{2}$ percentage point.) But the US banks were
already in trouble. The US stock market knew that Citicorp was a
heavy player in São Paolo and other emerging markets; so were

several of the big securities houses. None of them could now get their money out. It was also known that a large hedge fund with several hundred million dollars in loans from Citi had gone bust. Word now went round that Chase Manhattan, Citi's chief competitor, was refusing to lend it any money, perhaps as an aggressive move to damage its rival in its moment of weakness. Citi had been on the brink of collapse more than once before and the market took no chances: it deserted the bank. Citi's shares fell by more than half in forty minutes. Then the sellers turned on Chase and savaged its shares too.

At the same time, it emerged that one of the securities houses had underwritten a massive Brazilian bond issue which was still on its books when the crisis began. Informed market speculation put the securities house's loss at more than $1 billion. Together with losses it was assumed to have made in other markets, investors guessed the bank must be broke. Everyone knew that the US authorities had no obligation to prop up the investment bank sector because there were no deposits to protect as there were with the commercial banks – which meant, as far as anyone knew, that some or all of the investment banks might be allowed to go bust. The shares of every securities house on Wall Street more than halved by lunchtime.

The insolvency of the investment bank was confirmed almost immediately when it failed to make payments due that day to other US banks on hundreds of millions of dollars of interest rate and currency swaps. Several of the US banks which did not receive payments therefore refused to honour swaps payments of their own to other banks. As in the ordinary loan market, fear of bankruptcy made banks cut off their contact with each other, disrupting the flow of cash around the system.

As stock markets collapsed under relentless pummelling from the futures markets, many company executives bleated pathetically about how their businesses were sound and their shares undervalued. They were wasting their breath. The catastrophic fall in their shares had nothing to do with individual companies: investors were losing confidence in the economies on which those companies depended.

Governments and banking authorities struggled to come up with a strategy to stop the disaster, but they seemed like rabbits caught in the headlights, frozen with fear. Obsessed with fighting the crisis on their own doorsteps they achieved precious little international co-ordination. All attempts to organize a multinational bank rescue plan went by the board. The markets and the banks had always tacitly assumed that in a crisis the authorities would have a plan to bail them out. But when the crunch came, events moved so fast that no one knew where to start.

SATURDAY AND SUNDAY   With the markets shut for the weekend the authorities hoped they could cool the crisis down. The government of every industrialized country issued a statement saying they would stand behind their banking systems. Politicians appeared on TV every hour or so with reassuring statements about the markets, but hardly anyone paid attention. The public was mesmerized by accounts and analyses of the situation in the weekend media. Until now they had not fully realized how bad things were.

Reports leaked out that all of the British merchant banks were insolvent, that Castle Bank was on life support and that the other clearing banks were in trouble. Elsewhere in Europe, Italian banks had been slaughtered on the stock market because no one believed the Italian government could afford to support them if they went bust which, as far as anyone knew, they probably were. Spain was also in the grip of a banking crisis as was France, whose banking system had looked wobbly for years anyway. The European Union, meanwhile, was incapable of acting as a united force because the crisis developed too fast for its plodding bureaucracy to cope.

In the US, Citicorp was on its knees while a clutch of the biggest investment banks, which had been trading heavily on their own account, had seen their capital virtually wiped out. As for Japan, there was a mystery. Few foreigners knew how much Japanese banks used derivatives and their accounts gave little clue since they frequently seemed to be works of fiction rather than reflections of reality. Ever since its troubles in the mid-1990s the Japanese banking system had been regarded with suspicion by most non-Japanese. The Japanese banks and investment funds were, however, known to have been the largest players in the US treasury bond market and it was known that several took a pasting when the bond market went mad. By extrapolation, other banks concluded that the Japanese banking system was just as weak as those of the other industrialized countries.

No credit officer in any bank anywhere in the world wanted to be blamed for making the wrong decision, so they made no decisions at all. Banks, in other words, stopped lending money, credit was cut off. Companies which survived day to day on short term loans to pay their trade bills suddenly found the loans weren't available and they started to go bankrupt.

Late on Sunday, TV reporters got hold of a new story. Credit derivatives were a market that had developed in the mid-1990s to hedge the risk of default by developing countries. A counterparty – usually a bank – guaranteed to pay bondholders the difference between the bond's maturity value and its actual value if a country defaulted. If, say, a bond worth $100 was only worth $20 after a default, the bank would pay the bondholder $80. The TV news now reported that international banks had sold hundreds of billions of dollars worth of these guarantees. Following the default of Brazil they were therefore liable to pay their clients hundreds of billions for the massive fall in the value of their emerging market bonds.

THE NEXT SIX MONTHS As the new week began, therefore, the markets were as panicky as they had been the previous week. There was no let-up in the financial chaos. There were more losses as currencies went wild and several more developing countries announced that they were defaulting on their debt.

On Tuesday evening came the staggering news that a leading US computer company had gone bust. Unknown to the market, and possibly to its own board, its finance department had invested a chunk of the company's capital in highly leveraged and highly complex derivatives. Many people had thought these kind of instruments were things of the past but now it seemed that they were not. When interest rates fell, the value of the computer company's investments collapsed, leaving the company effectively insolvent. No one held out much hope for its survival because there was not a single bank that was willing, and few that were even able at this stage, to lend it more money to trade out of its difficulties. World stock markets braced themselves for more corporate failures like this one.

In Britain this was less of a worry because of the profound conservatism of most corporate treasurers. But the banking and credit crisis had already started to take its toll. Small and medium sized businesses that lived from day to day on credit started to collapse: six hundred on Wednesday, 1,100 on Thursday. By the middle of the following week, company collapses were running at around 2,000 a day. At the end of the month the government was unable to calculate accurate unemployment figures, but estimated that it had leapt by about 200,000 in the space of about two weeks. And it went on climbing. By the time winter came, Britain's unemployment rate had risen by a third to 13.5 per cent. In the US it had risen by about the same proportion, in Europe it was even worse and no one has yet had time to contemplate the suffering in developing countries whose economies had been thrown back two decades by the crisis.

The world, in other words, was sinking rapidly into a fully fledged depression. Economists bickered as always about what to do and why it all happened, but this helped no one. Within six months, general elections were held in Britain and the government was thrashed, but this was largely because the public wanted a scapegoat. The new government had no better idea of how to handle the situation than the old one did. Its first move was to outlaw all forms of financial derivatives which it claimed were the cause of the panic that caused the depression. The US government did the same. The futures and options markets – those that somehow survived the mayhem – were closed down. The public was desperate for scapegoats: several hedge fund managers who were accused of causing a speculative crash were forced to live incognito in the wilds of North Dakota for several years. There were flashes of social unrest: French farmers burnt down the Elysée palace; a drunken mob sacked the Bank of England but failed to get into its gold vaults; a US presidential candidate was assassinated; there was a coup in Russia. None of that changed the fact that companies had collapsed, millions of jobs had been lost and the world economy had been thrown into turmoil.

But that all came later. On a rainy day a week after his suicide, Jack Horner was buried quietly in the corner of a Kent churchyard with his grieving wife and children and a small gathering of former colleagues in attendance. His obituary in the local paper called him 'something in the City' and a man with a knack for making money. There was no mention of his job in derivatives and no word – because no one outside Castle Bank knew – of his role in precipitating the latest depression.

CHAPTER 2

A SHORT HISTORY OF DERIVATIVES AND SPECULATION

The rule is, jam tomorrow and jam yesterday – but never
jam today.

Through the Looking Glass

It was Aristotle who first recorded a suspicion that all might not
be well where derivatives were concerned. Around 330 BC, in the
first book of his *Politics*, he wrote down the first detailed
description ever recorded of an options contract in a story about
the philosopher Thales of Miletus. Aristotle claims that Thales
invented options, which is not exactly true since we know that at
least a thousand years earlier the ancient Babylonians used a form
of financing that looks remarkably like an option contract, designed
to cope with the danger of bandit attacks on trading caravans. But
whenever derivatives began, it is clear from Aristotle's description
that by his own time options were a well-developed financial
technique which would have been instantly recognizable to any
high-tech trader in London or New York today.

Thales had a problem: he had grown tired of his neighbours'
constant jibes about the uselessness of philosophy which, they
pointed out, had failed to make him rich. Unable to persuade them
that he was poor by choice rather than necessity, he set out to give
a graphic demonstration that if a philosopher decides to be wealthy
he can be.

Thales was expert at reading the stars and the weather (he is said, for example, to have predicted the eclipse of the sun in 585 BC) and one winter saw all the signs of a bumper olive crop the following season. Taking his meagre savings, he toured the owners of all the olive presses in the region of Miletus and Chios, paying them each a small premium for the exclusive use of their presses if he should ask for it in nine months time. He managed – 'in the absence of any higher offer', says Aristotle – to negotiate a low rent for the presses which he would only pay if he decided to use them. He had, in other words, bought himself the right to use the presses at an agreed price and time, but he was under no obligation to use them if he chose not to: a classic option contract. The delighted press-owners could probably not believe their luck. Here was someone giving them cash on the nail in return for the promise of a service that might not even be demanded of them nearly a year away. Everyone was happy – at least for the time being.

Thales sat down to wait. When the bumper harvest duly arrived the oil presses were naturally in hot demand but the farmers found to their dismay that Thales controlled every single one of them. Taking up his option to operate them at the prearranged low rent, he jacked up the pressing fees charged to the olive growers until the pips, as it were, squeaked. By the end of the year, Thales was an extremely rich philosopher and his neighbours fell silent – no doubt resentfully so since his actions would have sent the price of olive oil sky-rocketing.

This is as straightforward a case of market manipulation as you could hope to find, and it is no surprise that the first recorded description of an option should also be a story about speculation. And that is where Aristotle's doubts arose. He sadly points out that the tale proves the power of what he called a 'principle which can be universally applied to the art of acquisition': creating a monopoly. As Thales demonstrated, there is no better way for a speculator to gain a monopoly – or corner, as it is known in commodity markets – than by using derivatives. You don't even have to be rich to do it.

Which is why the history of derivatives is to a large extent also the history of financial speculation and why the heavy use of derivatives so often leads to severe market disruption or collapse. Not that anyone, after several thousand years of experience, has found a solution to this. On the frequent occasions when derivatives have caused chaos, misery and disruption there have often been attempts to abolish them. The attempts have always failed.

Given the chaos and unhappiness that speculation can cause, it is entirely natural that from Aristotle (who regarded making money out of money as morally degenerate) onwards, derivatives have rarely had a good press. Too often, they seemed to provide the tools for unscrupulous men to buy economic control over their neighbours and reduce important financial markets to the status of a casino. It is only very recently that attitudes to derivatives have undergone a profound change. Although they continue to get a rather bad press, the speculators who use them are no longer regarded as public enemies but as heroes of capitalism. Their machinations with derivatives are accepted as both inevitable and essential to efficient financial markets. Derivatives are no longer morally suspect. This crucial change in attitude has set the stage for the derivatives markets to become the biggest game of roulette the world has ever known.

The reason why society has never managed to abolish derivatives is that they are just too useful to give up. Even in simple farming economies, everyone stands to benefit. If, for example, you can find a way to set a fair price for a crop before the long process of bringing the produce to market, everyone is likely to be happier. The merchants are assured of their supplies at a price they know they can afford. The farmers have the comfort of knowing what they are going to be paid, and if the contract also involves some kind of cash payment in advance they have some extra working capital to tide them through until the crop is actually sold. By eliminating uncertainty and using capital more efficiently, the process of production itself should become more efficient. All because of derivatives.

The process of fixing prices in advance – otherwise known as forward or futures contracts – were widely used in the ancient world. Since it took about a month to ship a cargo of grain from Egypt to Italy, for instance, the Romans protected against price changes during delivery by agreeing a price with the merchants in advance.

Detailed evidence of derivatives is pretty slim during the Middle Ages although it is clear that various devices were in common use. The twelfth-century merchants of France and Flanders, for example, often contracted to buy wool from England in advance of delivery.

On the other side of the world, the Japanese evolved a more sophisticated method of trading commodities. To cope with social and economic instability they created the Dojima Rice Market in 1730 to protect planters from price fluctuations between harvests. This bore a remarkable resemblance to modern futures exchanges since trading was restricted to a certain place and hours of the day. The quality and quantity of rice in each contract was also standardized, which greatly simplified trading since dealers could for once be confident of exactly what they were buying in the future.

In Europe, financial lift-off occurred suddenly and spectacularly a century earlier, in Holland. In 1602 the Dutch East India Company invented the concept of the joint stock company when it sold shares in itself to the public. (Until then, companies had been set up for limited periods only with a few investors whose shares could not easily be traded.) The East India Company share issue worth 6.3 million florins was a spectacular success, selling out within a month to a public that responded as if it had been dealing in shares for generations. From that point, the Company was almost single-handedly responsible for the creation of the Dutch stock market which became the model for every other stock market in Europe.

Like a sudden conjunction of atmospheric conditions, the invention of shares produced a veritable tornado of wheeling and dealing that convulsed Western Europe's infant capital markets for the next century. Increasing wealth from growing trade and industry meant that more people had spare capital but there were few convenient ways to invest it. The invention of stock markets gave it to them. Suddenly they had something in which they could invest that did not depend on the weather (like crops) and which existed in a known quantity from year to year, could be easily bought and sold without requiring vast sums of capital (like land) and, above all, held out the possibility of quick wealth if the investor was lucky.

Before the century was half over the Dutch had become a nation of rampant speculators.

At the centre of this maelstrom were derivatives, which is why they were the focus of the first truly pointless financial crash ever recorded in Europe: the tulip bust of the 1630s.

Why tulips, of all things? It is never wise to underestimate the power of fashion in financial markets, whether it is Impressionist paintings in the 1980s or computer company shares in the 1990s. In early seventeenth-century Holland tulips were nothing if not fashionable. But once the mania got into full swing it really ceased to matter whether it was tulips, gold or horse shit that was being traded. It became a game not about flowers but about money.

Tulips were brought to Europe from Turkey, where they were already highly fashionable, in the 1550s. They are first recorded growing in a botanical garden in Vienna in 1559 but soon spread to northern Europe where they were taken up by aristocratic connoisseurs, particularly in Holland (the name comes from 'tulband', the Turkish word for turban, which tulips were said to resemble). The flowers were so rare and precious that sometimes a single tulip would adorn an entire flower bed.

There were tulips of all varieties and prices from plain reds and yellows to extremely expensive flowers with elaborately variegated colours. By the 1620s the most highly prized was the *Semper Augustus*, a white flower with flames of deep red and blue running all the way up the petal. In 1624 it sold for 1,200 Florins; in 1625 it was F3,000; in 1633, F5,500. (The most expensive Amsterdam houses on the central canals with a garden and coach house were worth around F10,000 each.)

When the mania really took off in 1634 the idea of buying tulips for future delivery appears to have been the key factor. The tulip trade was in bulbs rather than actual flowers which meant that the normal buying season was between about June, when tulip bulbs were lifted out of the ground, and October when they were replanted. For the rest of the year, the market died. To meet the rising demand, however, growers found a way of extending the trading season into the winter by selling bulbs for delivery in a few months' time: in effect, a tulip futures contract.

Although buyers could now trade at any time of the year few people wanted to wait months until delivery of their bulbs the next spring. Instead, they started selling their future contracts on to someone else for a profit. To play this game you didn't even need to own any tulips because the buyer almost never wanted to take actual delivery of a bulb. As long as he was confident he could find someone else to buy the contract off him at a higher price, he did not care. Futures, in effect, enabled a transaction to take place between a buyer without money and a seller without tulips. A growing number of contracts only vaguely related to the actual stock of real tulips began circulating, but as long as prices kept rising and the merry-go-round kept turning people continued to trade.

By the summer of 1636 prices for many varieties had at least trebled and were still accelerating. Feverish speculators desperate to get in on the action began paying in kind as well as cash to make up the prices as they rose to stratospheric levels. For a single *Semper augustus* an Amsterdam speculator offered F4,600 in cash plus a new carriage, two grey horses and a complete set of harness. Another buyer paid F2,500 for a Viceroy tulip by handing over four oxen, eight pigs, a dozen sheep, two hogs' heads of wine, four tuns of beer, two tuns of butter, two lasts of rye, four lasts of wheat, a thousand pounds of cheese, a bed, a suit of clothes and a cup.

As the price rise gathered pace in markets such as Haarlem, Rotterdam, Leyden and Hoorn as well as Amsterdam itself, all sorts of people, from artisans to aristocrats, were tempted to take a punt and turn a fast profit. A crucial feature of this trade, however, was that the contracts were unenforceable in law. The Dutch government had passed a regulation to deter speculation under which no one could sell futures contracts on goods they did not already own. Anyone who did so faced the possibility that his counterparty could renege on the deal with no legal consequences (known as an Appeal to Frederick, since the law was promulgated under the rule of the Stadtholder Frederick William). Most of the tulip futures now driving the market upwards were therefore literally not worth the paper they were written on if the market crashed (if they had ever been written down at all) and buyers who would otherwise lose heavily refused to honour their side of the bargain. Which is exactly what happened.

After eighteen months of developing craziness, the market finally lost touch with reality in the closing stages of 1636. The rising price of the futures contracts and the ease of dealing in them was like a self-generated fuel blasting the market into outer space. The hysteria may also have been boosted by a live-for-today, get-rich-quick mania resulting from an attack of bubonic plague that swept the Netherlands in the second half of the year. In the midst of the tulip euphoria people were dropping like flies: both Amsterdam and Haarlem lost about a seventh of their populations in the space of a few weeks. One wonders how many speculators bought or sold futures contracts not really expecting to live long enough to settle them. But whatever the psychological effects of the plague, it is not surprising that the worst of the inflation happened during the winter when the tulip bulbs were actually in the ground and the market was most reliant on futures trading – it had become a notional paper market which could conveniently ignore the actual flowers on which it was supposedly based, at least until the spring.

What triggered the collapse is unclear but in the first week of February 1637 collective doubt suddenly gripped the speculators. Prices fell, which instantly made the futures contracts virtually worthless, thus precipitating an even sharper fall. Many people were, at least on paper, ruined, but the courts refused to recognize the legal validity of futures trading. In the end, official tribunals accepted the *de facto* practice of allowing outstanding contracts to be closed out by the purchaser paying a mere 3.5 per cent of the full price.

It is doubtful whether the Dutch learned anything much from this painful experience. It certainly did next to nothing to dampen the national obsession with derivatives or the enthusiasm for speculation on the Amsterdam stock exchange.

In 1688, a Portuguese Jew living in Amsterdam wrote in Spanish the first treatise on stock market dealing ever penned in the West. Joseph de la Vega wrote the *Confusion de Confusiones* for the edification of the Portuguese Jewish community in Holland, most of whom had fled from the Inquisition at home, settled mainly in Amsterdam and become expert stock market speculators. It is a remarkable document. In describing how to profit from the market, he created the first systematic description of futures and options trading. His description of complex share dealing strategies makes it clear that well before the end of the seventeenth century the Dutch had discovered virtually everything of any importance there is to know about the basics of market manipulation. Most developments since then have been mere elaboration.

De la Vega leaves absolutely no doubt that the market floated on a churning sea of derivatives. An entire cross section of the community took part in the market, from the wealthiest aristocratic families to merchants and virtually anyone with a little capital who wanted to take a punt on shares. Even schoolboys pooled their pocket money to speculate. De la Vega describes their activity as: 'this enigmatic business that is at once the fairest and most deceitful in Europe, the noblest and the most infamous in the world, the finest and the most vulgar on earth. It is the quintessence of academic learning and a paragon of fraudulence; it is a touchstone for the intelligent and a tombstone for the audacious, a treasury of usefulness and a source of disaster . . .' As a judgement on derivatives markets, this has never been bettered.

The simplest deals were a straightforward exchange of shares for cash with settlement taking place towards the end of each month. But as in the tulip mania, speculators almost never took delivery of shares they had bought. They might, after all, not even have enough capital to pay for them. So the preferred method of purchase was the 'time bargain', a contract to buy or sell shares more than a month ahead. This was, in effect, a futures contract with the buyer paying a small margin as he would in today's markets.

In most cases, the seller and the buyer of the contract would then 'settle for differences' when the contract matured, which was no more than a straightforward bet on whether the price would rise or fall. If it was higher than the price agreed in the contract, the buyer was paid the difference; if it was lower, the seller got the difference. The convenience of this system was that no one was ever required to put up the full face value of the shares.

Options – 'opsies' as the Dutch called them – were also in everyday use. The principal behind them was precisely the same as that used by Thales. You could purchase a 'put' option which gave you the right to sell shares to your counterparty at a specified time and price; or you could buy a 'call' option which gave you the right to buy the shares at a particular time and date. For this right you paid a premium quite separate from the agreed share price. Unlike a futures contract which always had to be settled on the maturity date, you could simply decide not to exercise your option, in which case it lapsed and all you lost was your premium.

The pricing of options was an extremely imprecise art, open to the most blatant abuse and manipulation. De la Vega describes a merchant who wants to buy an option contract and is told the premium will cost 20 per cent of the value of the shares. The merchant haggles and is finally delighted to beat the price down to 15 per cent. Feeling pleased with himself he buys the option only to be told, on visiting a coffee house later in the day, that the proper cost of the premium was 9 per cent. The merchant, needless to say, feels like a fool but the anecdote makes clear that the tradition of ripping off uninformed buyers of options is at least 350 years old. Uncertainty over how to price options remained a problem until the 1970s when a breakthrough transformed the derivatives markets completely – but that comes later.

Like many governments before and after it, the Dutch States General disapproved of what it saw as dangerous speculation which distorted share prices. The power that futures and options gave to any tinker or cobbler in Amsterdam to trade his way to influence in the stock market was frightening the ruling class – a case of excessive economic democracy. Despite repeated attempts to stamp it out, however, nothing seemed to dampen popular enthusiasm for futures and options dealing.

And the problem spread. While the Dutch were blazing the trail, the English trotted in their wake, borrowing ideas shamelessly. The English East India Company did not issue shares until 1626 and even then it took time for an active market to develop. But as England caught up and then overtook Holland as Europe's top trading nation during the late seventeenth century, London began to replace Amsterdam as the chief financial centre. The City came of age in 1721 with a financial crisis of its own – the infamous South Sea Bubble – a full eighty-five years after the Dutch had succumbed to tulips. The difference was that the speculative buying of South Sea Company shares appears to have owed nothing to derivatives. It is as if the English still did not yet have the confidence or sophistication to mount a really complex market crash.

Not that they rejected derivatives. For the rest of the century London refined the strategies and legal underpinnings of futures and options trading, but the next big step in the history of derivatives came with the opening up of the American economy.

If there is a god of speculation, there is every likelihood that he resembles Benjamin Hutchinson, the super-trader of nineteenth-century Chicago's futures markets. Hutchinson was a Dickensian figure: well over six foot tall, fantastically thin, stooped and pale, with a beak of a nose, his head crowned by a tall black hat and his bony body swathed in a long black coat. 'All legs and nose, with the complexion of a liver sausage, and weighing only one hundred pounds,' wrote a contemporary. His voice was harsh and grating but he loved to quote Shakespeare. 'Old Hutch', as this apparently ageless man had been known since adolescence, was an obsessive dealer whose relentless and lifelong devotion to the grain futures markets made him one of America's richest men at the height of his career.

The American financial markets had been launched in 1791 with the creation of the New York stock market which borrowed most of its trading practices lock, stock and barrel from England. With Old World experience and New World pizzazz – some contemporaries called it rampant greed – the new market took off with a speculative bang that lasted for more than a century. With remarkable precocity it experienced its first crisis within two years when a speculator, William Duer, went bust trying to corner a stock using short dated futures contracts. By the early 1800s speculative deals driven by leveraged derivatives easily overshadowed ordinary share trading by investors. The usual suspects were in evidence: time bargains and settlement for differences (also called wager contracts because of their obvious kinship with pure gambling) and options were commonplace.

But while the suave speculators of the East Coast were obsessed

with their stock market manipulations, something more important
was happening among the rapidly expanding corn fields of the mid-
West. Derivatives were finding their modern home.

Ben Hutchinson may have been the biggest but was by no means
the only major speculator who helped to turn nineteenth-century
Chicago into the world's leading derivatives exchange. The rogues'
gallery includes P. D. Armour, Hutchinson's main rival in the high
stakes speculation game: John 'Bet You A Million' Gates, who
would lay $1,000 on which raindrop would race down a train-
carriage window first; James Keene, who manipulated the market
with fake telegrams; and E. L. 'Crazy' Harper, the former sewing
machine salesman whose failure to corner the Chicago wheat
market wiped out Fidelity National Bank of Cincinnati of which
he had become vice president. (Although the Fidelity scandal is one
of the earliest derivatives-induced bank collapses on record, it still
looks horribly familiar today. The year was 1887. As Harper later
explained in the Ohio state prison, each time the corner looked in
jeopardy 'it seemed as if just a few hundred thousand more dollars
would do it'. To this end he plundered the entire deposit base of
the bank without the other directors knowing until it was too late.
The board of Baring Brothers in 1995 presumably knew nothing
of this ominous pecedent.)

Hutchinson, however, stood out from his rivals partly because
he survived where most other speculators eventually went down in
flames. Born on a Massachusetts farm in 1829, he arrived in
Chicago in the 1860s after suffering a nervous breakdown from the
collapse of his first business manufacturing shoes. Chicago was
only just achieving any kind of pre-eminence in the Mid-West at
this time. It was a scrappy town of low wooden houses strung out
along the shore of Lake Michigan, bone-chillingly cold in winter
and sweltering in summer, and in the middle of pretty well
nowhere. Only a few of the streets, most of which were mud tracks,
were paved with timber. Buffalo, Detroit and Milwaukee all looked
just as promising as centres of commerce to serve the mushrooming
farming economy of the great plains. Buffalo and Detroit had even
established recognized grain exchanges before Chicago.

The Chicago Board of Trade was founded with no great

enthusiasm by a motley group of merchants and shopkeepers in 1848 as much as a meeting place for merchants as a place to trade corn. It was an almost immediate flop. Most merchants could see no advantage in allowing their activities in the free-for-all markets of Chicago to be regulated by anyone, least of all by a body that did not even have legislative backing. Weeks went by when not a single deal was transacted there.

It was eventually the sheer pressure of market forces that turned the CBOT into something important in the US financial system. The speed with which farm production grew in the Mid-West at this time was staggering. The mechanical reaper, the mower and the thresher had all been invented in the 1830s, more than halving the time it took to harvest an acre of wheat from an average of 27 hours to 11.5 hours. As more and more land was brought under cultivation, wheat production soared: 2.3 million bushels were shipped from the Mid-West in 1854, compared with 10.3 million a decade later. Thanks to the Eerie Canal, finished in 1828, linking the Great Lakes to the populous north-eastern states, Chicago began to capture most of the trade because it could send a larger tonnage by water than its landlocked rivals could by road or rail.

For a while, the hectic growth of the agricultural market made Chicago literally as well as metaphorically the Wild West of finance. A ramshackle system of warehouse operators, middlemen and shippers evolved but found itself in a state of almost perpetual chaos in a market that had no rules. In this financial free-for-all, almost anything was allowed. Virtually every season some merchant would attempt to corner the grain markets or buy up the available storage space or combine with others into a cartel that could overcharge competitors. And behind all this was the unpredictability of Nature. In years when there was a good harvest the Chicago market tended to become glutted and prices dived. In lean years prices skyrocketed, and people went hungry. There was no adequate smoothing mechanism to keep prices stable.

Inevitably, derivatives filled the gap. Futures contracts to buy an agreed amount of grain at an agreed price several months ahead helped to smooth out the supply problems that had once led to glut or famine. They even, arguably, sometimes helped to dampen

down wild price fluctuations on the Chicago markets that used to
cause terrible disruption to trade. Without them the development
of the Mid-West would certainly have been slower.

The CBOT gradually became the centre for this trade and the
system of dealing became organized. Each commodity had its own
ring or pit (because of the shallow circular depressions in the
trading room where each ring stood) in which the dealers could all
see each other. They shouted their prices – the so-called 'open
outcry' – so that everyone could hear and see what was going on,
and everyone knew where the market was going. The opportunities
for skulduggery were, in theory, reduced.

Most important of all, the CBOT standardized the contracts
traded on the exchange by enforcing standards of grain quality and
insisting that all futures and options contracts were for a set
quantity of grain and matured on specific dates. Traders could now
deal in wheat, corn, oats and rye in the reasonably secure knowledge that they knew what they were buying, and since the terms of
all contracts were the same they were easier to price and dealing
became more popular. The basis of all futures exchanges was
established.

It was on to this stage that Old Hutch stepped as a fledgling
'plunger' in the early 1860s, with the avowed intention of making
himself rich by speculation. After a profitable trial run in 1864 he
launched his first attempt at cornering the wheat market two years
later. Anticipating a bad harvest, he bought up a million bushels of
wheat in Chicago largely through the use of futures. The bears,
those who had sold short, spotted this too late – the wheat price
soared to a near record $2.85 per bushel and Old Hutch cleaned
up. Once the futures contracts matured the price of wheat dropped
50 cents within an hour. The effect on CBOT traders caught on
the losing end was spectacular: 'Men grew frantic, yelled, foamed
at the mouth, knocked one another down, tore off coats, hats and
shirts, broke up tables, smashed out windows and converted the
hall into a pandemonium until they were turned into the street,' a
local newspaper reported of one cornering episode.

Naturally, the public and the farmers hated the wild price
fluctuations that Hutchinson and his kind created. The price of

bread soared, while the farmers could never be sure what their grain was worth when prices raced up and down like this. Hutch was vilified for several months after his 1864 coup. But before long a familiar pattern of public behaviour asserted itself. Fascination at his success took over from revulsion; people started calling him a genius for having manipulated the market so effectively. This seems to be the fate of all really successful speculators, from Thales to George Soros. Soros was a figure of hatred to many people in Britain after he made his $1 billion profit in helping to force sterling out of the European exchange rate mechanism in 1992. But curiosity won out in the end: the public wanted to know about him. They could not help but admire a man who could make so much money so fast simply through the alchemy of derivatives. Within months, just like Old Hutch, he had been rehabilitated and was eventually accorded financial guru status.

The parallels between the two speculators go further. In response to angry attacks following his successful 1866 corner, Hutchinson objected that he had done nothing wrong. He had merely been following the rules of the market as they stood, and had violated no laws. If the public thought his actions were so bad, he declared, then they should change the rules. In an uncanny echo more than a hundred years later, Soros's standard defence of himself – this one uttered during a 1995 interview with *The Times* – uses identical arguments and almost identical language. After conceding that speculation is a necessary evil, he said: 'My defence is that I operate within the rules set by others. If there is a breakdown in the rules, that is not my fault as a lawful participant but the fault of those who set the rules. I think that is a very sound and justified position. I think that it behoves the authorities to design a system that does not reward speculators.' Soros knows, of course – as Hutchinson did – that such a system is probably impossible to design.

In 1888, the year after Crazy Harper blew Fidelity National to smithereens, Old Hutch cornered the wheat market again through a surreptitious campaign of futures buying. With a fortune estimated at $20 million and with the leveraging effect of futures and options, his power in the market was devastating. He came to

control the price in much of Europe as well as America and it was
only through the intervention of his son (who happened to be the
CBOT's chairman) that he relented and averted a market crash.

This unpleasant experience, however, failed to turn Americans
against the idea that everyone had the right to manipulate a market
if they could. Speculators argued, as they always have done, that
they were merely risking their capital as it is the right of every
capitalist to do. If their rewards often seemed excessive, that was
only because the risks they took were huge. That, too, was simply
capitalism at work.

Following this relentless logic with typical pragmatism, Americans converted the idea of speculation from something wicked into
something inevitable and beneficial. The courts were the first to
crack for the very practical reason that they found it impossible to
enforce the ban against options and speculative futures trading.
The only alternative was to accept them – for the first time in
Western history – as legally enforceable contracts. As a Federal
judge said in 1878: 'The truth is, men are speculative creatures as
certainly as they are eating and sleeping ones.' Therefore, he
concluded, 'commercial transactions must be left to be regulated
by the higher and more inscrutable laws which govern the trading
world'. Market forces, it seemed, counted for more than the laws
of man.

By the end of the century the historic opprobrium with which
derivatives had always been treated was fading away. Morally as
well as legally they were becoming respectable and the speculators
who used them were elevated to a position of veneration. It wasn't
going to be all plain sailing, admittedly. Yet another upset in wheat
prices in the 1930s, for example, brought about a further officially
sanctioned though temporary stop on options trading in America.
It was not until the final third of the twentieth-century that the
victory of free market theology permitted the conditions in which
speculators – and derivatives, their favourite tool – could flourish
truly unfettered by the moral qualms and legal constraints of the
past. Nevertheless, the Chicago futures markets of the nineteenth-
century had set the pace. They had institutionalized speculation as
never before, and thereafter it was impossible to put the genie back
in the bottle for long.

In its annual report of 1891 the CBOT gave form to the new creed: 'Speculation stimulates enterprise; it creates and maintains proper values; it gives impulse and ambition to all forms of industry – commercial, literary and artistic; it arouses individual capacities; it is aggressive, intelligent, and belongs to the strongest and ablest of the race; it grapples undismayed with possibilities; it founded Chicago, and developed the great West, which is the nation's prosperity and the impelling commercial power of the Continent.' This is strong stuff. To speculate was not only patriotic, philanthropic and spiritually uplifting, it was positively Darwinian. In this view, speculators were the true leaders of society. The men at the CBOT who wrote this declaration were, of course, talking about themselves.

And what of Old Hutch? Having helped to bring about this profound change in attitudes, he disappeared again. This time he was suffering from the market trader's traditional ailment: burnout. He was discovered years later in New York living like a hermit in a small store he had bought on a whim beneath the western end of Brooklyn Bridge. To fill his time he was writing articles for the *North American Review* in defence of speculation. He died quoting Shakespeare in a sanatorium in Wisconsin in 1899. With the new century, a new financial era was beginning.

In 1900, a few months after Hutchinson's death, a young French maths genius named Louis Bachelier published a seventy-page dissertation that laid the foundations of modern finance. He probably didn't know that's what it would turn out to be, and his contemporaries certainly did not because they almost completely ignored him. When he submitted his work to the Sorbonne for the degree of Doctor of Mathematical Sciences the learned professors awarded him only a '*mention honorable*', which was not good enough to make a reputation in the French academic world. His work languished unread and forgotten for sixty years until it was rediscovered by American academics in the 1950s who were starting to revolutionize the way markets could be analysed.

Using prices on the Paris stock market for a series of statistical experiments, he undertook some remarkable mathematics that included the basics of probability theory, a formula foreshadowing

Einstein's work on the behaviour of particles influenced by random shocks, and a clever attempt to find a method of valuing futures and options.

He noticed, for instance, that price movements got bigger over time and that the faster prices moved the further they were likely to go – a characteristic now known as volatility. Put a rabbit in your garden and the longer you leave it there the further it is likely to stray from its starting point. In the same way, over the space of a minute a share price is unlikely to fluctuate as much as it will over a day or a year or several years.

Bachelier found a formula to describe the movement which led him towards an attempt to price futures and options – both actively traded in Paris in 1900 – because they were simply bets on future price movements. For although people had been trading these things for centuries, no one had a theoretical basis for pricing them. Instead they used what traders always use – market savvy, past experience and a sensitivity to supply and demand – but it was always an ad hoc process. Since no one paid any attention to Bachelier in his own lifetime, however, they continued to value derivatives this way for another six decades or so.

By the 1960s, ad hoc did not look quite good enough, given the way financial markets were obviously going. The stable post-Second-World War world of fixed exchange rates was coming apart at the seams. The system had been set up by the Allies in 1944 in an agreement signed at a hotel in Bretton Woods, New England. It had pegged the world's major currencies to the dollar which in turn had been pegged to the price of gold. The aim was, among other things, to bring stability to international trade by enabling businesses to convert their currencies into foreign currencies at completely predictable prices. It was a political and bureaucratic solution to the problem of how to reduce exchange rate risk. But economies develop and grow at different speeds, and as they do so their currencies change value in relation to one another. Within a couple of decades, the values assigned to currencies within the Bretton Woods agreement no longer reflected the relative strengths of the economies the currencies represented. In particular, the dollar badly needed to devalue but the rigidity of the system would not allow it. Eventually the strains became too much and the Bretton Woods agreement fell to pieces in 1973 when the dollar was allowed to float freely and currencies were permitted to change value in relation to one another from day to day. At the same time, interest rates began to fluctuate more violently than before, under the impact of economic shocks such as the oil price hike of the early 1970s and government attempts to control the value of their currency.

The result was financial chaos. Companies that had once been able to forecast what they would have to pay for goods sold to them in foreign currency, for instance, now lived in a state of perpetual uncertainty. For companies and investors alike, the new environment was a nightmare because planning became almost impossible and there were few efficient ways to hedge the risks they now faced. For speculators, on the other hand, the new world was a godsend. Since uncertainty and volatility are what they thrive on, the opportunities to make money after the collapse of Bretton Woods were infinitely greater than before.

What was needed now was a free market solution to the problem of reducing exchange rate risk. With amazing speed the financial markets provided both hedgers and speculators with a way of coping with the new world. Two inventions in particular made the difference and caused the revolution that is the subject of this book. The first, which preceeded the second by a year or two, was the creation of financial futures contracts giving companies a cheap and easy way to hedge their risks while giving speculators an equally cheap and easy way to take on the risk in the hope of turning it into a profit.

The idea had actually first been tried on one of the New York markets in 1971, but they had got the details wrong and it died within months. The real progenitor was a young trader called Leo Melamed who had originally taken a job at the Chicago Mercantile Exchange as a runner (carrying orders across the exchange floor from brokers to pit traders) to pay his way through law school. The Merc had been created in 1874 by butter and egg dealers who broke away from the Chicago Board of Trade, but its trade had dwindled so pathetically that by 1970 the market was dying on its feet. The younger traders, Melamed among them, realized they needed to find a new business to keep the Merc alive.

It is hard to imagine now that the idea of a contract in currency futures was greeted with derision when Melamed first proposed it in 1970. Sitting in the office of his trading company, Sakura Delsher, fifteen stories above the rowdy trading floors of the modern Merc, Melamed has clearly found success. His office is roughly the size of a tennis court with glass walls on two sides overlooking Chicago; his desk is as big as a billiard table and tasteful art hangs on the walls. From the boardroom there is a stunning view of the skyscrapers of Chicago's financial district to the right and the endless flat horizon of the plains to the left. Physically compact, Melamed exudes energy and good-natured pugnacity; dressed in an expensive suit and tie, he has something of the air of a retired prizefighter who has made his fortune in the ring. Which, in a sense, he has. As well as helping to change the face of finance and becoming chairman of the Merc, he has made a lot of money in the robust free-for-all of the exchange's trading pits. But it has taken time and a lot of hard work to achieve this pinnacle.

Melamed was born in Bialystock, a town in north-eastern Poland. His father, Isaac Melamdovich, was a Jewish scholar and a staunch anti-Communist. To be either one of these was highly dangerous in Eastern Europe in the late 1930s, but to be both was likely to be fatal. The family first went on the run when the Germans invaded Poland in 1939, escaping at night on the last train out of Bialystock to Lithuania. Melamed was eight years old. When the Russians annexed Lithuania in 1940, the family had to move again because of its anti-Communist credentials, eventually fleeing right across Russia to Japan and finally to America.

They arrived just before the US entered the war. Leo Melamed says that his escape from wartime Europe left him with an abiding conviction that free trade is preferable to dictatorship, and a familiarity with foreign currencies which eventually stood him in good stead. After graduating, he studied law for a while before becoming a full time member of the Merc. But his skills as a trader were complemented by a prodigious talent for salesmanship and it is this that finally got his new idea accepted by his sceptical colleagues.

The catalyst was the Chicago economist (and eventual Nobel

prizewinner) Milton Friedman, who by 1970 was an outspoken critic of Bretton Woods. Melamed was captivated by Friedman's free market ideas. He was particularly impressed by an article in which Friedman described an attempt to sell sterling short in anticipation of a decline in the British pound. The point of the piece was that the great economist had failed because there existed no mechanism for individuals to sell currency short. Some large companies could do so through their banks, and a rudimentary interbank market in currency forward contract existed, but you had to be ICI or General Motors to use it. The trader in Melamed was scandalized. Shorting sterling was a potentially profitable trading opportunity, yet it couldn't be done. The answer was to have a currency futures contract that was as tradable as gold or porkbellies or wheat.

Realizing he had zero credibility among the politicians who would have to agree to the idea if it was to succeed, Melamed recruited Friedman to his campaign and within a couple of years the Merc set up the world's first trading pit dealing in a financial derivative.

Like commodity futures, a financial future is a contract to buy or sell a quantity of shares, bonds or currency at a specified price and time in the future. It *obliges* the holder to complete the contract at maturity unless he buys or sells an equal and offsetting contract that 'close out' his position. The beauty of futures contracts is that you only have to pay in cash a fraction – perhaps as little as one per cent – of the total value of the underlying goods. This is called margin. A contract to buy $100 of something in three months might cost you a mere $1 (known as initial margin). If the value of the contract rises to $101 before three months is up, you can sell it and get your deposit back plus the $1 profit. Clearly, you don't have to be rich to play this game, which is why it is so irresistible to speculators, but there are risks. If the contract falls to $99, the futures exchange insists that you put up an additonal $1 in margin (known as variation margin) to cover the loss: you have just doubled the amount of cash you have at risk. Repeated on a large scale, the requirement to raise variation margin to cover losses can wipe out a speculator overnight if the market goes strongly against him.

The alternative is to buy an option contract that gives the hedger the right to buy his currency at the price he wants when he wants it, *but he is not obliged to excercise his right if he doesn't want to.* There are no margin payments. If the market moves in the wrong direction and he decides not to exercise the option, all he loses is the one-off purchase price of the contract, called the premium. Like futures, this can produce large gains or losses and requires only small amounts of cash. Suppose you buy an option for $1 which gives you the right to purchase 100 shares at $10 each in three months but at the end of that time the shares have actually risen to $12, you would excercise your option and make a profit of two dollars a share or $200. All for an outlay of only $1.

But options are complex beasts and a great deal more difficult to price than futures. Without an efficient method of valuing them an active market was never likely to evolve.

The other great invention, therefore, that revolutionized finance as the world plunged into an uncertain era of constantly fluctuating currencies and interest rates was a formula for pricing options. The men who published the ground-breaking formula in the spring of 1973 became instant superstars in the hothouse world of the financial markets. They had come up with the financial equivalent of a cure for cancer.

Fischer Black and Myron Scholes were opposites in character. Black (who died in 1995) was taciturn, introverted and laconic, speaking in slow courteous sentences delivered in a soft mellifluous voice. Scholes is ebullient, always talkative and temperamental. Black's credentials as a 'rocket scientist' go back a long way: as a boy he experimented with rockets by pouring home-made gun powder into cardboard tubes and igniting them with a battery-powered remote-controlled launcher. He abandoned this, however, when a friend nearly blew himself up doing much the same kind of do-it-yourself pyrotechnics. Black turned to more studious pursuits and eventually graduated from Harvard in 1959 with a degree in physics.

During the 1960s he became interested in mathematical problems relating to finance and by 1970 was puzzling over how to price options and warrants (which are a form of call option usually sold by a company as part of a bond issue). By coincidence, so was Scholes who had recently received a Ph.D in finance from the

University of Chicago and now worked at the Massachusetts Institute of Technology. They teamed up but it took them the better part of two years to reach the answer.

What Black and Scholes, along with a growing number of other academics and a few bankers, were doing from the 1950s onwards was looking at the markets in a fundamentally new and different way from most people. The time honoured approach – whether by investors, brokers, dealers or bankers – was always to try to guess where the market was going. If they guessed right, they expected to make money. You want to buy some shares? Naturally, you buy those which you think will rise in price.

The academics didn't think that way. To them, the market was a patchwork of different risks to be quantified and guarded against. They didn't ask 'how much will that share rise?' like any ordinary person but 'how do I protect against the risk that that share won't rise?' Once you start posing awkward questions like that, you begin to think about things like options and how to price them, since the option price expresses the risk of the share moving up or down.

Risk, it has been said, is not getting what you want. What, for example, is the risk of being hit by a bus before you reach the other side of the road? For most of human history, people have been content to make rough estimates and the financial markets have always operated in much to same way: 'not much,' or 'quite a lot' has usually been a pretty acceptable degree of precision. Until now. Black and Scholes wanted a formula for calculating exactly – in dollars and cents – what the danger is that you will not get what you want in one set of circumstances compared to another.

This has come as a revelation to many financial folk – bank managers for example. In the old days – the 1980s, say – bankers would price a fixed interest rate loan intuitively, a process they liked to mystify as 'banking judgement' but which often boiled down to primitive predjuces such as never lending money to men with beards. This did not work well. In fact, banks all over the world have been incredibly bad at judging the risks in lending money: they lost billions lending to Latin America and billions more lending to property developers, to mention just two of the banking debacles in recent memory.

But with the new kind of analysis pioneered by men like Black and Scholes, bankers can analyse their loans as a series of separate risks such as credit risk (the danger that the customer won't repay the money) and interest rate risk (the danger that rates will rise above the fixed rate of the loan, in which case the bank will make a loss). Using derivatives, they can put an exact price on each risk and, if they want, get rid of one or both of them by selling them to someone else. Hedging, in other words. A bank could, for example, eliminate its fixed interest rate risk on the loan, purchasing an option to switch it into a higher interest rate loan if rates rise. Meanwhile, the risk itself has not vanished. It has simply been transferred from the bank to some other market player – a speculator, perhaps, or another bank – who happens to want to take it on.

It is hard to over-emphasize how revolutionary this process has been to the world of finance. After all, when you can fully understand your risks, you can control them. And when you can do *that*, you should be in a better position to get what you want.

A scientific method of pricing options was a crucial step in this process. Options, together with futures, are one of the basic building blocks of the derivatives market. Since options are contracts based on some event that may or may not take place in the future, they are not fundamentally different from betting on the score of a football game. To determine the cost of the bet, you have to know the likelihood of winning or losing. It's a matter of probabilities.

With options, the bet is on whether or not the share price (if shares are what you are dealing in) will reach the exercise price of the option. The more vigorously the share price moves up or down the more likely it is to reach your option's exercise price, which means the option will cost more to buy. This volatility is the crucial ingredient in the Black-Scholes formula, which also includes more mundane elements such as the time period of the option contract, the share price, the exercise price and interest rates. Volatility turns out to be a slippery concept. The number a dealer puts into his calculation is, in the end, nothing more than an estimate usually based on past experience. The historical record of a share's price movements becomes the basis for calculating its volatility – and this can be treacherous. You might, for example, calculate volatility for the S&P 500 stock index using historical data between 1988 and 1996. Fine. Except that if you had included 1987, the year of the last stock market crash, the S&P's historical volatility would suddenly look quite different and all your calculations would come out with very different answers.

The market generally reaches an agreement on what the volatility of a given instrument is at a given time by the usual process of supply and demand, but it isn't always perfect. For all the apparent mathematical precision in calculating what derivatives are worth there is still huge scope for guesswork, inaccuracy, obfuscation and outright dishonesty.

Given all these factors, an option price is too complex to work out in your head or even on the back of an envelope. If you tried to do it by hand you would probably find that the market had moved on before you were finished, so the only way to keep up is to use a computer which is why derivatives could only ever have flourished in the computer age.

These days there are many variants of the original Black-Scholes formula, and computers can churn out prices in fractions of a second. They can calculate options on futures, options on options and combinations of derivatives as bizarre as their names: knock-out options, barrier options, as-you-like-it options, binary options. As Leo Melamed correctly predicted, once the principle of trading financial risk was accepted, the sky was the limit.

Anyway, plain futures and options are only the beginning and are so simple many dealers don't even consider them to be derivatives. They have spawned a finance that has developed a mind-bending complexity which puts it well beyond the reach of most laymen. The whole process of mystification is helped along by the tendency of people in the derivatives markets to talk Greek. 'Delta' is the probability of an option ending up 'in the money' (in profit); 'gamma' measures the volatility of delta, the speed it is moving relative to the price of the underlying instrument; 'vega' measures the effect of changes in the volatility. And so on.

But the most crucial word in futures and options trading is not Greek, even though Thales of Miletus is the first recorded exponent of the technique. The word is leverage: the financial equivalent of lifting a boulder by placing a pebble on the other end of a strategically positioned lever. As Thales demonstrated, the beauty of derivatives is that you don't have to be rich to use them. With a little money you can control a great deal more money – or gold or porkbellies or Deutsch marks or shares, depending on your whim. You will have noticed in the examples above of futures and options trades that the dealer gets control of a large amount of whatever he is dealing in with a remarkably small down payment. And with the same small down payment he can walk away with a huge profit or loss.

That is leverage. It goes to the heart of what trading in derivatives is all about and why, even though they were invented for hedging, derivatives have become a speculator's delight. Instant and massive leverage is the great gift – if you can call it that – which derivatives have brought to the financial markets.

This is why they can make someone a millionaire overnight, or wipe them out. In the past it used to take banks months or years to make enough loans to achieve the kind of leverage they can now get in a matter of minutes by using derivatives. A few years ago a speculator like George Soros could never have taken a big enough market position to affect the future of an entire currency, but now with derivatives and the magic of leverage he can – and, arguably, did with the pound in 1992. With a few phone calls and the alchemy of leverage investment funds, corporations and banks can catapult capital around the globe with a speed and volume that was impossible before derivatives took control.

This is more than just a technical development; it is a conceptual change. The world works differently now. Governments can no longer dictate; they have lost the initiative to the markets where money ebbs and flows around the world with the irresistible power of ocean tides.

Most of this money passes through the so-called Over-the-Counter (OTC) derivatives market, a misnomer if ever there was one. It is massive and secretive and strictly for big league professionals sitting at their banks of computer screens and telephones, selling uniquely tailored derivatives to one another.

The other conduit for the world's capital flows are the derivatives exchanges in centres such as Chicago, London, New York and, increasingly, any other country with pretensions to financial sophistication. They grew directly out of the nineteenth-century Chicago commodity markets and it is there that the modern obsession with derivatives began.

CHAPTER 3

THE EXCHANGES

'What's one and one and one and one and one and one
and one and one and one and one?'
'I don't know,' said Alice. 'I lost count.'

Through the Looking Glass

The realization that a large chunk of your personal wealth has just vanished into thin air in the space of about ninety seconds is not something that most people either want, or expect, ever to happen to them. For Yra Harris, however, it was an occupational hazard on the Chicago Mercantile Exchange, and on this particular occasion it had just gone from being a theoretical possibility to a living nightmare.

The morning had begun normally enough. Harris had driven in early from his home in one of the more pleasant suburbs of Chicago to the gloomy modern office block that houses the Mercantile Exchange on South Wacker Drive. Reaching his office on the eleventh floor by about 6.30 a.m. as usual, he sat down to read the papers, contemplate the state of the financial world and devise a trading strategy for himself before the markets opened at 7.00 a.m. His office resembles a student common room more than a place of high finance. Most of the space is taken up by a couple of old leather sofas and a large, battered desk with an office chair whose seat is permanently stuck on a backward tilt of 45 degrees. A single, rather aged, computer screen stands on the desk; piles of yellowing newspapers lurk in the bookshelves. Clearly, this is a place of private contemplation rather than an office in which to impress clients. Harris does not, after all, have any clients in the conventional sense. The money he risks in the trading pits is his own.

He is one of hundreds of private traders, the 'locals', who supply much of the liquidity at the Merc and the CBOT. His ambition after leaving university was to go into politics but before he got sucked into Washington his father persuaded him to come and join him trading at the Merc. (Like many locals, who tend to be anything from former college professors to dentists to dustmen, Harris's father was a former soldier who had discovered futures trading as a second career.) Reluctantly, Harris joined, took to it and never left. Twenty years later he had graduated from being a humble pit trader to running his own trading operation. But while most of the locals typically trade by buying positions and selling them again within minutes to keep their exposure to large price movements to a minimum – 'scalping', as it's called – Harris tends to take longer term positions based on his view of how the market may move. Because he is the man with the plan he tends to have an edge in the trading pits since the scalpers, knowing he's done his homework, often follow his lead. When he buys, they buy, which pushes the price up so that when he decides to sell before the others he gets a better price than the scalpers whose selling drives the price down again.

Hence his need to be in the office early to pull up the price charts of the Merc's various futures contracts on his computer screen, update the prices from the day before and try to assess what might influence trading during the next few hours. Harris believes that the charts, over time, show recurring patterns that an expert can come to predict. Some traders view chartism as an offshoot of astrology or tarot card reading, but Harris swears by it.

On this particular day, the big news that was likely to move prices was the monthly US trade deficit figure. It was only one of a steady stream of official statistics fed out by government and industry on anything from the inflation rate to the state of the orange crop in Florida, any one of which might move the futures and options markets. By a process somewhat resembling psychic thought transference the market reaches a consensus on what it expects a given figure will be, and the effect the actual figure has in moving prices is usually in direct proportion to the degree that it disappoints this expectation.

The market had decided that the trade deficit figure was going to be fairly dismal. Since this would indicate a feeble trading performance by America the dollar would probably fall. Harris's plan, therefore, was to sell dollars and buy yen and marks (the currencies of more successful trading nations). It was a good plan, on paper.

Harris went to the lift and travelled down the ten floors to the trading area, expecting just another day's turnover and, with luck, another modest profit. As always when major bits of market moving news are imminent, the pits were unusually full of traders hanging around chatting, doing the occasional deal, trying to look cool although most were fairly keyed up. The trick in these circumstances is to be there, in position, when the news comes in. Turning up thirty seconds late might cost a trader a year's profit.

But when the announcement arrived on the huge electronic ticker-tape that runs around part of the wall above the pits, it blew Harris's plan to pieces. The monthly trade deficit was a couple of billion dollars less than expected which, in the greater scheme of things, made precious little difference to anything. Except the futures market. The expected figure had been missed, upsetting the finely tuned calculations of dozens of dealers and investors. In the couple of seconds it took for every trader to fill his lungs with air and let it out again at full volume, the market went berserk.

Sticking to his original strategy, Harris bought yen but found himself almost instantly swamped by a wave of programme selling triggered by computers that had been instructed by investment funds all across America to sell in these market conditions. He still remembers the despair of that moment with a chill. 'Computers are terrifying because they are not looking for value the way human traders would do. They simply follow the instructions they've been given regardless of anything else, and before you know it one price is melting down into the next price, and this drives the computers into more selling.' The process is self-generating and you can't argue with a machine.

The market's reasoning, if you can call it that, went something like this: a smaller than expected US deficit can mean only one thing – Japan is falling to pieces. Why? Because if Americans have spent two billion dollars less on imports it must be because the Japanese – the only country, as far as Chicago dealers were concerned, that exported anything to the US – had failed to sell them two billion dollars worth of goods. This showed that the Japanese export machine had broken down and there was only one appropriate action to take: sell the yen.

So the yen tanked. In the space of one and a half minutes Harris lost a substantial chunk of his capital. It meant that he faced ruin or something close to it. This, remember, was not the capital of some bank which could easily afford to lose a few hundred thousand, but his own money accumulated over years of labour in the pits. 'There was total emptiness in the pit of my stomach. You try to concentrate and keep your wits about you but it isn't easy when the world is caving in. There were a lot of white faces around me – others who must have been caught by the sudden move.' In general, whatever happens it's a bad idea to let your expression show your feelings in the pits because any sign of weakness puts a trader in much the same position as a wounded deer surrounded by slavering wolves. Harris tried to maintain a poker face.

But since his original strategy seemed to have led him to the edge of disaster, he let it go. He decided to keep his mouth shut and listen to the action to get a clearer idea of who was driving the market down. With practice, a dealer develops a kind of aural filter that cuts out the extraneous hubbub and only picks up the sounds of other traders shouting prices. By identifying the voices of individual dealers and what trades they are doing he can tell what is happening in parts of the pit he can't even see. He builds up a picture of the market, of who is selling, and how much, and how long the move may last.

It took Harris several minutes of listening and wondering how the hell to get himself out of trouble before he evolved a new plan. He decided to sell marks against yen. In reaching this conclusion, his thought process appears to have resembled a form of free association rather than ordinary logic and went something like this: if the yen's falling, it will overshoot and go too low (as markets almost always do in sudden price moves). When the market realizes this, speculators will start to buy the yen back but they won't want to sell dollars instead because the US trade deficit was better than expected. So they'll sell something else. Pick another currency. Pick the mark. By selling marks Harris was hoping to second guess the market and get in on the move before it happened. If he was right he might recoup his losses; if he was wrong he might be out of business by lunchtime.

About fifteen minutes after the yen had started to fall, the buying began. Somewhere out there, traders had realized that the Japanese currency had dropped too far and they came in to pick it up cheap. Eventually, their buying overrode the computer-generated selling and the yen rose again. When, as Harris had predicted, the mark started to dive he was already ahead of the game.

Even then, he had an agonizing wait to find out if he had survived. He had a sense that things were at last turning his way but, wedged in the pit amid flailing arms and bellowing voices, he couldn't be sure exactly where his trading had got him. Keeping a precise running total of gains and losses in your head while you are yelling and waving like a madman and scribbling prices on dealing slips isn't really a practical proposition. It was not until the trades were processed two hours later, at 9.30 a.m. that he found he had recovered his loss and come out slightly ahead. By then, however, having flirted rather too closely with personal financial disaster, he was emotionally drained. 'That's the problem with this business. You travel the emotional spectrum every day. Really, this business takes all the intestinal fortitude one has.'

A strong stomach, however, isn't the only physical attribute the average pit trader needs. On any given day, the Merc's Eurodollar futures pit – home to the most popular exchange traded contract in the world – resembles a scene that Hieronymous Bosch might have painted, one of his more apocalyptic visions of hell.

In a space hardly bigger than a tennis court more than a thousand people squeeze together in a heaving, yelling, jostling, multicoloured mob, waving their arms, flicking their fingers and scribbling furiously on small cards. The floor is deep in litter. It sounds like a riot and there is a distinct smell of sweating bodies in the conditioned air. Around the edge of the crowd stands a ring of yellow jacketed clerks, hanging over railings to shout at people manning telephones several yards behind them. At the core of the crowd, facing inwards, are others dressed in brightly coloured jackets shouting at each other.

It's at its worst early in the morning when most of the traders turn up to secure a good dealing position in the pit; they are jammed together elbow to elbow, so close that they can hardly move their arms. Occasionally, the pressure of bodies is so great that the railings around the edge of a pit have been known to give way and those at the bottom of the resulting heap suffer broken ribs or limbs. Sexism aside, women and smaller people in general tend simply to get shouldered aside or drowned out in the hubbub, so few bother to venture into it. The traders are almost all young men in their twenties and early thirties, built like rugby players with voices like foghorns, and robust enough to spend the entire day wedged in this crowd, trying to turn a profit from the billions of dollars that ricochet back and forth every hour across the over-crowded space. In the bowels of the building is a first-aid centre with stretchers to carry away anyone who collapses under the strain. If the financial markets are a war zone, this is the theatre of hand-to-hand combat.

It is said that in one of the pits one morning a trader died of a heart-attack in the crush but his body was wedged in so tightly it could not fall to the floor. Some time passed before the dealers around him noticed his demise but when they did, they took immediate action. They began feverishly filling in dealing tickets which gave them handsome profits from imaginary trades between themselves and the dead trader. Only when his pockets were stuffed full of tickets did they drag him away and call the medics. The problem for the exchange was to determine the exact time of death in order to judge whether the tickets in the dealer's pockets were genuine. Apocryphal? Whether it is or not, the story contains a grain of poetic truth. In full cry, the pits are merciless places where everything, including death, may be a market event.

'It's a war,' Harris says. Certainly, in comparison to pit trading, sitting at a dealing screen in the safety of a bank's trading room is for wimps. To survive in the pit you need the stamina of a marathon runner, the lungs of an opera singer and, preferably, the height of a professional basketball player. Travelling down in the lift from Harris's office to the trading floor, I didn't give him good odds: well under six foot, he was dwarfed by a scrum of twenty-four-year-old gorillas who barely noticed him in their midst: they never bothered to look down that far.

What he lacks in height, however, he makes up for in experience, which may be why he has survived as many life-and-death scrapes in the pits as he has. Some locals, like Harris, make a very healthy living indeed from the markets. But for all the stress and adrenalin and sheer terror at times, many never achieve massive riches. A scalper shaving a few cents of profit off each deal as he trades in and out of positions is never likely to become a Croesus. He may have to flip over several hundred deals a day simply to make a living and pay his modest overheads. So if the action in, say, the Eurodollar pit is too slow, he may wander over to a livelier pit – yen futures, perhaps, or T-bill futures – and try his luck there.

No trader ever made money out of a static market. Volatility is the key to wealth. As long as the market is moving up or down, there is the chance of making money. The markets are deliberately designed to encourage volatility. The options and futures contracts for the same month's delivery, for instance, never mature on the same day but usually about a week apart. There is no reason for this except to make it impossible to achieve a perfect hedge between the markets, which in turn creates uncertainty, which causes volatility.

And when all else fails, dealers start telling each other rumours. It is never clear where these stories begin. Someone with a short position in dollars, perhaps, is getting squeezed by a rise in the currency, so to turn things around he whispers to his neighbour that the US President has been assassinated. Within two minutes the story is all the way round the pit and spreading across the trading floor. No one is sure whether to believe it or not but that's okay because that in itself creates uncertainty. By now maybe people outside the exchange have heard the rumour by phone from one of the floor traders. They pass the rumour back to the exchange by phoning other floor traders who now conclude that since people outside the exchange know about it, it must be true. The dollar drops as if it's fallen off a cliff, and somewhere in the middle of all this the guy who started the rumour unwinds his position at a fat profit.

The rumour effect can be frightening. In another waltz with oblivion, Harris nearly ended his career in 1989 on a rumour that President Bush had been shot dead. To make matters worse, the story seemed more credible than usual (presidential assassinations recur with monotonous regularity on the rumour mill) because instead of arriving by a process of Chinese whispers it was put out by Telerate, a financial news service. Harris was long of sterling and short of marks, but when the news hit there was an immediate flight out of the dollar and into the German currency. Sterling slumped with the dollar, leaving Harris to face the prospect of huge losses – the kind that make you wonder whether you'll have to sell the house because you won't be able to afford the next mortgage payment. There wasn't much he could do except pray. In the meantime, most of the pit traders were like pigs in clover, trading off the volatility as if their lives depended on it.

It took the market about half an hour to discover that the story was completely wrong, at which point there was a flight out of the mark and straight back into dollars and sterling. The pound rocketed from $1.53 to $1.65 in about fifteen minutes. This extra dose of volatility came as a double bonus for the scalpers who couldn't believe their luck. Nor could Harris, who had barely begun to contemplate his own financial destruction when he found that he could sell out of his sterling position at a profit. By the time he staggered out of the pit a few minutes later he felt he had been through an emotional cheesegrater.

When their financial wellbeing hangs on something as unpredictable as a rumour, it is hardly surprising that pit traders, like gamblers, are profoundly superstitious. There are as many ways of propitiating Luck as there are dealers. One has a lucky tie – he owns a drawer full of the identical article but wears one tie until it is little more than a collection of ragged threads hanging around his neck before discarding it and starting on the next. Another always comes into work through exactly the same security turnstile each morning even if it means queuing. A third, when he is on a winning streak, wears the same underwear every day without washing it until the streak comes to an end.

But while traders may try to manufacture volatility on their own, they prefer it when speculators or corporate customers outside the exchange pitch in and move prices. Most of the dealing in the exchanges originates in the trading rooms of banks and corporations, although only about a quarter of it comes from genuine hedgers. The other threequarters is all speculation – and speculation is essential to any futures market because it supplies liquidity and ensures that hedgers will find someone to buy their risk from them.

The influence of players outside the exchange was illustrated in 1996 by the exploits of a mysterious speculator in sterling futures whom the pit traders nicknamed the 'hot-tub Sheik'. Although they did not know his identity they suspected that he was Arab and imagined him wallowing in a jacuzzi as he manipulated markets around the world from a mobile phone. Whoever he was, he had chosen to operate in the Merc's sterling futures market with such style that he often controlled the price of the contract. The sterling market is sufficiently small for a single large speculator to make a difference, which may be one reason the Sheik had singled it out. He first made his presence felt early in 1995 when he would put in one or two large orders a week. These turned out to be training runs for something far bigger. As the months went by he grew more confident, dealing more frequently and using increasingly complex strategies such as straddles and strangles, in which positions in futures are played off against options on futures which are traded in a smaller pit next to the sterling futures pit. He would deal almost every day in large amounts, sometimes buying 100,000 option contracts in an afternoon, or accumulating a futures position with a face value of more than $600 million.

By the middle of 1996 he became bullish towards sterling. His buying of futures was so aggressive that it began affecting the spot value of the pound and the Bank of England grew concerned. According to some traders, it tried unsuccessfully to persuade several major banks not to deal with the Sheik because of his disruptive influence on the currency. It had good reason to worry. In the space of about three hours on one afternoon in May, for example, the Sheik was instrumental in causing the cash value of sterling to rise by 1 cent. The standing of Britain's currency was, in other words, dependent on an anonymous speculator and about thirty young dealers in the Merc's sterling futures pit.

Not that the dealers cared much about the Sheik's identity. To them he simply meant pay dirt. I saw the effect he had on the market when I was standing beside the sterling pit as one of the Sheik's orders was phoned in. The clerk on the phone shouted something and started making frantic hand signals to a trader in the pit. As if by telepathy, every dealer in the vicinity sprang into action, aware that the Sheik was in the market. Dealers who had been loitering and chatting to friends just outside the pit leapt into the mêlée and within seconds were yelling with the rest of them. In an instant the small space erupted into pandemonium as if a fox had got into a hen coop. The price of the December contract began bouncing around like a ping-pong ball as the dealer executing the Sheik's order battled to buy at the lowest prices while the scalpers bought or sold for themselves on each upward or downward tick. The traders knew that the Sheik almost always moved the price of sterling when he came into the market. The trick for them was simply to guess which way he was going to move it. The pandemonium lasted for less than ten minutes before it died down as quickly as it had begun. Traders climbed out of the pit and wandered away, their breastpockets stuffed with dealing tickets. Others took up conversations they had broken off before the excitement, as if nothing had happened. And on the electronic screens overhead, sterling had crept up half a cent.

Yasuo Hamanaka was an unlikely hero. Watching him sing 'If I ruled the World' in the karaoke bars of Tokyo's Ginza red-light district during a night of heavy drinking, a few traders thought in retrospect that they should have guessed what was to come. Known as the Mad Jap or Mr Five Per Cent, he undoubtedly had a reputation. But that made him a puzzle to American and European dealers who never expected a Japanese trader to behave the way Hamanaka behaved. The received wisdom in the West was that Japanese traders are too much like cautious bureaucrats ever to put their heads above the parapet or make major waves in the markets. They have huge financial firepower, thanks to the oceans of cash still swirling around the Japanese economy despite years of severe recession, but they handle it like Vestal Virgins guarding the eternal flame. At first sight Hamanaka seemed like that too: he was quiet and usually self-effacing, with an unassuming charm and a penchant for grey suits. No one expected a guy who wanted to be a Big Swinging Dick, as they were called at Salomon Brothers, a Master of the Universe, a legend in his own time. No one suspected that he would perpetrate the biggest dealing disaster of all time, obliging Sumitomo to admit in 1996 to a loss of $2.6 billion.

He may have taken his employer by surprise too, although we may never know the truth of this. His dealing experience was extremely limited when he joined the metal trading desk of Sumitomo Corporation in 1987, so he was probably not expected to set the world alight. But in the copper market, the Sumitomo metals desk is a powerful place to be. With its copper producing, distributing and trading operations, Sumitomo is about the biggest force in the market right through from the point the ore is taken out of the ground to the point where the metal is sold to some manufacturer to be turned into something useful like wire or pipes. And Sumitomo is big – one of the largest trading conglomerates in the world. With that kind of financial clout behind him, an ambitious young dealer can do great things in the copper market.

What exactly sent him on his quest for glory is uncertain, although there are plenty of theories. One put forward by Sumitomo is that he inherited a bad trading position from his predecessor in the job and spent the next nine years trying to trade his way out of it. (This explanation tends to draw hoots of derision from other traders.) Another is that he was a megalomaniac who just wanted to control the market for the hell of it and didn't care about the consequences. Another conjecture is that he was operating with the knowledge of his superiors (strenuously denied by Sumitomo) and that his years of manipulating the market made the company billions before the strategy crashed.

Whatever the truth, Hamanaka *did* gain control of the copper market and treated it like a personal fiefdom for half a decade, until the summer of 1996 when it blew up in his face. During this period he never set out to be the kind of larger-than-life character that his counterpart in a Western company might have tried to be. He would, for instance, arrive late at social gatherings of copper traders and brokers, materializing so quietly many would not even know he was there until he drew them aside for a quiet chat about the market or their relationship with Sumitomo. This quietness was perhaps more effective than brashness in stamping his authority on the market. There was something mysterious, unpredictable and frankly creepy about him. Certainly, no one seriously questioned his power which he exercised with an unprecedented ruthlessness, earning him another nickname, the Hammer (a word play on his name), from the way he pounded anyone who tried to push the copper price against him.

He was obsessed with keeping the copper price high – higher, at any rate, than many people thought was warranted by the underlying demand from industrial users of the metal. He bought vast stocks of it, which were warehoused in Britain, the Far East and California. Sumitomo owned so much physical copper, indeed, that it had an effect similar to cornering the market. It was the first time anyone had seriously tried to do this with a commodity since the Hunt brothers, Texas oil billionaires, had made a celebrated attempt to corner silver in 1980. As with most such ventures they eventually ran out of cash before they had quite reached their goal and were ruined. Hamanaka did it a little more subtly. Instead of trying to buy all the copper there was, he simply made sure he owned so much of it that he could control the price of what was left on the open market. He bought so heavily on margin that he sometimes owned several times the amount of the official stock of physical copper held in the warehouses of the London Metal Exchange, the world's biggest copper market.

For years he made a great deal of money by using derivatives: all he had to do was buy futures and options contracts betting that the copper price would rise to a certain level in a few months time. Then he would manipulate the market to make sure that it did what he wanted. It was a strategy the nineteenth-century speculators of Chicago would have understood and applauded. Hamanaka's price support system also benefited Sumitomo's other activities of mining and supplying copper since, with a higher copper price, its profits from these operations were higher too. When anyone asked Hamanaka why the price was so high he would say that the Chinese were stockpiling the metal, a claim that was hard to refute since no one was ever sure quite what the Chinese were doing.

Sumitomo has since insisted that not even Hamanaka's immediate bosses knew about the thousands of allegedly clandestine deals he executed over nine years to carry out his often complex market manipulations. Hamanaka had the opportunity for fraud because as well as dealing, he controlled the settlements back office which monitors what the dealers do (the same lamentable arrangement as contributed to the Barings collapse). If he wanted to hide deals, therefore, he seems to have had the opportunity.

When he appeared in court in February 1997, then aged forty-nine, dressed in an open-necked shirt, casual jacket and green plastic sandals as if he had just strolled in from a beach bar, he dutifully admitted his guilt. He agreed to charges of fraud and forging documents that appeared to absolve the company itself from any blame.

Frankly, though, it strains credibility that he could have got away with manipulations for nearly a decade without detection by his employer, whose money he was losing so efficiently. And when you consider what he actually did, it becomes even less believable that no one at Sumitomo knew what was going on.

Hamanaka carried out his manipulation for so long by brilliantly exploiting the weaknesses and fault lines in the copper futures and options market. The LME is, like Lloyd's of London and other British financial institutions, a long standing market that has found it hard to adapt to the modern world. Unlike most futures exchanges it began as, above all, a spot market. With the growth of futures and options in the 1980s, however, it rapidly became predominantly a derivatives market, but the LME's structure did not change to cope with this.

While every other futures market in the world, for instance, requires players to put up variation margin at the end of each day to cover their losses or profits, the LME does not. Dealers can, in effect, run losses for months without ever having to acknowledge them. Players can give each other vast amounts of credit almost on a handshake, uncollateralized and therefore more freely available even to those who cannot really afford it, which makes the market more fragile when things go wrong. Although he could certainly afford it, Hamanaka tapped the banks for large amounts of credit, often using complex derivatives arrangements that disguised his loans as hedging deals and, incidentally, kept the loans off the banks' own balance sheets which they liked.

The world's leading metal exchange, in short, ran itself like a club. As long as a player makes enough friends in the club – an easy way of achieving which is to make sure that other members get plenty of lucrative business – he is welcome. He is certainly unlikely to be bothered by undue attention from the market regulators. The handsome commissions which Hamanaka spread liberally around the London market ensured his enthusiastic acceptance by the LME. And by using a network of brokers he gained the added advantage of disguising his market interventions.

The LME regulators took little notice of him. Even when a trader called David Threlkeld told them in 1991 that Hamanaka had asked him to illegally falsify a trade, the LME as well as the Savings and Investment Board (SIB) feebly accepted Hamanaka's bizarre explanation that the false trade had been necessary for a legitimate tax arrangement in Japan. 'The LME were pathetic,' says Threlkeld. 'They told me that when they met Hamanaka he had brought along his boss who assured them that there was nothing to worry about, so they'd let the matter drop. When I asked them how they knew the guy really *was* Hamanaka's boss and not some Sumitomo janitor pretending to be his boss, the blood drained from their faces. It hadn't occurred to them to check what Hamanaka said. The LME was a club, and once you were in no one asked any hard questions.'

As one trader put it, 'The LME made a business decision rather than a decision to regulate.' Too many members were making money out of Hamanaka. Threlkeld was one beneficiary of his business for a while, until the request to play along with a fake deal. In any case, Hamanaka's dealing was beginning to spook him. 'He knew exactly who had gone short of copper by selling call options expecting the price to fall. So he would force the price up, obliging them to cover their positions. Hamanaka could be vindictive. A good trader puts a squeeze on the market and then lets people out at a price. Not Hamanaka. If Metallgesellschaft drove the price down, he would drive it up again and keep it there so the Germans would suffer. He never had an exit plan, he never sold into the rally.'

Threlkeld believes Hamanaka launched a vendetta against him
after 1991, following which no one in London would deal with
him. At the same time, one of his former employees – Charlie
'Copper Fingers' Vincent – became a multimillionaire on the
strength of broking Sumitomo deals. He had parted company with
Threlkeld who disapproved of his close association with Hamanaka,
and set up his own company called Winchester Securities. In 1993,
he and his partner Ashley Levitt became the highest paid men in
Britain while they were still in their twenties. They eventually each
took £25 million out of the company and went into tax exile in
Monaco.

It's not hard to see where the money came from. In 1993,
Winchester and Sumitomo set up the biggest copper deal ever
seen, involving one million tons of copper – 10 per cent of the
annual global production. Codenamed RADR, the arrangement
included more than a hundred related futures and options trades
but the really remarkable thing about it was the fortune the
Japanese company lost as a result. The options were priced far
outside the prevailing market rates, giving Winchester, according
to some estimates, a profit of about $38 million at Sumitomo's
expense. Another broking company, Credit Lyonnais Rouse, which
acted as the conduit to the LME (since neither Sumitomo nor
Winchester were members) also creamed off millions from the
deal.

Hamanaka must have understood how much he was losing, so
what was he doing? The answer is that supporting the copper price
was more important to him than immediate profit. The RADR
deal seems to have been designed to give Sumitomo more firepower
in manipulating the copper market. Whether he gained personally
through payoffs from Winchester remains unclear.

But as the profits flooded in, many in London could hardly
believe their luck. The LME was benefiting from the fact that
Hamanaka had withdrawn almost all his business from New York's
Commodities Exchange, the other main copper market. The
intense rivalry between London and New York was another fault
line exploited by the Japanese trader. The problem with Comex,
from Hamanaka's point of view, was that it asked too many
questions that might have exposed him, such as how big were the

positions of the market's largest dealers – questions with which the LME never troubled him. The LME was already the larger market, but Sumitomo's business increased its lead over Comex as Hamanaka was certainly well aware. In 1995 the LME built its first warehouse in the US, at Long Beach, California, making it more attractive for US traders to buy on the London market since they could store their copper at home instead of in Europe. It was a direct challenge to Comex, which found within months that the stock of copper in its own warehouses was falling rapidly. 'It is as if they were trying to drive Comex out of business,' said a dealer. If this happened, no one doubted that the LME would be crowing with delight.

To add to the sense of gathering unreality, something very strange had happened to the copper price by 1995. It was in backwardation, meaning that the price of futures was lower that the spot price – an inversion of the normal order. The reason was that someone was buying huge amounts of spot copper and simply hoarding it, which made no commercial sense since the futures price was saying that copper was going to fall. The logical thing to do for anyone holding copper should have been to sell it immediately. Moreover, the market became so disjointed that copper on Comex, where it was becoming scarce, was often a great deal more expensive than on the LME. Yet still whoever was hoarding copper refused to sell on Comex.

In New York, bewilderment turned into frustration and then anger as it dawned on them what was happening. 'We were assured the copper was in safe, strong hands,' said Pat Thompson, head of the New York Mercantile Exchange which includes Comex. 'We figured this meant Sumitomo.' It seems, indeed, that the company owned almost all the copper in the new Long Beach warehouse but the LME appeared unconcerned by this market distortion.

Comex's complaints were at first dismissed as the sour grapes of a market that was facing oblivion, but by the end of the year it managed to convince the Commodities and Futures Trading commission, the US regulator, that the situation needed investigating. The CFTC sent senior people to London to goad the LME into action. The LME stalled, dragged its feet, whined and generally indulged in passive resistance until it was kicked into line by the Securities and Investments Board, the UK regulatory body. Only then, with the regulatory net at last beginning to close after nearly a decade, did Sumitomo deal with Hamanaka. In June 1996 the company sacked him, claiming that it had known nothing of his machinations.

And with brutal suddenness the copper market fell over a cliff.

At this point it is worth considering what other participants in the market – particularly those on the opposite end of Hamanaka's trading – were doing. Copper attracts an unusual amount of pure speculation because its price is unusually volatile. Some of the speculation is by companies, but a lot is by private individuals. Now, by and large, it is a lousy idea for private investors to dabble in the futures and options markets since about nine out of ten of them end up losing. But there are exceptions, one of which was Herbert Black, a Canadian scrap metal merchant. He won't say exactly how much he made when the market collapsed in the late summer of 1996 but it was probably in the region of $100 million. He admits it was the deal of a lifetime, the kind of one-off coup that could only come from an exceptional series of circumstances.

Black was a somewhat exceptional private speculator. 'I've traded on the LME since I was a kid,' he says, which gave him enough experience to recognize when something unusual was happening in the market. His Montreal based company, American Iron & Metal, was founded by his father and Black himself was already well-off when he made his windfall: he collects Georgian furniture and built himself a large Georgian-style house to accommodate it. He owns a Renoir and a Picasso and an extensive collection of Impressionists. He also used to collect Walt Disney cartoons, and once paid $20,000 for a guitar that had belonged to John Lennon. He had enough money, in other words, to speculate.

He and a number of other investors were convinced that Hamanaka had pushed the price so high that he could not possibly hold it there. Together with hedge fund managers such as George Soros and Julian Robertson, he began selling copper futures in the summer of 1995 to try to push the price down.

But they had misjudged Hamanaka who kept buying all the copper they pushed at him. By the end of the year when their short futures contracts expired, they were forced to buy back copper at a big loss because the price stubbornly refused to fall. Early in 1996 they tried again, and again Hamanaka fought them off. Then he started to squeeze the price upwards to frighten them away. At this point, Soros took his losses and dropped out of the game, but Black stayed in. He now went long because there were indications that the supply of copper was slowing down, which would push up the price naturally. But in the middle of May, everything changed once more. A strike at a Chilean copper mine ended and suddenly the copper price again looked too high, so Black started to sell. His broker patched him through by phone from Montreal to the LME so that he could hear what was going on in the pit. He sold 25,000 tonnes of copper which was immediately resold by a broker at a lower price. Black was amazed that the price had dropped since he could hear down the phone line that he was the only seller in the market. Guessing that Hamanaka's stranglehold was finally loosening, he sold another 25,000 tonnes, and the following Monday morning, as soon as the market opened, went short a further 50,000 tonnes.

He had, almost by accident, hit the market at exactly the right moment. His sales precipitated a copper price collapse of more than 12 per cent over the next few days. On 6 June, the day after Hamanaka had been sacked, an overhang of maturing option contracts on copper prompted the price to fall a further 15 per cent in the space of two hours. (Gold and silver fell in sympathy because many traders could only meet their margin requirements on copper by selling other assets.) The LME itself began to panic. It doubled the size of its variation margin calls to try to slow the pace of dealing – about the most heavy-handed intervention imaginable by a body that usually said it did not like to interfere with the market. Exchange officials admitted that they weren't sure what action to take because they knew so little about what was going on. Black, however, cleaned up in what must rank as one of the biggest killings in history by an individual punter outside of a casino.

The market collapse left the LME shell-shocked and Comex bitter. The LME's continued denials that it could have exposed Sumitomo any earlier infuriated the Americans. 'The LME says that if someone's manipulating the market, then that's just another market force which they need not be concerned with,' says Pat Thompson with thinly veiled contempt for the English laissez-faire approach. 'But the LME has to realize that when you're the central market place you have to have a surveillance mechanism to make sure you have reliable prices. When the LME makes decisions, does it ever consider the wider economic implications or simply the interests of its own members?' Under pressure from the SIB, the LME has said it will review some parts of its operation. Months after the affair, however, nothing had changed there.

Japan took an even more relaxed view. Since Hamanaka's dealing had taken place in a market outside Japan, the Japanese authorities said they had no reason or authority to investigate what had gone wrong or punish to the wrongdoers. Hamanaka himself vanished. There were press reports that he had fled from his unpretentious Tokyo home to a safe-house owned by Sumitomo. Finally, towards the end of 1996 when he was arrested and charged with carrying out unauthorized trading, it emerged that he had remained at home all along, living for four months with the curtains closed.

Is it possible that Sumitomo knew nothing of what Hamanaka had been doing in its name for most of a decade? To most copper traders, the answer is no. While the board and top management may have been in genuine ignorance, many find it impossible to believe that Hamanaka's immediate bosses did not know about the 3,000-odd unauthorized deals the company says he executed. For example, he opened several brokers accounts which Sumitomo says were unauthorized but which Merrill Lynch, where one of the accounts was held, says were fully authorized by senior Sumitomo executives. Even with control of the back office and the unstinting loyalty of the settlements clerks, it is hard to believe that someone in Sumitomo would not have wondered about the vast inflows and outflows of cash related to Hamanaka's trading.

Sumitomo's incentive to ask hard questions was probably somewhat blunted by the extra profits that Hamanaka's trading produced over the years. The company has never stated how much it made out of copper dealing before the final crash, and in the broadest sense this is probably impossible to know anyway. A high copper price would have produced extra profits all through Sumitomo's business in a way probably too complex to measure.

We will probably never know exactly what went wrong inside Sumitomo for all that time. So far, the company has shown no inclination to give a detailed explanation of how it blundered, and the record of openness in such things in Japan is not encouraging. It looks as though Hamanaka will have to carry all the blame by himself.

Yra Harris remembers Black Monday, 27 October 1987 – the world's first brush with a derivatives-induced cataclysm – as something akin to a funeral wake on the floor of the Merc. While the press and politicians were swept on a wave of hysteria as stock markets around the world collapsed, the traders themselves seemed to shrink into a huddle of fear. Their usual exuberance vanished, the atmosphere was sombre. 'After the first roar of trading when the market opened in the morning it was quite quiet. It was like a war zone: there were a lot of bodies around, metaphorically speaking. There was no happiness.'

Many firms simply did not dare join in the mêlée, but as one of the better capitalized locals Harris was asked by the Merc to trade in the S&P 500 stock futures pit to help keep the market functioning during the crisis. 'There was a very big volume of trading and some people were making a lot of money but there was no thrill to it. It was eerie: you thought you were witnessing a cataclysmic event, but at the same time you weren't sure what you were witnessing. You stood there thinking, "As I'm making all this money, are people out there jumping out of windows?" Then you went home and heard about the bankruptcies and you didn't feel good.'

The path to this unhappy juncture began ten years earlier with what Leo Melamed regards as the big breakthrough in financial futures markets: the introduction of the Eurodollar contract. This was a futures contract enabling the market to deal in the interest rates of dollars which existed outside the United States. Eurodollars are the currency of international trade and, thanks to technical banking regulations, they have slightly different rates of interest from domestic US dollars. But when it came to futures contracts, there was a problem with Eurodollar interest rates. 'The thing is,' says Melamed with a sly smile, 'they don't really exist.' What the contract bought and sold was a rate of interest and you cannot deliver a rate of interest. It is incorporeal, non-physical, it isn't palpably there in the way that Treasury bonds or commodities are there. The breakthrough for the futures market, therefore, was the discovery that it could trade futures in something that more closely resembled the Chesire Cat than a pork belly.

Until then the only thing according to US law that distinguished futures trading from pure gambling was the assumption that the seller of a contract actually intended to deliver the wheat or corn that underlay it. With the Eurodollar contract, however, the Merc definitively abandoned this idea. Instead, counterparties simply settled up their profits or losses in cash. If your Eurodollar futures went up in value after you bought them, your counterparty paid you the profit amount in cash; if they went down, you paid him – what was known in the nineteenth century as 'settlement for differences'. It meant that the futures markets had come full circle to the kind of futures contracts that had helped to cause the tulip mania in seventeenth-century Holland.

Once the markets had jettisoned the idea of physical delivery, all kinds of innovation was possible in contracts for things that had no material existence. What the markets had discovered was that anything is tradable as long as enough people think it is worth something. If you go to an exchange in Michigan, for instance, you can speculate on something as intangible as the sentiment of US consumers. The most important invention, however, was futures based on equity market indexes such as the Standard & Poor's 500, the FTSE-100 and the Nikkei 225. A market index is not a physical thing but a notional basket of shares that is meant to represent the market as a whole. The value of the contract is dictated by the value of the underlying shares in the basket. If the shares rise, so does the index futures contract; if they fall, it falls too. But no one expects, or even wants, a counterparty actually to deliver a basket of 500 different stocks at the expiry of an S&P futures contract. All they want is the profit in cash between what they bought and what they sold the contract for.

The stock indexes are an instant and easy way to hedge against stock market movements. If an investor thinks the market might fall, instead of selling his entire share portfolio which would be cumbersome and costly, he can simply sell some stock index futures short. Unfortunately, the ability to buy up or sell off the market at a stroke with this brilliant invention can produce spectacularly unsettling consequences.

The biggest – and one of the first – tests of the derivatives exchanges came on Black Monday. Without getting ensnared in the debate about the underlying economic causes of the crash, suffice it to say that it took most people by surprise and scared the hell out of everyone. Almost without warning, sellers stampeded into the market, flattening everything in their path. In Britain shares fell 12 per cent, in Japan 15 per cent, in Australia nearly 25 per cent. In the US the Dow Jones Industrial Average dropped 22.6 per cent which was nearly twice the fall on 26 October 1929, the first day of the century's most famous crash. More than $500 billion – roughly the same as the gross national product of France – was wiped off the value of US share prices.

By the end of the day's trading, the players who had held long positions owed the shorts $2.5 billion (compared with $120 million on an average day). The question for the Merc was would the longs pay up? If they did not, the market's clearing system would go bust. If it went bust, or even if one major institution failed to pay his margin calls, there was likely to be a crisis of confidence leading to financial gridlock where no one would honour their obligations for fear that no one else would either. It would also mean that the Merc would be unable to open the following morning which would cause, in Melamed's words, a 'dysfunction in the US market system', exacerbating the panic that had driven down share prices on Black Monday.

For the whole of that Monday night Melamed, who was then chairman of the Merc, and several lieutenants sat biting their nails in the market's clearing house. Gains and losses of hundreds of millions of dollars washed smoothly through the system until the inevitable hiccup: Morgan Stanley had lost $1 billion and had not paid up. It wasn't that Morgan Stanley refused to do so but that the interbank payment system had stalled. The investment bank's money had not yet made it through to Continental Illinois, its clearing bank in Chicago responsible for making its payments to the Merc. Melamed and his men called the Fed for help and then called Morgan Stanley's president, Richard Fisher. Neither could do anything about the problem. By 7.00 a.m. Melamed was getting desperate and called the Continental official in charge of Morgan Stanley's account. She could not help either – if the money had not come in, she could not pay anything out, period. She refused even to mention Morgan Stanley by name because of confidentiality rules governing client's accounts, so Melamed had to assume they were talking about the same customer. It was only the lucky coincidence of Continental's chairman, Tom Theobald, walking into her office in the middle of this conversation and giving her permission to pay Morgan Stanley's money on credit that saved the situation.

Had the money not come through, the Merc would almost certainly have closed. One of the great attractions of dealing on an exchange is that it guarantees that every trade will be settled, taking away the credit risk from the players in the market by standing liable if one side of a trade fails to pay up. But a shortfall the size of Morgan Stanley's would have bankrupted it.

Nine years after that near disaster another exchange nearly went belly up when Nick Leeson ran up $1 billion deficit for Barings Bank. With fewer reserves than the Merc ever had, the Singapore International Monetary Exchange reacted to the crisis by doubling the margin it required from firms with open positions on the exchange. But Merrill Lynch and other US firms did not see why their money should be used to shore up Simex's finances and threatened to withhold their margin payments. If they had done so, Simex would not have been able to clear the previous day's trades and might not have opened the following day, with the danger that the crisis might have deepened and spread to other markets. Fortunately, Merrill and the other banks paid up but it would be a mistake to assume that all banks will always do so in all circumstances. 'Markets,' Melamed observes, 'are not built for panics.'

Tuesday 20 October 1987, the second day of the crash, brought another problem when the anticipated avalanche of selling opened up a gulf between New York and Chicago. By lunchtime, the New

York market was in such disarray that it warned Chicago it might have to close. This terrified the futures traders because they did not want to have to face the full brunt of the selling on their own. So Chicago called a halt until New York made up its mind. Melamed recalls that when he walked into the bedlam of the trading pits to make this announcement the traders froze on the spot and the floor fell instantly silent. For many of them it was a make or break day. By the end of it, some traders were bust while others were millionaires but until the trading was finished no one was safe, and New York's decision would make all the difference. After fifteen minutes' deliberation, New York decided to remain open and Chicago followed suit. The bedlam resumed and the crash continued.

Once it was all over, however, the New York traders – who felt they had been sandbagged by Chicago – furiously accused futures traders of causing the crash. Until then people had tended to regard the New York stock market and the Chicago futures markets as separate. Now it was clear that they were closely linked, like Siamese twins who couldn't stand each other's company. Worse than that, the Chicago futures markets seemed to be the dominant partner because it had made most of the running on 19 October. Its trading volume was higher than the New York stock market's and it had led the price fall. To most people this seemed unnatural, an inversion of the proper order of things. Surely derivative markets were the junior partner; they should follow, or at best level peg, their underlying markets. If they led, was this not the tail wagging the dog?

The argument against futures went like this. There was a moderate downward pressure on prices on Black Monday which New York could easily have handled had it not been for the maniacs, speculators and gamblers in the futures markets. These had seen what was going on and had indulged in a disgraceful, self-interested and thoroughly unprincipled bout of arbitrage. Arbitrage is supposed to be a risk free activity in which a trader, seeing that the same stock or bond is priced differently in two different markets, buys in the cheaper one and sells immediately in the more expensive one. In the chaos of the crash, price discrepancies had emerged between stock prices in New York and the S&P stock index contract traded on the Chicago Merc. Moreover, the critics said, when the market began to fall institutional investors had done 'programme trades' – the same trades that so terrified Yra Harris – in which their computers had automatically hedged their share-holdings by selling vast quantities of stock index futures, thus driving down the market further than it should have gone. If index futures had not existed, this would not have happened.

A slew of official reports that came out after the crash proved that most of this was nonsense. There was, for instance, no real evidence that arbitrageurs had been buying futures in Chicago and selling shares in New York. For much of the day it wasn't actually possible to deal in many shares in New York which was not geared to cope with such a tidal wave of trading. Its computers kept breaking down and the traders found it hard to know what prices to quote, so they stopped quoting prices. In desperation, sellers turned to the more efficient markets in Chicago where they could at least sell futures contracts as a hedge. Chicago had appeared to lead the collapse simply because it was the only one working reasonably efficiently.

The question underlying this argument is fundamental: do derivatives create more volatility, and therefore instability, in the markets? Common sense suggests that they probably do – after all, since the derivatives markets are the preserve of speculators it seems logical that they might be more prone to volatile lunges in prices. But there is actually very little evidence that this is so. In fact, most of the evidence suggests that since the invention of the futures and options markets share prices in the world's main stock markets have been slightly more stable than before. This is probably because derivatives make the pricing of shares more efficient, so that in normal times they are actually less prone to speculative ups and downs.

In normal times. But when the going gets tough, the evidence is not so clear. The Brady commission, set up by the US government after Black Monday to investigate what had happened, decided that the Chicago markets had indeed encouraged the fall. This isn't very surprising. When a stock market starts to collapse, a large institutional investor is bound to have severe problems off-loading several billion dollars or pounds worth of shares. It is expensive in brokers' fees and hugely complicated with a portfolio of many different shares. It is far easier, quicker and cheaper to hedge the portfolio by selling large amounts of index futures or options. The ease and speed of selling futures will move the market faster than it would probably have moved if futures did not exist, simply because it would take longer to sell the individual shares. This is what happened on Black Monday and will undoubtedly happen in future stock market crashes.

The problem with that is the panic it creates. Investors cope far better with gentle market declines than sudden ones. A swift and extensive drop in prices causes fear. Fear leads to panic which can cause further declines, and so on. Before you know it, the market's in free fall.

To the question, therefore, can derivatives turn a market decline into a crash, the answer is yes.

The Merc's invention of currency futures set off a kind of arms race between it and the Chicago Board of Trade. Realizing that it was in danger of being left behind in the new world of financial futures, the CBOT invented the first interest rate futures contract based on mortgage bonds. It also set up a separate options market. The Merc responded with a contract based on Treasury bills; the CBOT set up a Treasury bond contract. And so on. The rivalry continued as the turnover in the new contracts on both exchanges grew exponentially, confirming Chicago as the unchallenged capital of exchange traded derivatives. Other cities, such as New York, set up their own markets and tried to compete but experience has shown that once an exchange has established itself, it is virtually impossible for rival markets to steal its business. By the middle of 1996 around two million contracts a day were traded on the Chicago exchanges. Of the $16.4 trillion worth of outstanding contracts on exchanges all over the whole world, Chicago alone accounted for about $6.5 trillion.

It took a decade before the rest of the world was willing to consider the idea of financial futures exchanges after Chicago's breakthrough. When Melamed first toured Europe to drum up support for his new currency futures, he spoke to almost empty meeting rooms. Throughout most of the 1970s, the Bank of

England's view was that the City needed nothing to do with the idea. Englishmen who went to view the bedlam in the Chicago markets concluded that it was all too unEnglish and uncouth to succeed in London. Only when Chicago's outrageous success could no longer be ignored did London start organizing its own exchange in part to forestall challengers from elsewhere in Europe.

When the London International Financial Futures Exchange (Liffe, pronounced life) finally opened in 1982 in the Guardian Royal Exchange Building, opposite the Bank of England, it had a different approach to that of Chicago. Instead of a crowd of locals in the trading pits, London preferred to have mostly institutions – mainly banks and other trading houses – as members. This, Liffe claimed, was to encourage less speculation and more underlying business. In Chicago they saw it merely as yet another manifestation of the British class system which refused to allow on the trading floor the kind of working-class lad-made-good who came to the Merc to make his fortune.

Liffe swiftly became the most important futures exchange in Europe, largely thanks to London's overall financial importance. It still accounts, for instance, for about 80 per cent of trading in German bond futures, much to the annoyance of the German authorities, who only got around to launching their own futures exchange in 1990. In 1997 Liffe even appeared to be overtaking the Merc in trading volume.

Exchanges began opening everywhere – there are now nearly sixty all over the world. As the rest of the world caught up with Chicago's innovations, the Windy City's share of world futures and options turnover slid from 80 per cent in the mid-1980s to about half that amount in the mid-90s. The over-all level of business everywhere, however, just kept growing.

By the mid-90s business has grown particularly fast in emerging markets. Developing countries with any pretensions to economic sophistication have been feverishly opening exchanges rather the way poor countries set up national airlines in the 1960s as a symbol of progress and national pride. Some, like the eleven exchanges which have sprouted like mushrooms in China, look like a severe case of overkill and may not survive. Others are proving hugely successful. The largest exchange outside the US and Europe is the

Bolsa de Mercadorias & Futuros in São Paolo which counts as about the fifth biggest in the world in terms of turnover. For many countries there is a logic to setting up an exchange. In a place where the local stock exchange may be somewhat primitive, where currency controls may still exist, where there may be problems for foreigners wanting to repatriate profits, there is also likely to be a serious resistance among outsiders to invest. Putting money into these economies and taking it out is often difficult, time consuming and expensive, and the markets may be unpredictably volatile. The liquidity may also be so bad that when an investor wants to sell there are no buyers in sight. Not so with a derivatives exchange. Countries like Malaysia, Taiwan and Korea want an exchange to give foreigners a cheaper, simpler and quicker way to invest money in the country. And players in derivatives markets positively welcome the extra volatility. It even gives them a way to hedge any investments in underlying shares or bonds, too. By dealing on margin in futures a foreign fund can make a substantial investment without having to commit large sums and with the reasonable confidence that the greater liquidity of a futures market will make it easier to withdraw money when necessary.

But that is the problem. Just as it is easy for overseas investors to put money into a country through a derivatives exchange, it is just as easy to withdraw it. The Mexican stock market collapse in 1995 triggered a panic that dragged down many other emerging markets which had no relation whatsoever with Mexico except in the minds of investors. The more money that goes into these countries through their futures exchanges, the more is likely to flow out again by the same route at a moment's notice. A wholesale flight of foreign capital will cause problems not only for the countries themselves as they watch their markets evaporate, but for the foreign investors who may suddenly find themselves caught up in a crash of their own making. In that case, liquidity would vanish far faster than in the larger US and European exchanges, prices would fall like the proverbial stone. The ability of many of the newer exchanges to cope in such circumstances is questionable: some would be likely to go bankrupt in the face of an avalanche of defaults. As always, derivatives are a double edged sword.

In Asia the exchanges are still battling for supremacy. The Japanese, ever leery of financial freedom, would not allow futures trading for years. Exchanges only appeared in Tokyo and Osaka in the 1990s. In the meantime, Singapore (with help from the Merc) had carved out a niche in Japanese stock and bond index trading, leading to the battle between it and Osaka to attract business, which helped Nick Leeson carry out his fraud at Barings. Meanwhile, Australia has built up a successful financial futures exchange in Sydney (which developed out of an older institution pungently known as the Sydney Greasy Wool Futures Exchange) dealing in US Treasury bonds and Eurodollars as well as the Australian dollar.

It is too early to guess the outcome of the battle for supremacy between the exchanges in the Far East. Given the size of the area, there is probably room for at least two large markets but the experience of America and Europe suggests that in each time zone market users prefer to concentrate their business in a small number of highly liquid markets. In the not too distant future, however, the idea of an exchange with traders bunched together in the hubbub of a pit may be outdated. Chicago and several other exchanges around the world are experimenting with electronic screen based dealing systems which would do away with the old open outcry method altogether. Electronic dealing would, in theory, be cheaper and faster. 'It has to happen,' says Melamed. 'Information travels faster electronically. When Chrysler recently split its stock the news didn't come to our trading pit for twenty minutes – long after the New York Stock Exchange knew about it. Twenty minutes is six eternities in trading. The pit can't compete with screens. Ten years from now open outcry won't exist.'

But the exchanges themselves will go on. However risky the markets, speculators and hedgers like to have the comfort of knowing that an exchange guarantees the settlement of their trade, just as when you win at a casino you are more likely to get your money than if you make a bet on a street corner with a complete stranger. Betting with strangers on street corners is more akin to dealing in derivatives off the exchanges. This is not a world that private investors or speculators would ever want to visit. It is undoubtedly the weirdest, most complex and most dangerous financial space ever invented, a kind of maze of mirrors in which reality gets bent and distorted to the point where no one is quite sure where they are. It is the over-the-counter market where most of the derivatives business in the world gets done.

CHAPTER 4

THE NERDS MEET WALL STREET

... The different branches of Arithmetic – Ambition,
Distraction, Uglification and Derision.

Alice in Wonderland

It was with much trepidation that a young man called Steven
Sykes turned up for his first day at work at a small Wall Street
investment bank early in 1992. Everything was new and strange
and Sykes had to admit that the place made him feel like a nerd.
He was an academic from a Mid-Western university, a professional
mathematician who was used to wearing tweed jackets with a row
of pens in the breast pocket, knitted ties and checked shirts. His
hair was, for Wall Street, unfashionably long. He came into the
office at eight o'clock – a time he would often have been still asleep
in his old life – and found the place already crowded. It was clear
people had been there for some time. The trading room smelled
faintly of coffee and muffins. He was shown by a friendly but
uninformative junior employee to a desk at one side of the trading
floor, away from the windows, and he was left there. For two days
he sat in his corner virtually ignored. Uncertain what to do, he did
nothing in particular except try with little success to strike up
conversations with his new colleagues. He thought this enforced
inactivity strange since the salary the bank was paying him seemed
to him a stellar sum – roughly three times what he was used to
getting as an academic. The chance to make some real money was,

after all, the reason he had taken this job. Yet the bank showed no particular hurry to get their money's worth out of him.

On the morning of the third day he felt like standing on his desk and shouting to get some attention but, of course, being an academic he did no such thing. He rang the personnel office but was told by an unhelpful assistant that the person who would know about him was away. Occasionally people on the dealing floor would wander over and chat to him but whenever he asked them what he should be doing they muttered vaguely and wandered away again. Finally the man in charge turned up in his glass office at one end of the room for the first time since Steven's arrival, and so Sykes went to introduce himself. The man looked at him expressionlessly and said, 'Who?'

'Steve Sykes.'

'So why are you here, Steve?'

'I thought you could tell me that,' Sykes said, growing bewildered.

The boss's face remained blank. 'I have no idea.' Reaching for his phone, he made a call and a minute later two large men walked in and sat down. The boss introduced them as dealers.

'This man says he has a job here. Anyone know anything about it?' he asked them.

The dealers looked at each other and solemnly shook their heads.

Sykes felt a tingle of panic. He explained that he had left his university job and moved to New York to work for the bank. Surely they were expecting him. Somewhere in his luggage he had a letter from the bank offering him the job.

'I think we'd know if we'd given you a job,' the boss told him. 'I can't understand how you've been allowed into the office like this. Stay where you are while I call a security guard to escort you out of the building.' The man reached for his phone.

'Wait a minute!' shouted Sykes. He wasn't just going to be dumped jobless on a Manhattan sidewalk without putting up a fight. He launched into a speech about how he had given up his old job to come here, how irresponsible they would be to kick him out when he had been promised a salary, how appalled he was at this treatment and how he would have to get legal advice – and so on. About halfway through he noticed that they were not hearing him with the seriousness which the situation seemed to merit. The two dealers, in fact, were snickering. The boss was fiddling with a pen and reading some document on his desk. As he finished, a broad smile spread across the boss's face. All three men burst out laughing. Sykes could feel what seemed like most of the blood in his body rush to his face. He turned to storm out of the door and noticed that most of the dealers at desks near the glass walls of the office were watching although they could not hear. Presumably they knew exactly what was going on because most of them were grinning like hyenas.

If he had got out of the office Sykes would probably have carried straight on to the Mid-West but he was stopped by one of the dealers who blocked his way. It took them forty-five minutes to pacify him. Welcome to Wall Street.

He had just gone through a ritual practised arbitrarily on new arrivals in the bank's dealing department for no particular reason other than the pleasure of watching a new victim writhe in discomfort. Who cared if their feelings were hurt. Dealers weren't supposed to have feelings. Sykes was told later that the two days he had waited before taking action was relatively short, which was good. One benighted recruit had spent two weeks drifting like a lost soul before quietly resigning and disappearing back to wherever he had come from. No one tried to stop him and no one regretted the way he had been treated. They figured that if he didn't have the initiative to sort his situation out sooner they must have made a mistake in hiring him.

But the sting in the tale of this story is that Sykes had the last laugh. Once he had calmed down he settled quickly into his surroundings. The dealing room was not large since the bank itself was not particularly big, and it had been slow in locking on to the new craze for derivatives. It was still a bond and equity trading operation on classic 1980s lines. Each dealer had a list of securities which he alone in the dealing room traded with banks, investment funds and other professionals. He had sole responsibility for making them cough up money for the firm. As the chief risktaker and moneymaker he was top of the dealing food chain with entitlements to eat anything beneath him. The main fodder were salesmen whose position between the traders and their customers in the outside world gave them split personalities: they were supposed to get the best prices for the client but enable the bank to make money out of him too. The interests of trader and salesman were inevitably in frequent conflict.

The bank had somewhat belatedly realized that it was being left behind in the derivatives market and was trying to catch up. It didn't take Sykes long to discover that the bank didn't really know what to do with a mathematician. Why had he been hired? To do the sort of calculations other people couldn't do. What were these calculations? His new colleagues weren't quite sure yet. The firm was starting up a mortgage bond operation but instead of hiring experienced and expensive talent away from some other bank they had decided to develop their own talent more cheaply. This meant switching dealers from other areas and bringing in novices like Sykes.

He was put to work with two other people – the two who had sniggered at him in the boss's office – both of whom were former bond dealers, which meant they were used to eating anyone in their path. Their problem, however, was that they did not see how the world was changing. They regarded Sykes, at first, as something akin to a Martian. They laughed at his clothes and made him feel like a country hick with straw still in his hair. They laughed at his lack of knowledge about the financial markets. They laughed at his ignorance about dealing. He had never in his life heard people with such loud voices. He had never met anyone before who could drink so much in the evening and still get out of bed at 6.30 a.m. to go to work. He felt completely out of his depth.

But then a strange thing happened. As he learned about derivatives in their more complex forms he discovered that within a few weeks he understood more about them than the bond traders did. The calculations required to work out the maturities and values of mortgage bonds can become extremely complex. It requires enormous statistical data on such things as how the average mortgage holder reacts when interest rates rise or fall; it requires calculus and a knowledge of Brownian motion and host of skills with which the average bond salesman is not equipped.

It wasn't long before it dawned on Sykes that his two noisy

colleagues were more out of their depth in these complexities than he was. They were used to the simplicity of ordinary bonds which were IOUs on corporate or government debt that could be bought and sold at a discount to the 'face value' of the loan, which would be repaid when the bond matured. Most bonds had fixed maturities and paid fixed rates of interest (known as the 'coupon'). Their behaviour in specific market conditions was well known. They were relatively predictable, familiar, easy to live with. The aim of a bond trader was simply to buy low and sell high, and the mental processes involved were not hugely different from buying and selling apples in a market. But now the bond traders were being asked to deal in complex derivative securities, and securities that were parts of securities, which seemed more like trying to buy and sell shadows. To Sykes, the bond traders seemed like a couple of cavemen who had been suddenly presented with a car and told to drive it. They walked around scratching their heads and grunting. They complained and made excuses. They never quite got the hang of the newfangled inventions. Eventually, overwhelmed by evolution, they left.

Sykes spent his early months in his new job tinkering all day with long mathematical formulae, much as he had done at university in the Mid-West, but this time there was a hard practical application for all his ingenuity. He would invent ways in which a customer could buy an instrument that paid him a 10 per cent coupon when ordinary bonds were paying 6 per cent, or borrow money at 3 per cent when bank lending rates were at 8 per cent. They were packed with options and futures and swaps, and they behaved quite unlike any financial instruments anyone had ever seen before. They bore as much resemblance to ordinary fixed rate bonds as Concord does to a glider.

Although Sykes didn't know it at first, he was part of a trend that changed the dealing rooms in London and New York and turned trading into something it had never been before. He was one of a new breed of mathematics experts colloquially known in the financial markets as 'quants' (as in quantitative analysts) or 'rocket scientists' who were sucked into the business by the need for a greater understanding of higher maths. Few so-called rocket scientist had literally been involved with rockets – although a few were – but the term reflected the fact that a lot of the maths required in constructing complex derivatives derived from the sort of physics used in rocket science. (For instance, a mathematical technique commonly used in derivatives called the Monte Carlo simulation – a method of altering variables in an equation to produce a required answer – was developed in the early 1940s by the Manhattan Project team working to produce the US nuclear bomb. Not quite rockets, but serious science.) The banks plundered the universities, the defence research companies, the armed forces, the computer industry – anywhere that employed anyone with the right training. They took on engineers, physicists, and pure mathematicians at salaries such people could not have got anywhere else. The demand for them became so intense that mathematics professors in Britain were heard to mutter that the best maths research had moved from the universities to the banks. The quants were the heirs of Black and Scholes, and they transformed the financial markets.

Within a year of joining his bank, Sykes found that the food chain in his part of the dealing room had turned upside down. With his superior knowledge, he moved to the top, with rights to eat all beneath him. Once the two loud bond dealers had left he was given a free hand to recruit replacements, so he brought in people like himself. With their specialized knowledge and the vast fees they charged their clients, the new derivatives team quickly came to regard itself as the highest stage of evolution in the dealing culture. The greatest failure for a derivatives dealer was to be thrown out into the aboriginal ranks of government bond traders who were regarded by Sykes and his team as closely related to baboons. As his group expanded rapidly it had a profound effect on the working conditions at the bank. The noise level fell several decibels in the dealing room, where the atmosphere changed from something akin to a street brawl to something more like a college library. Most of the new recruits were in their twenties and early thirties, as intensely materialistic as the old-style bond traders and, if anything, harder working. Twelve hour days were normal. But compared to the old lags on the bond desks, they were quieter, more earnest, lower key. They were not, in general, given to the extravagantly macho and egotistical behaviour that characterized dealers in some of the older markets. The quants didn't shout at each other and throw tantrums. Instead of bellowing prices across the dealing floor they communicated by phone and computer screen. Computers dominated their lives because without them they could not have done the complex calculations that enabled them to invent financial instruments of such unprecedented complexity.

As he gained control of the bank's newly born derivatives operation, Sykes watched himself change too. He got a haircut, the tweedy university clothes were ditched for Armani suits as he got used to spending his new-found wealth. When once he wouldn't have dreamed of paying more than $12 for a tie, he now bought silk designer ties for $50 at Barneys. He made the happy discovery that since he and his colleagues had the money but not the time to go shopping, the shops came to them. He could order shirts and suits at his desk without missing a minute of work: people would be measuring his arm length or inside leg as he constructed derivatives models on his computer. He perfected a technique of standing sideways to his desk with jacket off and feet apart as the clothes salesmen fussed around him with their tapemeasures. While they measured his left arm held stiffly out at right angles to his body, he could use his right hand to type on his keyboard or answer the phone. Food would also be delivered in whatever style or quantity he ordered. If the derivatives team stayed late working on an idea, it would order up to the dealing room a colosally expensive sushi dinner for everyone and let the bank pay. 'Someone said fish was good for the brain so we decided we'd get an edge on the competition by eating a lot of it,' said Sykes. 'Maybe it worked because we made a lot of money.' Sykes's beer consumption was replaced by a taste for red wine and champagne. He rented a two-bedroom apartment in Soho for a sum that made his stomach flutter, but he was proud to be able to afford it. Within eight months of arriving in New York he had lost all the trappings of academe other than his ability to do complex maths. Occasionally he had pangs of nostalgia for the days when he could get out of bed at 9.00 a.m. without feeling he had missed half the day, but then he looked at his pay cheque and realized that getting up at

6.00 a.m. was worth it. Wall Street swallowed him, and many others like him, whole.

The quants were crucial to the development of a whole new species of financial instrument: over-the-counter derivatives. The OTC market is not only several times bigger than all the exchange traded derivatives put together, it is a great deal more secretive. Every trade on the exchanges is visible and becomes a matter of public record within minutes of being executed. By contrast, the OTC market is to derivatives what the dark side is to the moon, and quants like Sykes made sure it stayed that way.

In the space of a mere fifteen years OTC derivatives grew from a standing start to a value of around $47 trillion in 1995, making it by far the world's largest financial market. In fact, no one is certain of exactly how large it is because there is no sure way of counting the number or value of all OTC derivative contracts. There are many other elusive things about this market, too. The name, over the counter, for instance, does not mean standardized contracts sold like aspirins over a store counter. It means exactly the opposite: specially tailored, bespoke derivatives cut to suit each customer. It is Saville Row to the futures exchanges' Oxford Street.

It began with the swaps market which was put on the map, appropriately enough, by the World Bank. Eugene Rotberg, the bank's genial treasurer, describes it as a matter of expediency to get round some very particular funding problems. Rotberg was responsible for borrowing about $8 billion a year in various currencies to fund the bank's lending to developing countries. Naturally, he was always looking for the cheapest interest rates at which to borrow, and in 1981 those happened to be in the Swiss franc and the Deutsch mark. 'The trouble was,' says Rotberg, 'that there came a point when we had borrowed so much in these currencies that we were in danger of saturating the market. But the rates were so low it was too good an opportunity to miss. I was talking to some people at Salomon Brothers about this one day when they said that one of their clients had large Swiss franc and Deutsch mark loans it no longer wanted but could not get rid of.'

The client was IBM which had taken out the loans some time earlier and then seen both currencies depreciate against the dollar.

In dollar terms, the loans were now worth much more than IBM had originally paid for them. If it could sell them, it would stand to make a handsome profit – except that there existed no market mechanism for selling them. 'I talked to IBM and we agreed that it would be silly if we couldn't do something about this,' says Rotberg. So the World Bank took out a dollar loan and swapped it for IBM's loans. IBM would pay the principal and interest on the dollar loan to the World Bank; the World Bank would pay the principal and interest on the Swiss franc and Deutsch mark loans to IBM. IBM got rid of its loans at a profit, while the World Bank got the foreign borrowing it wanted without upsetting the central banks of Switzerland and Germany. Although it wasn't the very first swap ever done, with two such blue-chip names involved the rest of the financial world sat up and took notice.

From there the market took off like a ballistic missile. Even if the details are fiddly, the concept is almost as simple as swapping sweets in a school playground. Each counterparty wants what the other has, so they do an exchange. A company that could not raise a fixed rate loan, perhaps because it was not a good enough credit risk, could raise floating rate money and swap it for another company's fixed rate loan. The other company, which had raised the fixed rate loan because it was cheaper than a floating rate one, might actually want floating rate money so that, perhaps, the three monthly interest payments would coincide with three monthly receipts from one of its businesses. In the financial markets it meant that, at a stroke, borrowers were liberated from their own capital markets by the ability to exchange their loans for ones at different rates of interest and different currencies with some company on the other side of the world. Everyone gained.

It took very little time for companies to see the advantages of such an international, unregulated and liquid market. International trade was growing rapidly and large companies were expanding their operations globally. If you wanted to build a factory on the other side of the world (as many Western businesses were doing in the Far East to cut down their manufacturing costs) you could borrow in your home market and swap the proceeds into the currency you wanted at the interest rate you wanted. And if the factory produced a particularly large income stream in a currency you did *not* want, you could swap that into a currency you did want. Applying capital at the right cost, in the right place at the right time had never before been so easy.

Or, rather, it should have been easy. The problem with the early swaps market was that two companies on opposite sides of the globe might have swappable loans but not know about each other. There was no exchange to go to, no efficient way for two compatible counterparties to find each other and get together in a deal.

Until the banks realized what the swaps market could do for them.

Soon after the World Bank–IBM deal, a few bankers began to realize that swaps could be big, lucrative business – the biggest poker game in town. Desperate not to be left out, they descended on the swaps market with dollar signs in their eyes. They didn't just want to join in, they wanted to take over the game, which they did in the space of about three years. At first they acted simply as marriage brokers, as Salomon had done for Rotberg and IBM. But they quickly saw that there was more money to be made by taking one side of the swap themselves. This also made things easier for companies. Instead of having to wait until some other corporate appeared with appropriate loans or currencies to exchange, a company could simply do the swap with a bank. The bank would then hedge its side of the swap with someone else – probably another bank. And so on.

This was convenient for everyone, but it was also a heaven-sent opportunity for the commercial banks which were grappling with the awkward problem of having lost billions of dollars in loans to Latin America. No one actually knew how much might eventually be lost, but it was clear that big borrowers, such as Brazil, Argentina and Mexico, had no intention of paying back their monster-sized loans when they were supposed to. This came as a shock to the world's bankers who had not long before that been congratulating each other on the incredibly efficient way they had recycled the billions of petrodollars that had accumulated in the Middle East and other oil producing areas during the 1970s. Now they realized that their incredible efficiency had consisted in pouring the money into a black hole, and they were suffering losses on an uprecedented scale. The banking industry looked over the precipice and shuddered to its foundations. Bankers started to look elsewhere for more reliable borrowers and found blue-chip multinationals such as IBM and BP. But the intense competition to lend to them drove lending rates so low that it became uneconomic for many banks, so the search was on for some other business that could rebuild their profits and their battered balance sheets.

To add insult to injury, the central banks made the quest more urgent by tightening the rules governing bank safety. The banking authorities had been frightened by the way the Latin American debt crisis had seriously weakened the world banking system, and as financial markets rapidly internationalized they also wanted a common set of rules to apply to all banks so that the whole industry would be playing the same game. The new rules required banks to have a higher level of core capital to underpin their lending than before, which made life more difficult for them. To comply, they could either raise more capital or make fewer loans. Most did both. But the effect of putting aside more capital against fewer loans was to reduce their profit from lending. Clearly, to keep up their profitability they had to find new ways to make money.

Swaps were the answer to the industry's prayers. Banks could earn handsome fees from selling swaps to exactly the same customers to whom they made loans – companies, other banks, governments – but the swaps are not loans. If a bank did a $100 million swap with a company, it did not actually hand over $100 million. The counterparties simply exchanged their interest payments. Since a swap was not a loan, however, it did not count against a bank's capital the way loans did. It was, according to the jargon, 'off balance sheet' and outside the new rules proposed by the central banks. A bank could theoretically do an unlimited number of swaps without ever worrying that it did not have enough capital.

At first Citicorp and one or two competitors did smallish swaps for huge fees. Then, as it usually does in banking, the sheep mentality took hold. The rest of the industry saw how much profit the pioneers were making and followed their lead. In the early days – around 1982 – $50 million counted as a large interest rate swap but the fees were so large that the first banks into the business made money hand over fist. As the market quickly became an orgy of swapping with the banks at the centre, the size of deal escalated. By the mid-90s a swap of $1 billion hardly causes comment and competition has driven the fees down to the point where banks regularly fight over hundredths of a percentage point to win a contract.

Which is how swaps came to be the most popular financial instruments in the world. The amount of principal outstanding on all swaps in 1986 was between $80 and $200 billion. By 1995, as far as anyone could count, it was around $30 trillion, or $30,000,000,000,000 making it easily the largest element of the OTC derivatives market.

New York and London share this massive business between them: New York for interest rate swaps, London for foreign exchange swaps because of its position as capital of the world's currency markets. Not that it matters to most companies where they do their swapping. There is nothing stopping you exchanging dollars for sterling in Frankfurt, or marks for yen in Sidney. The swaps market has no home and no boundaries.

Amazingly, Salomon Brothers, having played midwife to the new market in the World Bank/IBM deal, was slow to see the opportunities in it. 'On Wall Street you have a business if you make more than $15m a year,' says one of the few young traders who was assigned to the original swaps team. 'You have a good business if you make $50 million a year. Once you're doing over $100 million you're calling the shots on the management committee. We made $60 million which was a lot per trader but it didn't give us any clout in the firm.' At that time, while swaps hardly registered on Salomon's financial radar, the bank's legendary mortgage bond department was effortlessly tossing out profits of $200 and $300 million a year.

The Salomon swaps team in the early 1980s consisted of a total of six people – two traders and four salesmen – huddled in one corner of the dealing room. They were studiously ignored by the other dealers. For one thing, no one really understood what they were doing. Swaps weren't securities or money market loans or mortgages. To the bond salesmen, on the rare occasions when they gave the matter any thought, swaps remained a mystery. It was not an area for which ambitious young dealers aspired to work. 'They took the most junior guys and just ordered them on to swaps,' says one of the team of those days. 'No one with any stature in the firm wanted to go there so they picked on the most defenceless junior traders and just said: "You. You're on swaps."'

Another reason the rest of the dealing room ignored the swaps desk was that it did not recognize the way they worked. The normal mode of behaviour for a Salomon trader was aggressive individualism. In the end what mattered was how much money he personally made for the firm, because that would determine the size of his bonus. Traders would swell their own profit by quoting inflated prices to their salesmen, without caring if it meant that the salesman might never hear from his customer again. It was every man for himself on the trading floor. Over in their corner, however, the swaps boys didn't work like that. They couldn't. They worked as a team. 'People in the dealing room would look at us in disbelief and say: "A *team*? What's that?"' It was the same problem Steve Sykes later encountered at his bank.

Selling bonds, after all, is a simple business compared to derivatives. You buy a bond at one price, you sell it at another; deal done. A swap is far more complex. Rather than transferring a commodity like a bond from one owner to another, it is a matter of finding two counterparties of a similar credit rating, calculating a fairly complex cash flow structure on the swapped interest payments, putting a price on it and then doing the deal. This required traders and salesmen to work closely together. 'In general, we could all do each other's jobs,' says one, 'which meant you couldn't bullshit your colleagues.' You couldn't bullshit the clients either because most of them were, like IBM and the World Bank, as sophisticated as Salomon itself. When it came to handling clients, the swap team could not slash and burn their way through the client base in pursuit of profits the way bond traders often did.

With no precedents to follow in their new business the swaps traders invented their market as they went along. 'I was on my own,' says one. 'When I didn't know what to do, I couldn't just ask someone because there was no one to ask.' An additional problem was that they still inhabited the technological Stone Age. Few people can do calculus in their heads but there were no computer models or complex programmes to carry out the increasingly tortuous calculations involved in swaps and other derivatives. The most sophisticated piece of equipment the traders had was a pocket calculator. The Salomon swaps dealer's position sheets looked like the creation of some precocious kindergarten child: they were large pieces of paper showing a matrix of counterparties, swaps maturities and interest rates, stuck together with sticky tape. As each new deal was completed another strip was literally stuck on to the sheet. It was three years before the growing size and complexity of the business forced Salomon to promote its swaps team to the computer age.

By the mid-1980s no self-respecting derivatives quant, trader or salesman anywhere in the market could reasonably expect to stay in the game without a computer. Til Guldiman, one of J. P. Morgan's more promising young executives, discovered this when he was moved by his employer to the London office where the bank had set up a derivatives operation after realizing that this was a business it could not ignore. 'J. P. Morgan knew something was going on with derivatives but it didn't really know what. It put a group of young bankers together and said, "OK, now make some money." We weren't quite sure how at first but we discovered as we went along.' One day Guldiman found himself in the Milan office of Citicorp, talking to a currency trader whose computer contained one of the first spreadsheet programmes ever produced. The spreadsheet provided calculations at the press of a computer key comparing the forward prices of a handful of currencies and showing when any of them had got out of line. It was the ideal tool for spotting arbitrage opportunities which might last only a few minutes. 'He could key in the values of futures in any currency he wanted against the lira and the programme showed him which ones were overpriced and which were underpriced. Then he picked up the phone and made money come out of it. And he just sat there doing this all day long. He was making a mint.' Why? *Because he was the only dealer in Milan with a spreadsheet*. While the rest of the market laboriously worked out the price anomalies by hand, often missing the chance to deal, the Citicorp trader had already taken his profit. 'When I got back home,' says Guldiman, 'I bought five of these things.'

As the OTC market expanded to embrace all kinds of derivatives, options threw up particularly tricky calculations that demanded computing power. And options became increasingly popular during the 1980s, thanks to the mania for leveraged buy-outs and buy-ins. When some corporate raider got the urge to snap up a company he would almost always do it with borrowed money. He'd get it either in loans directly from a bank or by issuing junk bonds. These deals were often precariously balanced, like up-ended pyramids with some small company – the one being bought by the raider – at the tip, supporting a huge burden of debt once the purchase was completed. To prevent the whole thing crumbling under its own weight the cost of the loans had to be carefully controlled, so options were used to limit the risk. It became commonplace to include call options in buy-out financing which ensured that the interest rate on the loans would never rise above a guaranteed maximum. In many cases, it was these guarantees that made the buy-outs possible because without them the raiders would never have been given their loans. This spawned an industry on Wall Street of selling option contracts, and the options business demanded computers. As corporate America plunged into its buy-out frenzy, therefore, the quants took another step forward in sophistication.

Naturally, development was never even. Some banks evolved their technology faster than others, but whenever someone poked their nose in front it never took the rest of the market long to catch up in the technology race. It wasn't enough just to have a computer programme to maintain an edge; you had to have a *better* programme, able to calculate prices in different market conditions, predict market movements and take account of the credit quality of counterparties faster and more accurately than anyone else's. Although it later turned out that these programmes could sometimes be seriously, even disastrously, flawed the rocket scientists toiled to produce more sophisticated versions than their competitors. Whoever succeeded would have an advantage of a few months in which to make money before the rest of the market caught up and closed its profit window.

This was how Steve Sykes began his Wall Street career. He spent his days turning mathematical formulae into computer language. He constructed elaborate models for analysing and constructing complex mortgage securities so that by entering a few simple figures – an interest rate, say, or a price – a trader could get an instant valuation of a security on his dealing screen. Although he enjoyed the work for a while, he soon made an unpleasant discovery: rocket scientists in banks tended to get dumped on. Despite their key role in developing derivatives they were often paid less than salesmen or traders, were ignored by their bosses, and did not move on up the food chain. They were too quiet and introverted to play office politics effectively; in most dealing rooms the extroverts survive while the rest get trampled on. To avoid this fate, Sykes did what all his most ambitious colleagues were doing: he turned to the office e-mail system. He had noticed that whenever a particularly notable deal was put together the e-mail hummed with messages from people serenading their own key role in the transaction. Sykes was often astonished at how colleagues he had never heard of would suddenly emerge to claim credit for his deals. This was easy to do with derivatives because of the team nature of the game which allowed plenty of people to plausibly claim credit where none was due.

On one occasion, towards the end of the year as the bonus season approached, Sykes and two colleagues devised a fairly complex instrument involving the movement of US interest rates and DM exchange rates. It was duly sold for a handsome fee to a large corporate client. Word of the new instrument had got around the bank in advance because several trading teams had been consulted in its creation – interest rate specialists, currency traders, and so on – so that many people knew the details before the sale was made. When news got out of the profits involved and the likelihood that other clients would become buyers, the company e-mail system grew hot.

Within forty-eight hours the executive in charge of the division received a blizzard of correspondence. At least fifteen people sent him messages pointing out their crucial role in the triumph. About a third of them claimed to have had the original idea which had, in fact, been Sykes's. Most of the correspondents, it is true, had had some tangential involvement but office politics is office politics. You don't get anywhere without making it clear to your superiors how brilliant you are. In any case, the annual bonuses depended on the boss's perception of each individual's contribution. The boss, in this case, was bewildered. He did not actually understand enough about derivatives to be able to tell the frauds from the people who had really been responsible for the success. In this case, he solved the problem by ignoring it. No one got full credit. Sykes was furious but, for the time being, helpless.

Nevertheless, thanks to his specialized knowledge and the lack of competition on the small derivatives desk, Sykes progressed. Within a few months he moved from tinkering with computer programmes to dealing and meeting customers to sell his own deals. In most markets, the early days of a salesman's career are the hardest because he has no credibility, no customers and often precious little knowledge about the products he's selling. But no sooner had he started as a salesman than Sykes received another shock – this time a pleasant one. Selling complex derivatives was one of the easiest things he had ever done in his life.

One of the first clients he met was the treasurer of a medium sized corporation who was keen on esoteric financial instruments like derivatives partly because he knew his colleagues did not understand them. Using them gave him a degree of independence from the company's directors who also did not understand them, as well as a certain cachet among his colleagues as the only man who could handle derivatives. In any case, he had been fairly successful in pumping up his investment returns since he had begun using them a couple of years earlier. Interest rates were low and the treasurer wanted to get a higher rate of return for the company's spare cash than simply sticking the money in a bank deposit or buying a government bond. Derivatives seemed to be the answer since they frequently offered returns of several percentage points above the basic rates. Anyway, the treasurer had his own strong views about the financial markets. He was, for instance, certain that the German mark was about to sky-rocket. Germany had just been unified and the economic miracle was, according to the treasurer, about to happen all over again. He wanted to take a punt on the mark. The only problem was that his company's investment rules would not let him. Written in a quieter, less adventurous financial age, they forbade dabbling in any foreign currencies. The conservative directors steadfastly refused to change them. But it made the treasurer's eyes water to think of the killing he was going to miss if he didn't get an exposure, a really big exposure, to the mark.

Over lunch in a restaurant near Wall Street the treasurer told Sykes that if he could find a way for him to take a bet on the mark without appearing to do so, the treasurer guaranteed to invest $50 million. They shook hands over dessert. Sykes trotted back to the office, wondering if he was in Disneyland. He seemed to have a deal but nothing to sell. This seemed to him the wrong way round. How could the treasurer know that he wanted to buy something before he knew exactly what it was? And anyway, Sykes wasn't at all sure the mark was going to rise. He also wasn't at all sure the treasurer understood as much about derivatives as he said he did. But as Sykes stepped into the lift to go up to his office, it suddenly hit him: it didn't matter whether the mark was about to rise or fall, or what he thought it would do or how much the treasurer knew or how much money the treasurer might eventually lose if his bet went wrong. All that mattered was that the customer should get what he wanted. If the customer wanted to take an insane punt, the customer should be able to. Sykes spent the rest of the afternoon devising a relatively simple instrument that would allow the treasurer to pay dollars which the bank would switch into marks and then swap the resulting income stream back into dollars before it paid it to the customer. The following morning he called the treasurer with the deal which he sold immediately for $50 million, netting a hefty fee from a greateful client.

What Sykes had just sold was known as a structured note – a complex derivative instrument designed to do a specific job for a specific customer. Such instruments are the quintessential product of the OTC market. And because they are not standardized they can come in all shapes and sizes.

Almost from the moment they came into existence, structured notes had a tendency to grow more complex, more elaborate and ultimately more pointless as time went on. The trouble with 'plain vanilla' derivatives such as ordinary interest rate swaps is that when every international bank in the world is doing them the profit margins become horribly thin. New instruments, on the other hand, always command a premium price. Banks began selling futures and options to their customers, then options on futures, options on swaps, swaps futures with option attached, and on and on. There seemed to be no limit to the number of products they could invent. Among the most simple embellishments to a swap, for example, were caps and floors limiting the interest rate exposure of their clients. A cap sets an upper limit above which the customer's interest payments will not go. It is, in fact, a three or six month call option on interest rates which the customer exercises if rates have risen above the options' call rate by the time it is exercisable. Banks wanted to sell them because, of course, they could earn extra fees on top of the fees for the swap. The more bells and whistles were added on to a basic derivative, the more money a bank would make.

Creating a structured note was a matter of pure mathematics – stochastic regressions, Montecarlo Simulations, formulae so long they covered two or three pages of A4 paper. The banks turned themselves into financial laboratories, conducting increasingly complex experiments with new forms of derivatives. The rocket scientists pushed the mathematics of finance to greater and greater extremes of refinement. Like a laboratory full of mad biologists, the quants have spent the last decade dissecting the markets with the scalpel of mathematics, isolating and extracting different risks, then analysing them under the microscope to see what they consist of.

This is where the complexity of derivatives, which are the practical expression of risk in the market, really begins. Once you've isolated a particular risk and found how to put a price on it you can, of course, package and sell it individually, like cans of baked beans in a supermarket. A 'plain vanilla' exchange traded futures contract is like this. But the quants went further. Once they were able to take risks apart they could switch them around, mix 'em and match 'em, and stick them back together again in completely new structures. Suppose a British investor expects the Japanese stock market to rise and the US market to fall, and wants to profit from the difference. Instead of doing a long and expensive series of separate stock, option and currency trades, a bank can now sell him a single derivative instrument containing a call option on Tokyo stock market index, a put option on the New York index and a currency hedge that will produce his profit in sterling. The instrument links different assets and markets more closely than they have ever been linked before, yet the investor never has the expense and complication of having to buy actual shares in Japan or the US. What he has traded is the risk inherent in their movement. As well as the practical convenience, there is an attractive elegance to this.

Taking the lead in this enterprise in the 1990s was Credit Suisse Financial Products, a division of the investment bank Credit Suisse First Boston, created to invent and sell complex derivatives. It was headed by Allen Wheat, one of the outstanding figures of the early derivatives markets and one of the most ambitious financiers of his time. He learnt the business of derivatives at Bankers Trust which, as described in the next chapter, served as a kind of nursery and training ground for the new market in the late 1980s and early 1990s. Bankers Trust had an aggressive culture that suited Wheat's implacable and hard driving personality. While he won the respect of people who worked for him, he also scared them. Once, for example, when Wheat's father, with whom he did not have a close relationship, dropped by the office to visit his son Wheat refused to see him.

'When Wheat was running the CSFP office in London he would ring up Ben Weston who was running the New York office,' said one of the quants who worked for the firm in the US. 'There was always competition between the London, New York and Tokyo operations, but Wheat was something else. He was a close friend of Weston's, but the first thing he would say on the phone is, How much money did you make today? All he cared about was money.'

Wheat had left Bankers when he lost a power struggle for one of the top jobs and had to look elsewhere for a bank to run. He lighted on CSFB which was going through a bad time in the late 1980s and had been bailed out by its parent, Credit Suisse. Wheat told them he could turn the bank around. And he did. Operating first out of London, then moving to New York, he recruited young, motivated and highly numerate young business-school graduates and put them to work inventing new derivatives and selling them hard to the clients. 'Wheat was desperate to make a splash and sometimes the personal goals over-rode what's okay in business,' said one of his former employees. 'He hired a lot of smart kids and drove them to slash and burn the clients. His attitude was: be clever, be smart, but in the end I'm gonna bring round a bucket and you better fill it with money.' Which they did. By the early 1990s, CSFP was about the most profitable derivatives house in the world.

The twenty or so young turks in its New York dealing room would come into work by seven or eight o'clock in the morning and trade until the market closed at about 3.15 p.m. Then the real work began. They'd look, for instance, at the yield curve of seventeen or eighteen different currencies and try out combinations and permutations of different currencies together in a single instrument – swapping out of one and into another, with options or futures attached to give guaranteed rates of return or caps and floors on possible losses. 'We were looking for inefficiencies or unrealities in the market,' says one of them. 'Maybe 20 per cent of our ideas were worth looking at in more detail. We'd discuss them, refine them, work them into something usable. In the end we'd squelch it all into about three really good ideas which we'd try to sell the next day. It was about 9.00 p.m. before anyone started to leave the office.'

Next day the dealers would return to their desks to try to sell their ideas to forty or fifty clients. 'That's when things got interesting. It's the interface of the nerd culture with the rest of the world. You're fired up because you say to yourself, "I've spent all night coming up with this idea, now I want to sell it." It was not always easy, but a hell of a lot easier than it should have been.'

As Sykes had found, it was a matter of giving the customer what he wanted. 'We were structuring ideas to find business, and we were doing it well. We would mix all these elements up, polish it into a single instrument and sell it to you, and guess what? It would embody exactly what you wanted to hear. You think dollar interest rates are heading down and the yen is going to rise? We'll sell you something that exactly reflects your view. And that really is alchemy.'

It wasn't really that difficult either. It was an era when the customers had strong opinions and were willing to back them by betting hard cash on derivatives. They just didn't always understand what they were buying or how to put a price on them. There was a bravado among investors who seemed to think that structured notes were like any other asset and that they could price them by gut feel. Most of the time they actually couldn't because they did not have the computer models and advanced maths to do so but they only discovered this later. 'There was also a trust factor then that doesn't exist any more,' says a former CSFP salesman. 'We'd say this is the price of the thing we're going to sell you and the customers would usually just take our word for it. Occasionally they would query a price and we would say, in effect, "Shut the fuck up; your contract will say X." And we'd charge them X, which was always a lot of money. If banks didn't get a double digit return selling this stuff, they were hopeless.'

Allen Wheat encouraged his young employees to herd the market in front of them and make as much as they could out of it. One of his traders recalls a hot July afternoon, when he and his colleagues were sitting chatting in the dealing room after the end of trading for the day. They were congratulating themselves on having made $60 million in profits so far that year which was more than they had ever made before and more than the rest of the bank had made – and the year wasn't even over. They felt like the élite of the élite, sealed off from the rest of CSFB by a special door and security arrangements that included a separate telephone switchboard in case they transgressed the insider dealing laws. As they talked, the door opened and Wheat walked in. Apparently sensing an atmosphere of incipient complacency, almost before the door had closed behind him he delivered a brief and simple message. If they did not make a profit of $120 million by the end of the year, he said, they would all be sacked. Then he left.

In the event, the derivatives team made more than the required target but no one for a moment doubted that he had meant exactly what he had said. Firm but fair is a phrase often used about Wheat. It means that a dealer who does not produce the big profits Wheat demands knows that he will lose his job. 'At least you always know where you are with Allen,' they say. (In 1995/96 he decided to pay bonuses that many CSFB executives thought were too small and more than 50 of them left the bank in the space of about a month. Most managers would have panicked at such a huge loss of personnel, but not Wheat. He never recanted, apologized or suggested he had made a mistake. He simply hired new people and carried on.)

Under his direction, CSFP led the finance industry's charge into ever more complex derivatives. But huge and profitable though this experiment was, it had its dangers. Like Dr Frankenstein, the quants had a tendency to get carried away with their own research. Just as Frankenstein chopped up bodies and reassembled them into something that was less than a total success as a human being, the quants managed to create complex derivatives that did not in the end do what they were created to do. The danger was that sooner or later these monsters would get out of control, escape from the laboratory and cause mayhem in the real world. And that would turn out to be unhealthy, to put it mildy, for anyone who got in the way. Anyone, for instance, who invested in mortgage backed securities.

There was nowhere in the structured note market that indulged in more spectacular and unnecessary innovation, and which in the end caused more financial pain, than the US mortgage bond market. It is a classic example of how the quants systematically solved one set of problems only to find they had created a completely new set. Spurred on by competition and the drive for bigger profits among the banks the process took on a momentum of its own, resulting in some of the most complex and incomprehensible financial instruments ever invented.

In the beginning, back in the early 1980s, mortgage backed securities looked relatively simple. To create a mortgage bond groups of home loans with similar maturities, interest rates and credit risk were gathered up and packaged into a single instrument that looked and acted something like an ordinary bond. Then they were sold to investors who wanted a nice safe place to put their money. There are, after all, few lower credit risks than mortgages. The reason for creating mortgage bonds was that they expanded the pool of investors in mortgage securities, increasing the amount of capital available for home loans and thus lowering their cost. They were sold to pension funds, insurance companies, municipal funds, even private investors. Whether home owners knew about the mortgage backed securities market or not, they certainly benefited from it with lower interest rates. It all seemed easy and beneficial, but it wasn't. In fact, it was a nightmare because mortgage bonds quite definitely are not like ordinary bonds.

Most of the bonds were issued by Fannie Mae (Federal National Mortage Assocation) or Freddie Mac (Federal Home Loan Mortgage Corp) which gathered up loans from the Savings and Loan companies, the US equivalent of building societies, and packaged them. These agencies were backed by the US government, giving investors the invaluable security of a guarantee that the principal on the bonds would be repaid. That was phase one in the development for the mortgage backed bond market.

The trouble with mortgages is that they have a built in call option: people can, and frequently do, pay them back early. If interest rates fall, for instance, they may redeem their mortgages and refinance them at a lower rate of interest. This is splendid for the home owners but a nuisance for the holders of mortgage backed bonds, who cannot be sure how long their bond is going to last. If enough home owners refinance their loans, the mortgage bond may shrink suddenly or possibly vanish altogether, leaving the bondholders with nothing but a handful of cash from the paid-off loans just when interest rates had fallen and it was least profitable to reinvest it. This created uncertainty for investors, and if there is one thing investors hate it is uncertainty. To get around this nuisance two banks, First Boston and Salomon Brothers, invented something new in 1983. They collected mortgages together in the same old way but put them into a trust that paid out interest and principal derived from the mortgages. Investors could buy a slice of the trust, an entitlement to a share of these payments. Their share was called a Collateralized Mortgage Obligation.

The beauty of CMOs was that they were so malleable. You could bend them and knead them, chop them up and reconstitute them like plasticine. To put it another way, the mortgages poured money into the trust, creating a pool from which the money could be ladled out again by the bank at different speeds and in different amounts to different investors. As long as you could do the maths, you could do anything with them. So began phase two.

The rocket scientists sliced CMOs into 'tranches' with different maturities: one tranche might cover the principal and interest payments on the underlying mortgages for their first five years, the next for years six and seven and so on. The riskiness of your investment depended on which stream of income you had bought within the CMO. The longer the maturity of a tranche, the greater the danger that the owners of the underlying mortgages would pay off their home loans early, so the interest rates on each tranche reflected the different levels of risk. On a typical $200 million deal there might be anything between four and seven tranches. The tranche stuck on at the end called the 'Z', would be the riskiest and often behaved like a junk bond paying little interest but with a very low purchase price compared to the principal that would eventually be repaid to the investor. Like a junk bond too, its value could fluctuate wildly. Such bonds were so risky they were referred to as nuclear or toxic waste. In financial markets risk does not disappear; it simply gets redistributed.

But this was only the beginning. The real fun started when some tax rules were changed in 1986 which made it easier for Wall Street banks and investment funds to get in on the action alongside Freddie Mac and Fannie Mae.

On Wall Street, this set off something akin to a gold rush. There was tons of business to be done: the US housing market was booming, people were flocking to buy houses so the mortgage market was mushrooming; and interest rates were low so investors were looking for bonds that paid above average rates of interest. Even more important, like many new financial products, CMOs were incredibly profitable for anyone who underwrote them (guaranteed to buy new CMOs from Freddie Mac or Fannie Mae if other investors refused to buy them). If you underwrote a CMO issued by Fannie Mae worth $500 million and then sold them on to investment clients your profits might be as much as 2 per cent or $10 million. And $500 million was only a fraction of what many of the big underwriters such as Kidder Peabody or Bear Stearns were doing. Underwrite a few billion dollars worth of this stuff and you were rolling in money. From $29 billion outstanding in 1985, the CMO market surged to $335 billion in 1990 and kept on racing until it hit a brick wall in 1994, so for a while there was plenty of business to go around.

But as more banks saw the profits and piled into the market to get a slice, the extra competition drove down the profit margins relentlessly until they became only fractions of a percentage point. To keep the money rolling in, however, the banks simply accelerated the deal flow. But that meant finding new customers to whom to sell mortgage securities, which in turn spurred the quants to fresh feats of inventiveness in creating instruments that would appeal to the new investors.

For example, they would 'strip' out the cash flow of the interest payments and the cash flow of the principal payments and offer them to investors as separate investments. When interest rates fall the 'principal only' strips tends to rise because they are being paid off faster. The 'interest only' strips, on the other hand, tend to fall in value, or vanish altogether, because the underlying mortgages are being paid off and are therefore no longer paying interest. The different strips suited the strategies of different investors.

The banks were home and dry as long as investors don't notice that these bonds could totally self-destruct: if the rate of mortgage repayments go above or below the expected levels the bond will not just fall, it will completely tank. Other creations included 'inverse floaters' (which rise in value as interest rates fall, and vice versa) support tranche floaters, turbo and WAC floaters, soft-bullet maturities, and sticky jump 'Z's. All the most toxic stuff left over was swept up into yet another bond, appropriately called a 'kitchen sink'.

The more complex the inventions of the rocket scientists, of course, the more difficult it was to put a value on them. It was all a matter of determining how much cash flow would go to the derivatives in different market conditions and different rates of mortgage repayment. A particular bank may be the only institution in the world capable of unravelling a particular derivative – a process known in the business as 'reverse engineering' – because it was the one that created it in the first place. Among those who did not, and could not, understand it were most investors. They frequently had no clue as to the real value of what people like Sykes were selling them, which made it easy for the banks to impose enormous charges on their new instruments.

Sykes was well aware that his bank, with its small and relatively weak derivatives operation, was not particularly sophisticated by the standards of the time. In the jargon of the market, its manufacturing capability was limited: it couldn't construct very sophisticated derivatives because it couldn't have handled the risk created by more complex instruments. Sykes and his colleagues were like mechanics who were able to understand the beauty of a Ferrari but who knew only how to build bicycles. After a while it worked out how to put motors on them. Then Sykes would see a Ferrari glide by and be blown out of his socks.

Yet the inability to produce the most sophisticated deals in the market did not mean Sykes lacked customers. Quite the opposite. The clamour for high yielding securities was deafening and the banks did their best to provide them. Sometimes the production line became clogged. By 1993 the Federal mortgage agencies were issuing dozens of deals a day worth hundreds of millions of dollars. Queues developed with dealers waiting on the phone to talk to the agencies about the next mortgage security issue while the agency wrapped up the previous issue with some other bank. The details of the trade would then be laboriously read over the phone by the agency in a ritual that could last twenty minutes or half an hour. In that time the market might be moving either in the bank's favour or away from it. If prices were falling – which meant the bank's dealing fee was evaporating – the dealers would try to hurry the agency along or cut it short. Usually they failed.

Nevertheless, everyone was making money and no one was making more money than the leaders of the mortgage bond market such as Kidder Peabody and Bear Stearns. No one was bigger or more expert at CMOs in the early 1990s than Mike 'The Arm' Vranos, a former weightlifter who had come to greatness early in life as Mister Teen Connecticut in his home state and had worked as a bouncer while still a teenager. Vranos's passion for pumping iron was matched only by his passion for maths. He joined Kidder Peabody in 1983 and quickly found his niche among the dealers trading in esoteric bonds that required more than a knowledge of long division to work out the prices. CMOs became his speciality.

Vranos was energetic and he spotted an opportunity. By the mid-1980s Kidder was in bad shape after Martin Seagal, one of its corporate finance executives, was arrested for participating in Ivan Boesky's illegal insider dealing ring. In a fit of self-righteousness, corporate America shunned the firm whose traditonal corporate advisory and underwriting business duly withered. Kidder therefore needed gainful employment and, if possible, a saviour. Vranos supplied both.

He made the rest of Wall Street look like a bunch of ageing maiden aunts when it came to CMOs. They would buy $500 million dollars or so of a new issue while Vranos would gobble up three times as much. They would genteelly underwrite only one issue at a time, making sure they had sold off the first lot of bonds to their clients before starting on the next. Vranos, in contrast, would underwrite whatever was there – at one point Kidder brought five deals to the market in a single week, with a total face value of $9.2 billion. And while most firms would sell off the whole of an issue as fast as possible, Vranos would sell on 20 per cent and hold the rest for a profit – which he got as long as the market went up.

His philosophy, colleagues recalled, was roughly this: 'We're not trying to outsmart the smart guys. We're trying to sell bonds to the dumb guys.' Which is what everyone was trying to do, of course, but Vranos did it on a spectacular scale. When the rules got in his way, he changed them. On one occasion he went to Freddie Mac with a list of demands about the way the agency structured its deals and threatened to give his business exclusively to Fannie Mae if the agency did not comply. Since he was, quite clearly, king of the market Freddie Mac gave way. The payoff was that Vranos appeared in one of the agency's advertisements wearing fishing waders to make the point that Freddie Mac bonds were highly liquid.

He was, indeed, not a man to cross. He once apparently punched a colleague in the stomach, doubling him up, when the man brushed against Vranos on his way to pick up a phone. On another occasion Vranos asked a trader for the price of a bond he wanted to buy and grew annoyed when the trader did not reply. When the bond's price rose a few minutes later, Vranos exploded, whacking his telephone receiver repeatedly into the desk and then smashing a swivel chair until the wheels broke off. People tended to stay out of Mike 'The Arm's' way.

But he was strikingly successful at finding the dumb guys to sell to. Kidder became undisputed leader in mortgage bonds – in 1993 it underwrote $81 billion of mortgage securities, giving it a quarter of the entire market and roughly ten times the volume of business it had been doing in the late 1980s before Vranos took over. With sales figures like that Vranos inevitably prospered. In 1993 he was paid $15 million by his grateful employers, almost four times as much as Jack Welch, the chief executive of General Electric which owned Kidder.

Vranos's determination to sell sometimes meant that customers received securities they hadn't actually bought. A client who had contracted to buy a certain type of mortgage bond would find Kidder trying to deliver something completely different, or it would be the right bonds but too many of them. Some complained to Freddie Mac about this but Kidder was unfazed. It was making millions out of the business – indeed, mortgage bonds *were* its business for a while, they so completely dominated its profit line.

But no one in the derivatives markets stays top of the heap for very long. Nemesis, in one form or another, has a habit of catching up with them. Part of the problem this time was a market crash which caught institutions like Kidder, with its large bond inventory, by surprise. Another was the sheer mind-boggling complexity that CMOs had achieved. This was probably the first time in its history that Wall Street had managed to evolve a species of financial instrument that not even it, apparently, could understand.

Every bank in the market, of course, had a computer model of greater or lesser sophistication to tell it what would happen to the value of mortgage securities in different market conditions. Most banks had formed their models long ago, in the mid-1980s, using assumptions that seemed reasonable at the time but many of which in the event turned out to be completely wrong. Just because the computer programmer told them what had happened to CMOs the last time interest rates hit, say, 5 per cent, the bankers assumed it would tell them what would happen the next time rates hit 5 per cent. Nothing could have been more mistaken.

For instance, when interest rates fell in 1991 and 1992 mortgage holders scrambled to refinance their loans at lower rates. The 1980s computer models, however, failed to predict just how fast they would do so. Unexpectedly, some bonds vanished before the eyes of their owners as the home loans on which they were based were paid off. Interest only strips were annihilated as the interest payments dried up and nuclear waste, whose special characteristic is a hypersensitivity to interest rate changes, had a tendency to blow its owners to hell.

This did not stop the sale of more and more CMOs, however, as investors looked for something that would offer a better return than cash deposits which were now paying some of the lowest returns in living memory. For the next two years the market boomed, despite the highly uncertain nature of CMOs caused by the high level of mortgage repayments. The banks found ever more creative ways of enhancing the apparent returns on the bonds and reducing their riskiness. At the height of the bull market there were at least a hundred different varieties of instrument backed by $1.7 trillion US domestic mortgages.

The next shock was even bigger than 1991. It came in February 1994 when the Fed unexpectedly raised interest rates. Suddenly the repayment binge stopped dead. This time it was the principal only strips that blew up – again, unforeseen by the computer models. Overnight, their maturity dates shot out from, say, two years to twenty years and their values collapsed. Many investors who had switched out of interest only strips in 1991 had bought principal only strips instead and now got hammered for the second time.

Much of the profit banks had made in the last eight years went up in smoke. And then the CMO market hit another snag. People could not get out of their positions: their bonds were unsaleable, the market's liquidity had dried up. This was a problem that almost never happens in the futures and options exchanges, thanks to the

standardization of contracts: buyers and sellers always know what
they are dealing with. The very diversity of the OTC market, on
the other hand, acted like a kind of booby trap.

Consequently, when the panic began Wall Street turned its back
on investors. 'Most banks were only interested in selling the bonds,'
says Ted Dumbold, a dealer who worked with Bear Stearns,
Kidder's big rival in the CMO market during this period. 'They
would not buy them back, except occasionally ones they themselves
had packaged. They didn't like the bonds because they knew they
weren't good bonds to begin with. But they had another reason for
caution. Different banks were in the habit of issuing almost the
same bonds as each other except that they would build in some
tiny, almost invisible difference which made their value completely
different. They would sell them to investors at the same price as
the old bonds because superficially they looked the same even
though they were actually worth less.'

The bankers, in other words, knew what was going on and did
not trust themselves to understand any other bank's CMOs. So
they refused to buy them.

Inevitably, the Wall Street banks that owned the most CMO's
lost the most heavily, and few probably lost more than Kidder,
which tended to have billions of dollars of mortgage bonds on its
books at any given time. The bank said its portfolio was fully
hedged in the market but rumours of huge losses persisted. As the
CMO market dried up in the wake of the crash, Kidder's profits
dropped to $40 million from $300 million in 1993. Some experts
believe the mortgage-backed debacle ultimately cost the bank more
than $1 billion. When the bank was also hit by a separate scandal
over what it claimed was a rogue trader on another form of
derivative bond, General Electric gave up on it. It sold Kidder to
Paine Webber for a fraction of what it had paid for it a few years
before. In 1995 Mike Vranos left to run his own hedge fund
investing in mortgage bonds.

But investment banks were not the only sufferers in the CMO
market immolation of 1994. Investors all over America could only
stand and stare in bewilderment as instruments that they had
thought were reasonably safe exploded before their eyes. One
mutual fund manager watched in astonishment as the maturity of

some inverse floaters he had blithely purchased a year or two earlier shot out from 3.75 years to 57 years. Pension funds in California, American Indian reservations in New Mexico, insurance companies in the Mid-West all lost money in spades. Often they were small organizations – school or college funds, local community investments, and the like – which could not afford the losses. Many of them, it turned out, should never have bought the CMOs in the first place.

How did they come to have them? They were the dumb guys whom the investment bankers had been searching for and had eventually found. They were mainly investment fund managers seeking ways to jack up their performance to the high levels they were used to in the 1980s, and this had given them an addiction to high-yielding bonds – or things that *looked* like high yielding bonds until market conditions changed and they detonated like handgrenades.

But although Wall Street had mounted a bravura marketing campaign to shift so many CMOs, it had not actually had to dirty its own hands by dealing with most of these small-town customers. The investment banks had enlisted the help of numerous local broker-dealers – investment companies that operated at a regional level with the host of small investors that Wall Street never saw.

The role of the broker-dealers became increasingly important as the rally wore on, when more sophisticted investors – the big institutions which deal directly with Wall Street – started to back out of the market. As they stopped buying, the sales effort further down the scale increased to keep up the deal flow. The investment bankers could sell CMOs in chunks to the local broker-dealers who would then shovel them out in smaller packages to their clients.

Although the regional brokers were not the kind of people the average Wall Street investment banker would choose to have lunch with, their presence was a relief to bankers who were having qualms about the CMO explosion and the frankly bizarre nature of some of the bonds. 'We don't know who the regional dealers were selling to,' one banker said after the market had collapsed and the dust was beginning to settle. 'If the investors blow up, it's not our problem. We don't get the liability.' (Several of the regional dealers did, however, and were sued so heavily by their former customers that some went out of business – not that Wall Street cared unduly about that.)

While the selling binge was on, not even the New York bankers entirely understood how the regional brokers were shifting their nuclear waste to the small investment funds. Ted Dumbold was amazed at what the funds were willing to buy. 'I'm supposed to be an expert, but even I didn't understand a lot of these structured notes. Many of them were designed with the temptation at the front end – say, the promise of 10 per cent interest for two years when the normal rate was 4 per cent. The investor was up by 6 per cent – but only for two years. After that the note was structured so that he'd be under water for the next ten years. Why would anyone buy this stuff? It didn't make sense. So one day I asked a regional broker and he told me. "Here's how it is. I'm selling this stuff to guys – corporate treasurers and so on – who are retiring in a year to eighteen months time. They buy the notes which no one else in their organization understands. For a year or so, it earns a fantastic rate of interest so the guy who bought it is a hero. He goes out on a high. Then he retires. He doesn't care, of course, what happens after that." And neither does the bank which designed and sold him the structured note.'

Much of the time funds just did not understand what they had bought. They didn't have the expertise to do so, and the brokers – many of whom probably did not understand any better than their clients – did not explain.

The wreckage was impressive. One of the most spectacular crashes was the failure of the Granite Fund, run by a soft-spoken but egotistical manager called David Askin. He told his investors that he was using a market neutral strategy which meant that the fund would make money whether the market rose or fell. In fact it was anything but market neutral because the fund turned out to hold more nuclear waste than Windscale. How this happened remains somewhat mysterious; it also remains the subject of a court case in which investors accuse banks such as Kidder and Bear Stearns of colluding with Askin to sell the fund the scariest kinds of mortgage derivatives because of the high fees they earned by doing so. As the market collapsed, Askin could not sell his nuclear waste and so the banks were eventually forced to close him down.

But while the investment community was bleeding it did not take Steve Sykes and his colleagues back on Wall Street long to figure out a way of profiting from the mortgage bond disaster. They were the only people in the world who knew how the original bonds had been sliced into derivatives, which meant they were the only people who knew how to put them back together again. Yet again, Sykes couldn't believe how easy it was to make money in this business. He found himself wallowing in a sea of cheap mortgage bonds that the investment funds were willing to sell at almost any price. Having sold a bond to an investor a year or two earlier he could now buy it back at a lower price, reconstitute it into a plain mortgage bond, and then perhaps even sell that at a profit back to one of the federal mortgage agencies.

The equation linking knowledge, power and profit has rarely been applied as ruthlessly as it has in the derivatives market and the banks used their knowledge and power to profit quite ruthlessly from their customers. It took the customers a few months to understand what had happened and realize that the banks had not been acting as advisers, as many had thought, but as predators. It deeply damaged the trust between investors and bankers – probably permanently.

George Soros, famous as the 'man who broke the Bank of England' in 1992, summed up the problem of complex derivatives in testimony to the House Banking Committee in April 1994, as the dust settled on mortgage security disaster. 'There are so many of them [complex derivatives], and some of them are so esoteric that the risk involved may not be properly understood even by the most sophisticated investors, and I'm supposed to be one. Some of these instruments appear to be specifically designed to enable institutional investors to take gambles which they would not otherwise be permitted to take.'

The rocket scientists had truly made their mark. While there is no doubt that many investors were greedy and took foolish risks, it is also true that thanks to the new financial instruments being offered to them they frequently did not understand the risks they were taking. Hardly anyone did. Sometimes not even the rocket scientists did. In a market of kitchen sinks and sticky jump Zs, everyone seemed to have lost their bearings.

To many investors it seemed as though they and the banks now spoke different languages and no longer understood each other. Few institutions did more to widen the fracture between banks and their customers than Bankers Trust, where the creation of complex derivatives was elevated to an art form and gave the phrase *caveat emptor* a whole new dimension of meaning.

CHAPTER 5

GET IN THE MIDDLE AND RIP 'EM OFF

'Contrariwise,' continued Tweedledee, 'if it was so, it
might be; and if it were so it would be; but as it isn't, it
ain't. That's logic.'

Through the Looking Glass

f the character of a company is set by the example of its senior
executives then Charles S. Sanford Jr, chairman and chief
executive of Bankers Trust, was the embodiment of his bank.

In 1989 Sanford cut bonuses at Bankers by 10 to 15 per cent
because of losses that had depressed the year's results. To show his
solidarity with his troops, Sanford, as well as his four-man management committee, took a combined pay-cut of $650,000. It was,
everyone agreed, typical of the chairman's intensely competitive
spirit: if you make profits you get rich, but if you lose you don't
deserve to be rewarded.

It was not until three months later that the truth came out: while
publicly cutting his bonus, Sanford had quietly issued 1,200,000
restricted Bankers shares to himself and the management committee – the equivalent of a $3.4 million raise. It was a graphic
demonstration of the ethos he had fostered at Bankers Trust: while
you give with one hand, make damned sure you take away more
with the other.

The story of Bankers' transformation from a rather second rate
commercial bank into the world-dominating derivatives powerhouse

of the 1990s is about the creation of a particular kind of corporate spirit. Sanford liked to call it entrepreneurial; others who worked there call it simply amoral. 'There was a single-mindedness about making money,' recalls a former vice-president of the bank. 'Anything that was not explicitly illegal or prohibited, the message from senior management was: go for it.'

Sanford created Bankers in his own image, producing the most aggressive derivative sales and trading bank in the world. In the process, he also created a bank which cut corners in a spectacular way to get profits. Up to a point, the transformation of Bankers was an exaggerated version of what happened at many hitherto staid commercial banks in the 1980s and 1990s. There seemed to be so few rules to break in the new derivatives markets that there was nothing unusual in banks taking a freewheeling approach to their products and their customers. What made Bankers stand out was the sheer scale and arrogance of its dealing, and the enormous size of its profits.

It began in the mid-1970s, when Bankers was a lowly ranked New York commercial bank with a portfolio of lousy real estate loans and no particular place to go. It was never likely to challenge the big boys like Citicorp and apparently had a future of dogged mediocrity to look forward to. Then came Alfred Brittain III. Appointed chairman in 1975, he decided that the only way to deal with the problem was to reinvent Bankers. It would no longer be an ordinary commercial bank with boring old high street branches and retail customers. Instead it would concentrate on the glamorous end of high finance, doing business only with big companies and governments, and it would make its money by dealing in things. What things, people wondered on Wall Street? Whatever things happened to be good to deal in, said Bankers. Things that would make the bank money. It didn't really matter what they were exactly, as long as there was profit in them.

So Bankers sold off its retail banking operation and most of its loan book too. By packaging its loans to big companies as bonds, a process known as securitization, it could sell them to someone else and use the capital for something else. By the early 1990s Bankers had a mere 19 per cent of its assets in loans ($14.5 billion) compared with more than 50 per cent for most normal banks. In 1992 Sanford called loans a 'discontinued business'.

Instead it dived into new business such as foreign exchange trading and junk bonds. One of Banker's best customers was Henry Kravis, the leveraged buy-out king who perpetrated the largest and arguably the most unnecessary takeover in history when he bought R. J. R. Nabisco in 1989. Bankers used to lend his company, Kohlberg Kravis Roberts, so much money that it was affectionately known at KKR as 'The Wallet'. In return, Bankers would not only sell the loans as junk bonds but get a slice of the equity on each KKR deal, in effect making it a business partner rather than just a banker.

Brittain's lieutenant in this radical change was Charles Sanford, a sandy-haired southerner from Savannah, Georgia. After leaving the Wharton School of Economics in Pennsylvania in 1960 he tried a brief stint as an economics teacher (his grandfather had been a university professor) before heading into banking (his father was a banker) by joining Bankers in 1961. 'Teaching,' he later claimed, 'was too political. Banking sort of fit the bill. It was a place where I could be measured.' He began as a credit analyst, rose fast to become head of the bank's Southern Division and then moved over to its sales and trading side, of which he became head in 1972.

'Mr Charlie' as he was known to those who sweated in his employ on the Bankers trading floor, spoke in a startlingly high-pitched and rather clipped southern accent that somehow belied his fearsome ambition. 'He was a killer businessman with a veneer of southern charm,' says one former employee. Acquaintances paint a picture of a man unable to stop competing whether he was at work, playing golf or cards, or simply holding a conversation. No one seems to have escaped this all-encompassing competitiveness. Not only did he relish being measured, he relished measuring all those around him. He and Brittain overturned the old system of paying commercial bankers by seniority in favour of bonuses based on performance. The better the performance, the higher the bonus. Performance, of course, was measured by how much profit an employee brought into the bank. An individual's pay could fluctuate wildly from year to year depending on his profitability. If he was any good, though, it went up and up. A typical case would be a salesman joining on a salary of $75,000 for the first year, rising to $200,000 the second and thereafter, if he was good, to $500,000 or more than $1 million.

This was great for the salesmen and the traders whose impact on the bank's bottom line could be measured pretty exactly month to month and year to year, but for everyone else, from back office nobodies to the people in investment banking, measurement was not so simple. Nor so remunerative. The place to be in Bankers, it became clear, was in sales and trading. Anywhere else was nowhere.

The boiler room of the bank was the thirty-third floor of its offices on Liberty Street in the heart of New York's financial district. More than 400 people were crammed into a single large trading room. Each dealing position, complete with computer terminals, was incredibly small – a couple of feet wide in many cases – although mere proximity did not stop them conducting conversations by phone with people sitting only a few feet away. The ceilings were low, the air circulation poor, the conditions cramped and sweaty. As if to remind him of his roots, Sanford kept an office there even after he became chairman of the bank and was often seen striding among his troops exhorting them to greater efforts.

And who were the foot-soldiers willing to work in such conditions? 'They were really nice kids, basically smart nerds, mostly guys without girlfriends,' said one former managing director. They were willing to work all hours of the day and night because they believed Bankers was the best and because they hoped to hit the financial jackpot. They were men with degrees in physics, chemistry and engineering who were comfortable with complex formulae and who wanted to get rich quick. Competitors admitted that Bankers probably had the highest collective IQ on Wall Street.

Sanford's young troops readily absorbed the inferiority complex that formed the bedrock of Bankers's culture. The dealing room was not in the traditional Salomon Brothers style, full of swagger and shouting and testosterone. It was usually quite quiet, the atmosphere almost academic and scholarly but with a killer instinct. Bankers was the underdog; it couldn't compete with the likes of Morgan Stanley, Salomon, Goldman Sachs or J. P. Morgan on their own terms so it would find a different way. 'The approach was "we're smarter than everyone else and that's how we'll beat them". That's what Sanford preached,' says a former dealer.

Given the direction Bankers had taken, it was entirely natural that as head of the trading empire Sanford should succeed Brittain as chairman, which he did in 1986. By then the bank was relying on trading for more than half its profits and it looked remarkably like one of the investment banks such as Salomon Brothers or Goldman Sachs, whose business was securities trading and underwriting rather than lending. In 1989, recession killed the leveraged buy-out boom stone dead, leaving Bankers without its main business. Something else had to take its place.

Derivatives were ideal. They were little understood; there was very little competition to sell them; and they offered massive profit margins, particularly on leveraged deals. Opportunistically, Bankers piled in. Its target was to make a clear profit of 30 per cent on derivatives, but former employees say the figure was more often closer to 50 per cent.

Under the new philosophy employees were encouraged to be, in the jargon of the bank, *entrepreneurs* – to find new areas of business and exploit them. The old management structure had been replaced with a more fragmented system that allowed this more freewheeling approach, and after two weeks at the firm any nerd straight out of business school could see that the big money was in derivatives. In any case, the bank had no particular expertise in anything else that could give it an edge over its rivals.

Bankers became expert at devising more and more complex instruments in which fearsome levels of leverage might come into play without the client even knowing about it. Bankers was so far ahead of the field that few of its customers had the mathematical sophistication, let alone the computer models, to understand these instruments in detail. It adopted an advertising slogan: 'Risk wears many disguises. Helping you see beneath its surface is the strength of Bankers Trust.' In the early 1990s between a third and a half of the bank's profits came from derivatives business, while about half of the staff on the thirty-third floor were involved in it.

The business of making money was enormously simplified by Sanford's philosophy that employees weren't to worry about relationships with clients any more. The new game was called transactional banking – each deal was what counted. You didn't have to worry about looking your client in the eye the next time, since without a relationship there might not be a next time. You did what you had to do to get the business today. Tomorrow was a different matter. This was a 'counter-party culture' in which the client, whether he knew it or not, was an adversary. It did not take long for Bankers's salesmen and traders to discover that what this really meant was that clients were geese waiting to be plucked. And that the more plucking they did, the better they got paid by Bankers.

The imagery of physical mutilation peppered the badinage of traders on the thirty-third floor. Clients were forever having their eyes ripped out or their faces ripped off or their lungs ripped out by Bankers Trust executives who would boast of having just screwed them on a deal. When a client 'came back for more' it was the mark of a true blue idiot, and an indication of the salesman's skill that the client had not even noticed that his eyes had just been ripped out. In Bankers's parlance, a client who could be taken undue advantage of was known inexplicably as a 'mullet'.

An in-house training video for new derivatives salesmen made the point. An instructor called George Mimura gives an example of a hypothetical swap transaction in which Bankers acts as the agent mediating between Sony and IBM. 'What Bankers can do for Sony and IBM,' he says, 'is get in the middle and rip them off – take a little money.' In this officially encouraged hot-house atmosphere, the client's interests in any particular deal did not just take a back seat to Bankers's own profit – they didn't even count. Some of the staff took to referring to the ROF, the Rip-Off Factor, in deals. This was the amount of money the client did not even know he was paying to the bank, either because he was too stupid to work it out or because Bankers simply hadn't told him. The ROF was something to be proud of. It meant profits, and profits meant bigger bonuses. And that was what counted.

As his new bank took shape, Sanford was hailed in the media as the new intellectual leader of the banking sector and a worthy successor to Walter Wriston, the former head of Citicorp who had once claimed that role. With hindsight, the comparison is ironic.

It was Wriston, after all, who had memorably declared that 'Countries don't go bust' as he led the rush to lend to Latin America in the 1970s. His leadership was no more successful than Lord Cardigan's charge at the head of the Light Brigade: it resulted in the debt crisis that nearly broke the international banking system. On the whole, history teaches that the fewer intellectual leaders in the banking sector the better.

But at Bankers, the revolution continued unchecked. Sanford concentrated power in his own hands and reduced the top management committee to only four people. Not everyone liked the new-look bank. A stream of senior directors was soon flowing out of the door, including the heads of corporate finance, mergers and acquisitions, the corporate advisory group, and private equity investing, as well as the chairman of the London operation and the vice chairman of the bank in New York. Defectors said that Sanford was too abrasive, demanded too much of employees, and had no idea how to organize teamwork.

To turn up the pressure still further, Mr Charlie decreed that he was aiming for an over-all return on capital at Bankers of more than 20 per cent, a rate so high it was almost unheard of among US banks at the time. To meet these demands, Bankers became a ruthless selling machine and a fearsome speculator in the markets.

In 1986, for example, it had hired a young currency options trader from Salomon Brothers called Andy Krieger who had graduated from the Wharton School after studying Sanskrit and philosophy at the University of Pennsylvania. He quickly became one of the most aggressive dealers in the world, with the full sanction of Bankers. While most of the bank's currency traders had an upper dealing limit of $50 million, Krieger's was in the region of $700 million – around a quarter of the bank's capital at the time. By using options, Krieger could leverage this exposure to many times that size ($100,000 of currency options would buy control of $30 to $40 million in actual currency). In 1987 he did this to launch a speculative attack on the New Zealand dollar. If his own claims can be believed, he sold short the entire money supply of the country. In a matter of hours, the NZ dollar plunged 5 per cent against the US dollar. It was enough, at any rate, to draw an angry complaint from the New Zealand central bank. But with typical arrogance, Sanford later turned this on its head. 'We didn't take too big a position for Bankers Trust,' he grumbled, 'but we may have taken too big a position for that market.' It was New Zealand's fault, in other words, for being too small to cope with Bankers.

Krieger resigned the following year in disgust at the ingratitude of his employers who had paid him a mere $3 million for his efforts which had netted the bank a profit of more than $300 million. But after his departure an odd thing happened. Regulators discovered discrepancies in the way Bankers valued its currency options portfolio. The bank was forced to admit that $80 million of foreign exchange trading income had disappeared and that it had deliberately overstated its 1986 earnings. It seemed, on the face of it, that the bank had been simply unable to understand Krieger's complex options positions. Dealers in other banks, however, wondered how it was that Krieger's options portfolio only maintained its value as long as Krieger himself was in charge of it. Whatever the reason for the readjusted profit, the whole episode was a serious embarrassment. An even bigger embarrassment, though, should have been that Bankers had been willing deliberately to publish figures that were inaccurate by $80 million as if it didn't matter. But the bank showed no sign of blushing.

This was yet another warning of its attitude: anything goes as long as the suckers don't find out. Bankers was lean and very, very mean and there were no bigger suckers in sight than in the derivatives markets.

Two of its clients, Gibson Greetings and Proctor & Gamble eventually took Bankers to court when they realized what had happened to them. The claim submitted by P&G mentioned several other alleged victims of Bankers's derivatives business: Sandoz, Sequa, Jefferson Smurfitt, Equity Group Holdings, Adimitra Rayapratama, Air Products & Chemicals, and Federal Paper Board, although these did not resort to legal action. The bank also became embroiled in court cases in the Far East, with Dharmala Group of Indonesia.

The conversations quoted in the following accounts are taken verbatim from tape recordings made by Bankers of its own dealing and sales staff. The recordings were originally made to protect the bank against disputes over deals but ended up being filed in court as evidence of how it handled its customers. They provide a fascinating insight into the way some people in Bankers's derivatives operation worked. None of the dialogue is invented.

Gibson Greetings of Cincinnati was exactly the right kind of customer: big enough to pay its debts but not sophisticated enough to know what it was doing. It was ripe, in fact, to have its lungs ripped out.

As the second biggest greeting card manufacturer in the US it was medium sized and solid, with annual sales of more than $500 million and profits of about $20 million. Having survived a leveraged buy-out and refloatation in the 1980s, it had settled comfortably into a groove, supplying the world with Christmas cards, mother's and father's day cards, anniversary cards and get-well cards. Until, that is, a couple of young Bankers Trust salesmen turned up at the door in November 1991.

Jim Johnsen, the treasurer, remembers them as forthright and honest, the opposite of the kind of hard-sell securities salesmen who interrupted you during dinner. They had a reassuring patter about derivatives, a new kind of instrument which had apparently been invented recently on Wall Street. Their computer models showed how simple and safe derivatives were. They could save the company money too.

Johnson liked their pitch and decided to try some. He had no inkling that he was embarking on a course that would lose him his job and Gibson an entire year's profit. The only condition he laid down was that if – heaven forbid – the company lost more than $3 million the bank would cancel the deals. He frankly admitted that he didn't know how to price the derivatives he was buying or how to calculate the exact risks. He left this to his new friends at Bankers.

The two salesmen handling the account were Gary Missner and Mitchel Vazquez. In charge of them was Jack Lavin, the head of corporate derivatives sales. Lavin, like Missner, had worked for several years in Chicago where he had taken a job at Continental before suddenly jumping ship a few weeks later to join Bankers. His ambitious and hard-driving ways had gained him a reputation for being, as one business acquaintance put it, a 'low hanging fruit picker'. The phrase can have different meanings in different contexts but it is never complimentary. It often means someone who sells deals that look riper than they really are. It's easy money, as easy as picking low hanging fruit. He fitted effortlessly into the Bankers ethos and drove his sales team hard.

As well as Lavin, two senior commercial bankers also oversaw the Gibson Greetings transactions. The bank, in other words, knew what was going on with Gibson at a high level, and no one had any illusions about the relationship with this client. As Missner told Lavin: 'From the very beginning they just, you know, really put themselves in our hands like 96 per cent ... And we have known that from day one.'

To start with, everything went smoothly as Gibson's first two derivative contracts – very simple 'plain vanilla' deals with no hidden leveraging effect – turned in a profit of $260,000. After that, as Bankers sold them more and more complex derivatives, it was all downhill. Gibson entered into what Bankers called an 'interest rate ratio swap' in October 1992 which almost immediately made a loss. Missner and Vazquez told the company in February 1993 that it was down $975,000, even though Bankers's own internal calculations showed a loss of about $2 million. They also understated the loss on another Gibson derivative that went under the bewildering name of a 'periodic floor basis swap'.

With touching faith in its bank Gibson accepted these figures, incorporated them in its company results and therefore, however inadvertently, lied to its shareholders – an action for which it was eventually rebuked and fined by the Securities and Exchange Commission.

Nor apparently was it the only customer who was unaware of its real position. At around the same time, Bankers's tapes caught a conversation between two of its employees about another client that goes like this:

'What are you telling them [the client] their mark is today?'

'Today I gave him a value of 12.9 million.'

'And it's really what?'

'It was really about four and a half higher than that.'

Still blissfully unaware of the full extent of its losses Gibson entered a string of linked derivatives deals, each designed to mitigate the deficit on the previous deal while actually (although Gibson did not understand this) increasing it. To reduce the risk contained in the ratio swap, Gibson did a deal called a treasury linked swap. It was a pity that Bankers omitted to tell the company that this was structured so that Gibson would make an immediate loss: far from reducing its risk, the company's position promptly deteriorated by a further $1 million. Another deal – a so-called 'wedding band' that triggered dire losses if interest rates wandered outside agreed maximum and minimum limits – pushed Gibson's dealings a further $1.4 million into the red.

At the end of 1993 Vazquez told Gibson that its cumulative loss so far was $2.9 million – magically just short of the $3 million limit at which Gibson would stop playing with derivatives. In fact, the true loss was closer to $7.5 million, more than twice Gibson's limit. By now, though, the company had done twenty-six different transactions with Bankers and was probably so confused that it had no idea whether it was getting any financial benefit, let alone what risk of further loss it was running.

Then came the 'Libor linked pay-out' deal in January 1994 that finally sank the whole leaky vessel of Gibson's dealings. The aim was to lower the interest costs on a $50 million fixed rate bond issue, so Bankers agreed to make the fixed rate payments to the bondholders if Gibson paid Bankers a floating rate. If interest rates fell, as Gibson confidently expected them to, it would end up paying less than the fixed rate, thus saving itself some money. But the way Bankers designed the deal meant that it would only work in its client's favour if short and long term interest rates moved in tandem. If they did not, Gibson's loss would sky-rocket.

Jim Johnsen admitted later that he and his department hadn't understood this. Missner revelled in this knowledge: as he told a colleague soon after the Libor deal was struck, 'These guys ... have done some pretty wild stuff and probably don't understand it quite as well as they should. I think they have a pretty good understanding of it, but not perfect and, um, that's like, perfect for us' (laughter).

In February the trap snapped shut on Gibson: the Fed raised short term interest rates but long term rates refused to follow suit.

At the end of the month Missner dropped the bombshell on Kevin Rice, Jim Johnsen's deputy: 'The total CMV [value] right now is about $8.1 million,' he said.

'Okay,' Rice replied, probably too stunned to say anything more.

'In any case, that was really the point of the phone call, to just make you aware of where things are right now, number one; number two, don't, you know, don't think it's a time to panic or start pulling out,' said Missner.

Yet again he was understating the matter because the actual loss as calculated by Bankers was $14 million – not that this worried Missner and Co. unduly. What concerned them was that now Gibson's loss was at least triple its original $3 million limit, it would stop dealing. If the company pulled out at this stage, Bankers would have had to hand back around $5 million in profit it had made from its gullible customer.

As Gibson's loss escalated daily, Missner plotted tactics with his colleague Vazquez: 'We should call Kevin [Rice] and maybe chip away at the differential a little more. I mean, we told him 8.1 million when the real number was 14. So now that the real number is, you know, 16, we'll tell him it's 11. You know, just slowly chip away . . .' Their problem was that having so grossly understated the loss before, they now somehow had to get it to match reality before they revealed the actual loss to their customer.

Unfortunately for this strategy, interest rates just kept rising which made the losses bigger and bigger. Bankers finally bit the bullet and told Gibson its loss had gone from $8.1 million to $13 million. A few days later the figure was $17.5 million.

It was lucky for Bankers, however, that Gibson was unable to shake off the gambling habit. The company had acquired a new chief financial officer, William Flaherty, who thought he knew about derivatives. Lavin, Missner and Vasquez flew to Cincinnati to meet him and pitch him one last deal. Gibson could have settled there and then to limit its losses at around $18 million. Instead, Flaherty agreed to a new deal that would cap the losses at $27.5 million.

Just consider that decision for a moment. He could have got out with an $18 million loss but instead agreed to risk another $9.5 million. Like a gambler who can't leave the tables, he was still hoping that Gibson could win in the end; he was willing to raise his stake for one last spin of the roulette wheel.

But it didn't. By the time Gibson's losses topped $20 million the company changed its attitude and sued. Mr Charlie and his lieutenants were not impressed and denied culpability. 'We decided these guys are nuts,' declared one bank executive. Soon the regulators took an interest and began investigating. The banking industry mounted a powerful lobbying effort to kill the investigation but failed. Then the taped conversations fell into the hands of the Securities and Exchange Commission. The SEC and the Commodity and Futures Trading Commission declared that Bankers had failed to inform Gibson of its losses, had caused the company to report untrue information to its shareholders and had failed to supervise its derivatives unit properly. It also fined the bank $10 million, while Bankers said that it would only demand $6 million instead of $20 million from Gibson in settlement of its deals.

The bank never admitted that it had had any responsibility to advise Gibson of the foolishness of what it was doing. It still believes, along with every other investment bank, that bankers have no obligation to warn customers that they may be doing stupid derivatives deals. That is the customer's lookout, they say.

Bankers also denied that it was wrong to quote two different prices – one for itself and one for the client – for the value of derivatives contracts. Missner has always claimed that in understating Gibson's losses he did nothing that was not sanctioned by the bank or that was not common practice on Wall Street. It is true that banks tend to apply two different values to over-the-counter derivatives. One is the value they give it for their dealing book. This, in effect, is the deal's basic value. The other value is the one they quote to the customer, and since these deals are purely between the bank and the client, the bank can put any value on it that it thinks the customer will accept. The difference between this and the first value is the bank's profit on the deal.

This system, of course, puts the client at the mercy of the bank – but that is the nature of over-the-counter derivatives. The dual quotation technique is not illegal. But there is a fine line which banks are not supposed to cross – even though many of them do when it suits them. Bankers Trust did this. The profits it tried to squeeze out of Gibson were excessive. And it withheld information from the company about its losses when Gibson asked for it. That was Bankers Trust's crime.

To prove to the regulators that it was turning over a new leaf, the bank said that it had sacked three directors involved in the Gibson debacle. This was not exactly accurate. Lavin became an advisor on new products to the Chicago Board of Trade but remained on Bankers's payroll. Vazquez had already left to join CS First Boston as a derivatives salesman. Only Missner was fired. In 1996, an SEC inquiry into the conduct of Bankers Trust officials resulted in a $50,000 fine for Vazquez and a $100,000 fine for Missner, plus a five-year ban from the securities industry.

At Gibson Greetings, Johnsen, the treasurer, was sacked. He left the firm a wiser and sadder man, wishing he had never heard of derivatives or Bankers Trust.

The story of Bankers Trust and Proctor & Gamble, the soap conglomerate, is a little different. P&G is a big company and a sophisticated investor with the resources to run a large derivatives book. The comedy of its encounter with Bankers is that both companies had the arrogance to think they knew better than the market and each other. But it turned out that P&G knew far less than it thought it did, while Bankers Trust made matters worse by employing its familiar economy with the truth. They both ended up as losers.

Raymond D. Mains and his team in the treasury department of Proctor & Gamble reckoned they were pretty good. So they should have been. With hundreds of millions of dollars to look after they were in a different league from Gibson Greetings. As far as financial sophistication went, they were among the élite of corporate America.

In his mid-fifties and beginning to think of retirement, Mains still kept abreast of the latest developments in the financial markets even though they seemed to change faster than computers these days. The department used derivatives to reduce the company's funding costs – in the early 1990s, for instance, it had swapped large amounts of fixed rate debt into floating rate debt in the belief that interest rates were on the way down. That belief turned out to be right and P&G paid a lot less for its loans as a result. But more than that, the treasury department – with the blessing of the main board – had increasingly used its expertise to punt some of P&G's capital on the markets to turn a little extra profit. As the years went by, the amount allocated to pure speculation rose while the limits constraining what the department could actually do became fewer. By 1993 it had a speculative fund of around $1.3 billion devoted to making profits from dealing in the financial markets.

And then the Bankers Trust salesman came knocking. Kevin Hudson, in the opinion of several of his colleagues, was the very image of the young super-polished Wall Street investment banker. He is well built, charming, well spoken, the kind of guy who never has a strand of fair hair out of place. He was a southerner and many of his customers seemed to appreciate his southern manners. He was well educated. And he also seems to have been extremely pliable. When Bankers Trust in general and Jack Lavin in particular urged aggressive sales techniques, Hudson eagerly complied.

By the time he called on P&G in May 1993, he had considerable experience selling derivatives. He offered the P&G team a special interest rate swap. In his favour, Hudson had the fact that P&G had used Bankers services for more than seventy-five years but had not apparently caught up with the new churn 'em and burn 'em ethos at the bank.

The swap Hudson was peddling was governed by a complex formula tied to changes in the yields of two different US Treasury bonds and was leveraged so that any increase in the T-bond rates would multiply the reduction in P&G's return many times over. There was, indeed, virtually no limit to the potential loss. Judging it too risky, P&G told Hudson to go away. But you couldn't get rid of a Bankers salesman that easily. Hudson was back again in July with a similar proposal, and yet again in August, and was each time sent packing. Then in October, P&G cracked.

It wanted to renew an expiring interest rate swap that achieved two objectives: it changed fixed rates to floating rates, and it squeezed those rates to a minimum – specifically, 40 basis points (0.4 per cent) below the prevailing commercial paper rate that P&G would normally pay for its borrowing. The swap had also involved minimal risk for P&G. Suddenly, here was Hudson claiming that he had a solution specially designed by Bankers to meet all P&G's needs (standard banking jargon meaning 'we happened to have this idea which we've been peddling to every client we can think of, and you're one'.)

The idea was a five-year swap with an option included. The bait was that P&G would pay not 40 but 75 basis points (.75 per cent) below the commercial paper rate for the first six months of the deal. For the following four and a half years, however, the floating rate would be calculated using a mind-numbingly complex formula including the five and thirty year Treasury bond rates – hence the designation of the deal as the 5/30 swap.

P&G was betting that the general level of interest rates would fall. In effect, it believed it knew better than the market which way they were headed. If everything went P&G's way, it would save $7.5 million in total over five years or about 0.3 per cent of the group's entire interest bill. Not, in other words, a deal that would transform the group's profits if all went well. The risk of loss, however, was completely disproportionate to this meagre potential gain. If interest rates rose, particularly in the first six months of the swap, the company would end up paying well above what it would have done if it had borrowed by a conventional method.

For a while, P&G worried that the potential downside looked too big. Hudson sent them a reassuring table purporting to show possible changes in the rate P&G would have to pay if general interest rates moved up. As a clincher he said that the company could reduce its risk by locking in its rate after three or four months at 40 basis points below commercial paper rate, assuming general interest rates did not move significantly. Reassured, P&G doubled the nominal amount of the deal from $100 to $200 million, then signed on the dotted line on 2 November 1993.

P&G thought it was being clever, but Bankers knew better. There were large profits from this deal and they weren't going to the soap-maker. Hudson knew he had pulled off a big one. He immediately did a lap of honour – figuratively speaking, since it was all by phone – around the Bankers dealing room to acknowledge the applause.

The first stop was a colleague called Schindler, who was agog. 'This has got what in it, like, percent-wise?'

'It's sick ... you're looking at an eight million dollar trade,' gloats Hudson, referring to Bankers profit.

'That's so unbelievable ... It's just mind-boggling. It's like our, our greatest fantasy.'

'I know,' smirks Hudson. 'It is. It is. This is a wet dream.'

He also talked to Jack Lavin, head of derivatives. 'I think my dick just fell off,' was Lavin's tribute.

Hudson then checked in with Ari Bergmann and Guillaume Fonkenell, both Bankers managers who had to know about the deal as part of their job. Fonkenell allocated $7.5 million in profit from the deal to Hudson. 'Kevin, you are unbelievable,' swooned Bergmann in admiration.

'This is a new customer,' purred Hudson. 'That's the key. A customer that has never done structured leveraged proprietary trades before. This is it.'

At last Hudson got to Alison Bernhard, another experienced saleswoman who also happened to be his fiancée. He never let an opportunity go by to pump up his prowess in front of her. 'I was so smooth,' he boasted. 'I'm wallowing in a little glory right now. Yeah. In fact, I don't even have the desire to call my other clients and beat them up this afternoon.'

At which point the conversation naturally turned to the size of Hudson's bonus. They calculated that the sale would make him the number one or number two bonus earner on the trading floor.

Bernhard pressed her fiancé on how he managed to sell anyone such a lousy deal. 'How ugly can it get?' she wanted to know. Hudson said that he had given P&G information that showed they would actually be paying the commercial paper rate plus 20 basis points but that they could not work this out for themselves. 'That's the beauty of Bankers Trust,' he gloated. 'They [P&G] don't know, they don't understand selling leveraged options and stuff, I mean that's not their job to understand that. Their job is to say here's my funding target and here's the risk I'm willing to take.'

'Oh my ever loving God,' gasped Bernhard when he explained that the put option P&G had just sold to Bankers leveraged P&G's

$200 million by 17 times. 'Do they understand that? What they did?' she asked.

'No.'

'They didn't?'

'No. They understand what they did but they don't understand the leverage, no.'

'But, I mean, you know,' spluttered Bernhard, 'that's what I don't understand, like where, where did, how much do you tell them? What is your obligation to them?'

'To tell them if it goes wrong, what does it mean in a pay-out formula ...' He mimicked breaking the bad news to P&G's treasury department: 'Here it is. It went wrong. You were wrong, you were really wrong. Do you understand how wrong this is.'

Taking his contempt for his gullible clients a stage further, Hudson said that he had paid them only half what the option was really worth, leaving P&G with even less potential benefit from the deal than they should have had. 'This could be a massive huge future gravy train,' he chortled.

Over the next two months, he repeatedly assured P&G that he was monitoring the deal to find the best time for his client to fix their funding rate and close out the option. The soap company frankly admitted that it did not have the expertise to do this itself. 'We're sure happy you're keeping on top of this deal,' Dane Parker, a P&G treasury officer, told Hudson at one point with unconscious irony.

But Hudson wasn't monitoring the deal in quite the way Parker imagined. By mid-January, P&G was losing around $17 million on the swap. It was bound to lose heavily if interest rates rose, and between early November 1993 and early May 1994 the five and thirty year Treasury bond rates both did so. A colleague rang up Hudson to point out the current level of loss and ask if Hudson felt comfortable telling his customers about it. 'Depends on who they are,' said Hudson.

The colleague pointed out that another customer, Air Products, was losing $20 million on a deal almost identical to P&G's. 'I can definitely tell 'em that,' said Hudson and then said he could probaby also tell P&G about its $17 million loss.

But he didn't. Nor did he tell them that thanks to the complex formula which P&G did not understand, the company had in fact been millions of dollars under water from the day the deal was signed. Having wrongly guessed that interest rates would fall instead of rise, P&G had never stood a snowball's chance in hell of making money.

Instead, Hudson started talking to P&G about extending its option period by two weeks, effectively increasing the customer's risk and potential losses. As he bragged to Bernhard, it would mean another two million profit to Bankers.

'You're headed for trouble,' she said. 'It's gonna blow up on you. You got a stronger stomach than I do.'

'I'm a glutton for punishment, and, well, you know, I'm rollin', man, I gotta make money here,' said Hudson.

'You're not gonna have a job, you're not gonna have customers to make money with if you do stuff like that all the time, you're gonna bow 'em up . . . You're getting greedier as the days roll by,' his fiancée cautioned.

But Hudson was deaf to her warnings. He was high on adrenalin and the thought of his bonus. And he was already working on selling P&G another deal that would lose them still more money and swell his bonus further.

This new derivatives scheme, which Bankers had already sold to a number of other clients, was a bet on German interest rates. P&G would again swap fixed rate funds into floating rate in the hope that interest rates would fall, thus cutting its interest bill. Although the Federal Reserve was raising US rates, P&G believed that the move was overdone and that world interest rates, including those of Germany, were still going to drop.

So it bought $95 million of Deutschmark in a swap deal which, if everything went perfectly, promised savings of just under $1 million in interest charges. The savings would only result if interest rates stayed between 6.1 per cent and 4.05 per cent before 14 April 1995. This was a form of swap deal that Bankers liked to call a 'wedding band'.

It was a hell of a risk to take for the sake of saving $1 million since P&G would lose if, even for a day, interest rates broke out of the band. In that case another complex formula that P&G did not understand would kick in and multiply the company's losses many times over. A second booby trap lay in another formula which would also greatly increase P&G's costs if the swap rate rose. However one looks at it, and without even working through the formulae, it is not hard to see that this was a deal designed for outright gambling rather than hedging.

Back at Bankers, Hudson was almost beside himself with excitement. He and Bernhard calculated that the profit he had made for the bank now stood at $25 million and that was not counting the money he expected to make from the DM trade with P&G. As usual, Bernhard took a cooler view of things while her intended behaved like a hyperactive child.

'You got to calm down,' she scolded him once when they were talking about the DM trade.

'I'm not calming down, man, I'm on a roll.'

'Are you letting your greed get in the way of business decisions? ... I'm amazed ... I just hope that you're right. I hope these people don't get blown up. 'Cause there's the end of the gravy train.'

'Yeah, well,' said Hudson, 'I'll be looking for a new opportunity in the bank by then anyways.'

Early in February, Hudson urged Parker at P&G to go ahead with the DM trade in anticipation of a German rate cut. But he knew they never would if they understood how large their losses were on the 5/30 trade. Solution: don't tell them about the losses.

On 4 February Hudson told Bernhard that P&G was down $17 million but that it had been as much as $25 million at one point.

'Are they dying?' she asked.

'They don't know.'

'They're not asking?'

'Never.'

'Oh shit. God help you if they do,' Bernhard said.

'That's okay. Let me just get the DM trade done first, then they can ask,' Hudson replied.

A week later he was talking to Jack Lavin, his boss, discussing the mounting losses of clients such as P&G and Air Products. The two agreed that they would keep quiet about the losses until the new DM deal had been done. By 14 February he was laying the hard sell heavily on Parker: the DM swap was 'a great trade ... I think all of our positions are very good positions, but this one, I think, has the potential to be a winner very quickly . . .'

To be fair to Bankers, there were some qualms. A manager asked Hudson if P&G really understood what they were doing and Hudson insisted that the company was a very sophisticated investor and had approved the deals at the highest levels in its treasury department. Both of these statements were true which is why the manager went away satisfied. But as Hudson admitted to Bernhard later, the deals he was doing weren't quite that simple: 'It's like Russian roulette, and I keep putting another bullet in the revolver . . . every time I do one of these.'

The same day, 14 February, he loaded the revolver and spun the cartridge again: P&G signed the DM swap.

By mid-February the controllers at Bankers, the people who watch over trading positions, were getting agitated. By then P&G was losing $38 million on the 5/30 deal but still did not know. Thanks to the rise in US interest rates and the deal's strange formula, the company was paying not 0.40 per cent below the commercial paper rate as had been its original aim, but 4.6 per cent *above* it. Hudson explained his problem to Lavin, his boss.

'I've got to call P&G and give them their mark. See, I've got controllers crawling up my ass on that.' He explained his strategy: 'So I'm going to tell them this morning, I'm not telling it's $38 million, I'm telling them it's CP plus four and a half per cent.'

'That translates to what?' asked Lavin.

'$38 million.'

'They can figure that out.'

'Yeah, they can figure it out, but that's the way I'm presenting it. I'm not telling them that . . . they owe me 38 million dollars.'

(Hudson employed a similar technique with other clients too. In a conversation with a colleague about the Swiss pharmaceutical group Sandoz, he said: 'We're telling Sandoz about 13.5 million, but it's really down about 18 million.')

Through numerous phone conversations with Parker, Hudson miraculously managed to smooth over the situation. P&G agreed to hang on to its position in the hope that things would improve while Hudson made reassuring noises. But he was playing Jekyll and Hyde: while he sounded optimistic to P&G, to his fiancée he presented a darker picture. He told her it was the worst month in the history of world financial markets. 'Here's the positive side. I've buried my clients so much that it's going to take me four years to trade them out of this loss. P&G, well, we're down twenty million a year for the next five years, how are we going to trade our way out of that one?'

He was laughing when he said this: the situation was now so bad it was funny. In any case, it didn't matter too much if P&G lost heavily because there was no obligation for Hudson to maintain a relationship with them. That was not Bankers's policy. And besides, there was no suggestion that he would lose his bonus if P&G lost its shirt – so why worry unduly?

And interest rates continued to rise. By the beginning of March the 5/30 trade was down $53 million and the DM trade was down $40 million. Belatedly, P&G's treasury department began to realize that it was getting killed. Hudson had told them about the loss on the 5/30 trade but hadn't got around to mentioning the DM loss. P&G now began trying to lock in its rate of interest for the full term of the deals to forestall further losses, as it claims Bankers had said it could. But it had not reckoned with the formula for calculating the interest rate spread. It was stunned when Bankers gave it the rates at which it could lock in or sell out. On 3 March, Hudson told them they could lock in at 8.51 per cent above the CP rate, or somewhere above 12 per cent – some 10 per cent above their original target. 'Holy crudola,' spluttered a bewildered Parker. 'This is unbelievable.' And as well he might, he began to wonder what effect this would have on his 'performance rating' inside P&G. Predictably, it wasn't good.

By then the 5/30 trade was $120 million underwater and P&G was at last getting suspicious of Bankers. Parker had heard a rumour that the bank was making a $10–$12 million profit on the swap even though it had always maintained that it had nothing to gain. Hudson blustered so effectively when Parker accused him of this that the P&G official rang back later in the day to apologize.

On 10 March, however, P&G finally bowed to the inevitable and unwound $50 million of the swap at a margin of 10.55 per cent over the CP rate. Four days later it unwound another $50 million at a margin of 11.98 per cent. But when the company asked about cancelling the other $100 million it got a shock. Bankers said that to unwind the positions would require such massive money market operations that it might actually drive up interest rates still further. This puzzled P&G considerably, until it concluded that to cover its position when doing the original swap, Bankers had put on $3 billion in hedges. Unwinding all of that was what threatened to push up interest rates.

But by now, at least, everything was out in the open. Then came the time for retribution. Faced with the embarrassment of having lost the company so much money, P&G's treasury department did the obvious thing: it covered up. The board was kept in ignorance of the actual level of losses for months, while the treasury department sweated over the knowledge that it had played a very large game of roulette with the banks and money markets and had suffered the indignity of having its face ripped off. As a measure of the size of its gambling, it had entered into thirty derivatives contracts with several banks, having a total nominal value of $3.8 billion. Several deals were so highly leveraged they risked losing nearly half their nominal value.

When the truth finally came out, Ed Artzt, the group's famously short tempered chairman, blew a fuse. He wanted a good explanation of what had gone wrong, or he wanted blood. Or both. Faced with massive losses and the fury of a man like Artzt, the treasury department did what most people would do: it passed the buck. It said Bankers had duped it. The treasury officials had thought they understood the derivatives until Bankers unexpectedly sprung its formula for calculating losses on them. If they had known about the formula, they claimed rather implausibly, they would never have done the deals.

This is a lame excuse, to say the least. P&G is a large conglomerate and its treasury department is nothing if not a sophisticated investor. It knew perfectly well what it was doing, in the sense that it was deliberately speculating in the market. Its officers probably did not understand the detailed internal workings of the derivatives Bankers sold them, and it is true that Bankers lied to them about the losses. But for a player the size of P&G to claim that it was duped is simply absurd. It had a duty to understand what it was doing, but it didn't.

Artzt, for one, was not convinced by his own officials' arguments. The treasury executives had acted 'like farm boys at a country carnival', he fumed. Mains himself 'simply went to sleep' over the whole affair. In Artzt's view the Deutschmark deal had not even been particularly difficult to understand. Heads, inevitably, began to roll. Mains retired early. Parker felt, probably correctly, that his career at P&G was hopelessly compromised, and left. Two other treasury employees were reassigned within the company. Erik Nelson, the chief financial officer, had his bonus docked for a year.

Fearful of lawsuits from angry shareholders, meanwhile, P&G embarked on the only damage limitation option left open to it: it launched a law suit against Bankers to recover its losses. Both sides rattled their sabres up to within a week of the trial starting in the summer of 1996. Then they abruptly settled out of court – no one, after all, really wanted to wash their dirty linen in public. P&G paid Bankers $30 million – less than a third of what Bankers said it was owed – and both sides went home claiming a victory. The settlement means that none of the numerous banker-client disputes over derivatives in the last few years has ever been settled in open court, leaving many of the murkier issues of morality and business practice untested by the law.

These public disputes, however, were only the tip of an iceberg. Hundreds of other companies that lost money from investing in complex derivatives found ingenious ways of disguising the fact in their accounts. Scared by all this, company directors vowed never to touch derivatives again. Dealing in the complex instruments dreamed up by Bankers Trust and other banks slumped during 1995 and 1996. Salesmen like Kevin Hudson went quiet for a time. But if one thing is certain in finance and banking it is that memories are shorter than a pair of hotpants. By the second half of 1996, the salesmen were on the warpath again and company treasurers were lending them a willing ear. It was not long before sales of complex derivatives were back at the heady levels of 1993.

And Bankers Trust? True to form, it remained unrepentant. When P&G first complained, it refused to offer a penny in compensation. When it finally settled out of court, it refused to admit any wrongdoing. No one lost their job. Hudson got his opportunity elsewhere in the bank and was moved to London where he continued to sell financial products. He married Alison Bernhard. And, of course, he received his bonus.

Charles S. Sanford Jr – Mr Charlie – retired from his bank at the end of 1995, a year earlier than planned, saying he intended to learn ancient Greek in order to read the Bible in the original. He denied the early retirement had anything to do with the furore over Bankers's derivatives trading. But his successor, Frank Newman, immediately went about settling all the outstanding claims by hurt corporate customers and has switched Bankers's policy back towards long term corporate relationships. 'Transactional banking', in theory at least, is history.

CHAPTER 6

DO YOU PLAY POKER?

'But I don't want to go among mad people,' Alice
remarked.
'Oh, you can't help that,' said the Cat: 'we're all mad
here. I'm mad. You're mad.'
'How do you know I'm mad?' said Alice.
'You must be,' said the Cat, 'or you wouldn't have come
here.'

Alice in Wonderland

'The derivatives department resembled a sandpit full of kids
where the adults had wandered away. We did our own thing,
made our own mess and made new kids feel miserable. It was
the natural order of things.'

As a new kid Terry Grove was, as a matter of course, terrorized
when he arrived in a British bank dealing room as a raw university
recruit. Knowing virtually nothing about trading swaps – buying
and selling the interest cashflow payments on different loans – he
was given about a week's grace in which he was allowed to sit at a
dealing desk next to the experienced swaps dealers, sip coffee, trade
jokes and watch what they were doing. After that the truce ended.
They'd start throwing him deals to execute, which was fine except
that while he tried to execute it the dealer next to him would
continue to shout prices or obscenities in his ear until Grove's
brain became scrambled. Prices would start coming out of his

mouth backwards and he would have to break off, explaining embarrassedly to his counterparty that his confusion was because he was a trainee, at which point all six traders on the swaps desk would rise to their feet and jump up and down, pointing at him and gibbering incoherently like a troop of overexcited gibbons. The effect, according to Grove, was strangely humiliating. Was there any point to this behaviour? 'After a while it made you focus your mind on the deal you were about to do on the phone and block out everything else. But was that the reason they did it? No. The reason they did it was to scare the shit out of you. Why did they want to do that? Because they could.'

Trainees were treated like dirt on principle: they deserved nothing better because they hadn't earned it. To Terry Grove this seemed like simply the next stage in an increasingly bizarre process that had begun with his job interview. In one of these, an executive had asked him to solve a puzzle with matchsticks laid out in adjacent squares on the desk. He was told to turn four squares into five without using extra sticks. While he tried to solve it, they fired questions at him. After several minutes he came out with the right answer more by luck than judgement and the interviewers were impressed. 'What was the point of that?' Grove wondered afterwards, when he had time to think. 'What did it show about me?' He never found out.

Different companies, different selection techniques. Some US banks took to advertising in chess magazines. The idea was to attract people who liked solving intellectual problems, although it was never entirely clear why anyone skilled in planning a chess strategy should necessarily be good at designing inverse floaters. The result, though, was that several banks ended up with powerful chess teams in their derivatives department. Bankers Trust's team claimed to have come close to beating Gary Kasparov in a friendly match.

Another interviewing technique was to fire mental arithmetic questions at the candidate – what is 14×17, say – and then time how many seconds it took to get the answer. Or there were questions like: if it's a quarter past six, what's the angle between the minute and the hour hands? To answer 90 degrees is no good but, then again, too much delay in considering an answer is no good either. A better reply would be along the lines of: 'It'll be just over 90 degrees because the hour hand won't be exactly on the six because it's quarter past ...' At least this answer shows some vestigial ability to think through a problem.

'Frankly, the people who interviewed me didn't seem to have a clue what they were looking for,' says Grove. 'They had to go through the motions, of course, and one of them would get a bee in his bonnet about what sort of traders they needed and would start asking a load of irrelevant questions. It kept them happy.' 'The only question my interviewers seriously seemed interested in,' said one New York trader, 'was: Do you like gambling? Do you play poker? They had obviously decided that good gamblers made good dealers, that the qualities were the same. And maybe they were right. Actually, I don't play poker but since the answer they obviously wanted to hear was yes, I told them that I did and everyone was happy.'

Once hired and on the trading floor, a rookie dealer is like a landmine ready to go off at any moment. 'It took me a while to learn accuracy on the details of trades,' says Grove. 'At first I could not take seriously the idea that one hundredth of a percentage point mattered to anyone.' Even simple orders can get scrambled in the soft tissue of a trainee's brain as, for example, when the traders at Bankers Trust in Tokyo wanted to square their position at the end of a day's trading, a straightforward operation, simple enough to be entrusted to someone as stupid as a trainee. It was near to the 3.00 p.m. market close on a Friday and in reckoning up their positions in Euroyen and Japanese Government Bonds (JGBs), the dealers found they had to sell some Euroyen. A trainee was sent off to do this. A few minutes later, shortly before leaving the office, one of the senior traders noticed that the JGB market was collapsing. Then it dawned on him that the trainee a few desks away was selling JGBs, not Euroyen, and single handedly moving one of the largest capital markets in the world. The trainee had in fact unloaded $500 million JGBs in the space of a few seconds and would have sold more if the senior dealer had not pounced on him and stopped him. With the market now collapsing like a heart-attack victim, Bankers was able to buy back its JGBs at a lower price and ended up making a profit of $100,000 from the mistake.

But how do you select good dealers and keep out the bad? It is a question to which every bank chief executive in the world would like to know the answer. Nick Leeson, the young man who reduced Barings Bank to rubble looked like a good trader to his bosses until it turned out that they had badly misjudged him. He is in plentiful if undistinguished company, so it seems fair to say that the process of selecting reliable traders – let alone good traders – is extremely difficult.

How, for example, do you explain why a bad trader can, without warning, turn into a good trader almost overnight. It happened, for instance, at Lehman Brothers which recruited a young man in his mid-twenties to trade in its New York dealing room who, after more than a year on the job, turned out to be hopeless. He never seemed to get the hang of the markets or the instruments he was supposed to buy and sell or the ability to make profits. He consistently lost money whenever he was allowed to deal, and so after a while his employers came to the inevitable conclusion: he had to go. They did not do anything as crass or potentially expensive in severance payments as sack him. Instead, as was usual with unwanted staff, they simply decided not to pay him a bonus and hope that he got the message to leave of his own accord. The trader was lingering on in his last weeks in the trading room while his fate was being decided, when a junior job fell open in the bank's Tokyo office. A low paid menial was needed urgently to help the traders with some of their number crunching and clerking, some-one who would not be missed from anywhere else in the bank and probably wouldn't progress anywhere beyond the unpromising position on offer. Feeling the milk of human kindness surging in their veins, the young trader's managers decided to give him a second chance. They sent him out to Tokyo. Realizing that his career was not exactly taking off in New York, he readily agreed to go and within forty-eight hours was climbing aboard a plane to the Far East.

Shortly after arriving he was given a heavily loss-making position in futures and options left by his predecessor and told to clear it up. It was a cruel move by his colleagues since his almost certain failure to turn a profit would simply complete his humiliation within the firm. But the young trader was suddenly blessed with the kind of luck for which all traders pray but few are ever granted. The market went unexpectedly in his direction. Had he been more experienced or had the faintest idea what he was doing he would have hedged his positions, but he hadn't because he didn't know how to. As a result he got the undiluted benefit of the favourable market move and produced by the end of the year a profit of $50 million for Lehman. Suddenly the firm loved him. He was a star, the favourite of his bosses and the envy of his colleagues. His pay went from $50,000 to $1 million the following year. With the extra time and confidence this gave him he went on to become a consistently successful trader.

What does this prove? Probably nothing more than that picking successful traders is more akin to pinning the tail on the donkey blindfolded than it is to a scientific exercise. Even the best traders are not necessarily intellectual giants, and luck is a more crucial ingredient in trading success than most dealers would like to admit. But how does a manager spot a lucky trader among the crowd of post-business school applicants filing through his office every year. The solution to the question 'what makes good traders?' remains stubbornly elusive.

Are they, for example, born or made? Richard Dennis, one of the legendary futures traders of Chicago during the 1970s and 1980s thought relatively ordinary people could be taught how to be good traders and set out to prove it with a unique experiment. He himself had been spectacularly successful as a 'local' in Chicago and his qualifications for understanding how to create a successful trader – if such a thing was possible – were impeccable. He had started trading as a teenager in the 1960s, long before Chicago had heard of financial futures or had become an international market. For the first few years he lost money – small amounts which he earned doing odd jobs like delivering pizzas. Every time he earned some more he went back to the market and lost it again. Since he was under the legal trading age of twenty-one he persuaded his father to take time off from his several other jobs to stand in the pits for him while he gave instructions from the sidelines. 'It was like the Marx Brothers,' he once commented. By the age of twenty-three he had made $100,000 in trading profits on the Mid-America Exchange, which he converted into half a million in 1973 by following the rise in soy-bean futures. By twenty-five he had made his first million. In 1977 he left the pits and moved to an office upstairs where he sat in front of computer screens, giving his orders down the phones. This enabled him to follow more markets simultaneously which, from a trading point of view, is a kind of hedge. Instead of trotting between two or three pits on the floor of the CBOT he could now cover fifteen or twenty markets, which meant less chance that all of them would go sour at once and more speculative opportunities in some of them all of the time.

It proved a hugely lucrative move. Some years later his net worth rose by 200 or 300 per cent. In 1981 he was wealthy enough to lose $50 million without going out of business, and the following year he made it all back. In 1983 he made $23 million in six months and in 1984 another $20 million on the back of a rally in bond futures. In 1986 he made another $80 million. And so on.

Dennis evolved a system of following market trends. He reckoned it was impossible to outdo the big banks and investors in the quality of research into the markets, so the best bet was to ride the market wherever it led. The skill was in getting in on a trend early and getting out before it reversed. His other main rule for good dealing is to play it safe. Whatever you do, never take positions that can wipe you out if they go wrong. Always live to fight another day.

Since it worked so well for him, he reasoned, it should work for other people if he taught them how. He felt so strongly that he bet his partner, William Eckhardt, that he could turn a group of ordinary people with no appreciable financial experience into successful futures traders by training them in his system. The stake was one dollar for every candidate.

Advertising in *The Wall Street Journal*, he weeded ten lucky candidates out of several thousand applicants. It may be that the selection process somehow identified naturally talented dealers, but the diversity of their background suggests this is unlikely. The candidates included people with no market experience, such as a man who had worked for the game company that produced Dungeons and Dragons, as well as people with some experience of futures trading. Anyway, once Dennis had made his selection, he put the students into class. The name for these protégés derived from a trip to Singapore, where he saw a vat full of baby turtles being raised on a turtle farm. He regarded himself as raising a similar shoal of baby dealers and the name Turtle stuck to his protégés ever after.

Their training took a mere two weeks, after which Dennis provided each of them with $1 million of his own money to trade and sent them out alone for a year to see how they would do. They were so successful that he repeated the experiment the following year. Several Turtles achieved returns of 30 per cent to 60 per cent for several years after being launched from Dennis's financial laboratory. About half of them are still actively trading and several have become extremely rich. Although they are sworn to secrecy about the details of Dennis's trading method, their success suggests that good dealers can indeed be made.

For the average trader in a bank, however, it is rarely as easy as this. Once a dealer has survived the inevitable torture of the early years, things don't necessarily get much better. There is a widespread and erroneous view among people who do not work in finance that dealing is a glamorous business, but for most dealers nothing could be further from the truth.

Clare Gervat joined Chemical Bank as a trainee straight after university at Cambridge, and then spent two years at BZW in the late 1980s as a swaps dealer. 'It was fun as long as you didn't mind not having a life outside work. If you leave for work at 6.30 a.m., you fall asleep at 10.30 p.m. – even if you are in the middle of a dinner party. The people you spend time with are those in the same sort of business, as they are the only ones who find your arcane knowledge and jargon-laden conversation even remotely interesting. I bought a flat and hardly ever saw the inside of it except to go to sleep in. The fridge was empty most of the time apart from a bottle of vodka in the freezer and a couple of half-bottles of Veuve-Cliquot for when it had been a bad day. Drink featured heavily in a trader's life: to blot out a bad day or celebrate a triumph – the talk getting bigger and more aggressive with every glass. At work, though, traders spend a lot of time at their desks. They probably even go to the loo less often than anyone else. Our team had a junior whose four main duties were the four 'Fs': filing, faxing, photocopying and food – especially food. At 8.00 a.m. she would order breakfast, and at noon buy huge expensive sandwiches for lunch. None of us saw daylight in winter except for a few hours at weekends.'

On one wall of the department facing most of the desks was a board with the names and phone numbers of major clients and counterparties written out in felt tip pen to act as an instant reference for the traders. The board also included a perpetually changing roster of women's names. These represented the department boss's latest conquests, and their names were placed on the board to warn staff that the women were out of favour. If a dealer answered a call from anyone owning one of these names they were to put them on indefinite hold until the woman went away.

It wasn't a lifestyle calculated to nurture rounded human beings with broad experience and diverse interests. It was excellent at breeding rich, neurotic people who saw the world in terms of numbers to be bought and sold, as if it was all one massive video game. If there is any glamour in this life it is all in the pay cheque. No one goes into investment banking to make the world a better place. They go in to get rich. Since money is the reason they are there, they make sure they get it.

Dealers, salesmen, quants and their managers are, like door-to-door salesmen, paid by results. The more profit they make the more bonus they earn. A successful dealer or salesman can expect to get more than £1 million in basic pay and bonuses per year. Nick Leeson was waiting for a bonus of around £450,000 when his multimillion pound losses came to light. That was a handsome sum, but not particularly large by global standards. Barings was not a large bank. A dealer at Morgan Stanley or Salomon Brothers who was as well regarded as Leeson had been by Barings would have been getting two or three times what Leeson was paid.

It took Terry Grove almost no time to discover the simple equation that led to higher pay. The bigger the profit he made for the bank, the bigger his bonus. Bigger profits are easier to make by taking bigger risks, so the incentive was always to push things to the limit. 'You look at your position and you look at the market and you think you see the chance to make a bigger profit than you have already. You have to make a decision: do I or don't I? And you look at your screens again, thinking "What the hell, it's only numbers." So you increase your bet and hope you haven't done anything stupid.'

The frantic competitiveness of the banking industry makes it impossible for banks to change the bonus system even if they wanted to. The few who have tried have always failed. Salomon Brothers made a brave but misguided attempt in the early 1990s after it had been hit by scandal in the government bond market. It was caught trying to rig prices in the regular government bond auctions, resulting in the expulsion of most of its senior management, including the legendary chairman, John Gutfreund, who was one of the arch exponents of the bonus incentive system. Warren Buffett, the famous investor who already owned some shares in the bank, stepped in with extra capital to save it (a move which turned out to be a less than brilliant investment). Buffett, a down-to-earth Mid-Westerner, did not like the inflated salaries at Salomon and so he and Deryck Maughan, his English appointee as chief executive, tried to institute a limited bonus system. Within weeks there was rebellion. Executives began leaving in droves because it was so easy for rival banks to offer them more money. If anyone needed proof that investment bankers' only true loyalty is to their wallet, this was it. By the time fifty managing directors had left, Buffett got the message. The old system was reintroduced whereupon three men – the heads of the bank's securities operations in New York, London and Tokyo – were paid $40 million between them in bonuses. And this was in a year when the company made an over-all loss.

The same high-minded attempt to limit bonuses backfired horribly at another investment bank in London, when a warning that the staff were not happy with the plan was delivered in the form of a freshly laid turd that turned up one day in the desk drawer of one of the senior managers. In keeping with dealing culture where numerical accuracy is paramount, the turd was measured before a secretary was summoned to dispose of it. It was found to be nine and a half inches long, but not even this gave a clue as to the perpetrator's identity or how he had deposited it undetected. Refusing to be intimidated, the management stuck to its small-bonus policy but nemesis came swiftly. Within weeks seven top traders had defected to other banks, leaving their former employer to replace them at even greater cost than if the bonuses had been paid in the first place.

The effect of a massive pay cheque on the psyche of the average twenty-seven-year-old is by now pretty well documented in the literature of financial markets. The feeling that he is invincible and possibly divine seems to be almost automatic. The desire for an equally big pay-cheque the next year is only natural. He knows all too well that the way to achieve that is to play the video game in the markets with even greater intensity and *élan* than before.

Aware that money is the only thing that keeps traders loyal, managers are careful to stimulate their greed. Take the example of the chief executive of Chemical Bank, a lifetime commercial banker who hardly ever set foot in the dealing room. Chemical had recently set up derivatives trading terms, and to supply some of the desired incentive to its newly recruited traders the CEO decided to give them a taste of just how generous Chemical could be. He appeared like visiting royalty in the trading room one lunchtime, called the dealers together and singled out one of the 'star' traders. He then handed the lucky dealer a bonus cheque for $500,000. The applause was thunderous. No doubt about it, the troops were encouraged. (Unfortunately for Chemical, the trader went on to lose a lot of money the following year.)

The trouble with the gambling that the bonus system encourages is that the dealers are playing with someone else's money. This gives the game another dimension of unreality. It is axiomatic that losing someone else's money is never as bad as losing your own. It can even be fun. And if a dealer loses heavily this year, he does not have to give last year's bonus back. The system positively encourages greater risk taking.

Theoretically, a dealer who loses a lot of money suffers the sanction of being sacked. But it is a curious feature of the financial markets that losing money – as long as it is does not break the bank – rarely makes a dealer unemployable. He will almost certainly find a similar job with another bank within a few weeks, and often at a higher salary. Take the example of Howard Rubin who started on Wall Street as a mortgage bond trader at Salomon before moving on to head Merrill Lynch's mortgage bond department. It was in this capacity that in 1987, at the age of thirty-six, he made the largest trading loss anyone had ever seen on Wall Street – a thumping $250 million. He made it on POs, the principal only components of mortgage bonds. Having sold $500 million worth of IOs – the interest only component – he was unable to get rid of the POs before interest rates rose and beat the hell out of his bonds. Merrill accused him of doubling up his bet and losing so much that he hid his trading slips in his bottom drawer rather than admit to them. Although it was never proved that this is what Rubin had done, Merrill kicked him out. Did this ruin his career? Not a bit of it. Hardly had word of the loss hit the headlines of the *Wall Street Journal* than Rubin was hired by Bear Stearns.

You could argue that Nick Leeson's tragedy was that he never understood this principle. 'His problem,' remarked one English investment banker after the Barings affair, 'was that he allowed himself to lose so much. If he had stopped near the beginning and admitted to some smaller losses he'd have been sacked by Barings but he would have got another job.' But while the lack of accountability for trading losses is a phenomenon that everyone in the financial markets has encountered, it is not easy to explain why it happens. Part of the reason is that banks hate to admit to losses, so they rarely announce to the world why they have sacked a dealer (Rubin's case was unusual in this respect), or an entire department of dealers, as quite often happens. On the other hand, if anyone asks the dealer what happened, he can almost certainly find plausible ways to lay the blame on his former managers. And in the US an employer may actually get sued for giving out negative information about a former employee. No one outside the bank, in other words, ever really knows what, if anything, went wrong.

The system, therefore, encourages thousands of young people to sit down every day in the hermetically sealed security of their bank dealing rooms to play roulette with the financial markets. This is not unique to derivatives. It happens in almost every major financial market in the world. But it is with derivatives that the greatest danger lies because of the speed with which massive risks can be accumulated and magnified through leverage.

And for the traders involved it offers enormous improvements on mere gambling in a casino. As one young dealer in London observed, 'It beats playing roulette. The numbers are bigger, it's

not your money at risk and you always get paid whatever happens.'
Unlike ordinary gambling, you win even when you lose.

What is needed, of course, is a system of controls within banks
to stop the risk-taking getting out of hand. Every bank on earth
insists that their control systems are good. Most insist that they are
state-of-the-art. Many insist that theirs are head and shoulders
above everyone else's.

They can't be all right, and most of them are wrong. After
Barings collapsed, all major international banks insisted that the
same thing could not have happened to them. It was a predictable
reaction from people trained never to admit mistakes and always
reassure the markets about their financial health, whatever the
truth might actually be. In many cases their protestations were
more like ritual formulae; they did not really *mean* anything – as
the chairman of the New York Federal Reserve Board knew when
he went around for weeks afterwards urging banks to improve their
control systems.

There is no doubt that banks have better risk and management
controls than they did a few years ago. Hundreds of million of
pounds and dollars have been spent on sophisticated computer
systems and training to try to minimize the number of things likely
to go wrong in a dealing operation. One argument in defence of
the concentration of risk in the derivatives markets on a few big
banks is that at least these institutions are better equipped to handle
the risk than anyone else. Smaller banks – such as Barings – cannot
afford the massive investment it takes to have state-of-the-art
systems. Banks also argue that it is simply in their own interests to
have the best systems to cope with the markets. No one wants to
go bust.

But there are several reasons why banks do not control their
risk-taking as carefully as they would have you believe. Several
powerful factors are at work in most dealing operations which may
undermine considerations of long-term safety. Chief among them
are greed and ignorance.

No system of controls is better than the managers who look
after them, so if the managers have as much incentive as those they
are controlling to take unreasonable risks, there is reason to worry.
The bonus system in investment banks does not stop with the

trader in front of the dealing screen; it goes all the way to the top. Indeed managers are usually the biggest beneficiaries when those they manage make a lot of profit. When Leeson got his bonus of a few hundred thousand pounds, Peter Baring, the chairman, got £1 million and Andrew Tuckey, the chief executive, got £1.4 million. When Joseph Jett, the alleged rogue trader of Kidder Peabody, received $3 million in bonuses during a period when the bank thought he was making huge profits, several of his bosses got bonuses of around $10 million. Everything in the bonus system that distorts the judgement of traders works exactly the same way on the managers in charge of them.

The prospect of bigger bonuses seems to have an almost magical effect on some managers. The sight of a dealer making large profits is guaranteed to make him the darling of his bosses. His success goes into their bonus. The temptation not to ask too closely how the dealer is making such extraordinary profits is as powerful as it is understandable. Like Nelson, the managers put the telescope to their blind eye and do not see what they do not want to see – excessive risk, suspicious trading patterns, unexpected losses. At best it is wilful ignorance, although when transgressions get really bad it is little better than complicity in fraud.

It is a fine line, often difficult to judge, between encouraging a profit centre and allowing a rogue dealer to get out of hand. For example, banks always impose dealing limits on their traders to prevent them going wild in the market, but in many banks the more successful traders habitually overstep their limits. They could not do this without the tacit approval of their managers. The logical conclusion of this process is that a trader is cut more and more slack until his trading limits, in effect, cease to exist.

The other reason for inadequate controls – ignorance – usually stems from the sheer complexity of derivatives and the speed with which they have grown. It is a characteristic of these markets to run ahead of the vast majority of their users. They develop so fast that there are always new instruments or trading strategies or market conditions that the participants are not prepared for. Market practice, on the other hand, has always been, and still is, to plunge into a new area of business first and work out the accounting, back office and computing problems associated with it later.

Moreover, most dealing desks are manned by young men whose entire banking career may have been spent concentrating on one kind of derivative or another. They are not only proficient in the intricacies of their markets; they are the only insiders. Anyone who did not grow up with derivatives is highly unlikely to have the same familiarity and proficiency with them – anyone such as their managers, who are older, and grew up in the old world. The senior executives may lack the mathematical ability as well as the training to comprehend what the people supposedly under their control are doing.

This has produced a kind of generation gap in many banks not unlike that created by computers, between kids who grew up with them and their parents who never felt comfortable with them. The generation gap in derivatives has caused untold problems. While no one expects the chief executive of a bank to grasp every detail of, say, options hedging, it is important for him to understand the nature of the risks his dealers are playing with and to be able to recognize whether they are being properly controlled. Managers who do not understand cannot manage effectively. Time and again this has led to disaster: it is most unlikely that the senior management at Merrill Lynch, for example, had any understanding of what Rubin was doing with his POs until they saw the results.

Managing the risk in a bank's proprietary dealing operation is one of the most difficult jobs in the business and one that is frankly beyond some bank executives. The point was made by Eugene Rotberg, inventor of the swap and former member of the World Bank, the SEC and Merrill Lynch. He told *Risk*, a financial magazine that is not afraid of jargon:

On the risk-management side the bank runs five separate books: a spread book, a volatility book, a basis book, a yield-curve book, and a directional book. The spread book trades swap spreads using Treasuries to hedge medium-to-long-dated swaps and a combination of futures and treasuries for the short term. The volatility book makes markets in caps, floors, and swaptions as well as captions, floortions, and spreadtions. The basis book deals with the spread between different floating-rate indices, such as prime and commercial paper vs. Libor [London interbank offered

rate, the basic rate at which banks lend money to each other].
The last two books are structured to arbitrage changes in the
steepness of the curve as well as overall movements in interest
rates.

'I doubt,' added Rotberg drily, 'that the CEO of that bank was
equipped to supervise that operation.'

One bank that evidently was not so equipped was National
Westminster which, in the spring of 1997 discovered a massive loss
on the options book of its investment banking subsidiary, NatWest
Markets. The bank's chief executive, Derek Wanless, was actually
serenading NatWest's achievements in a series of meetings with
investors in New York when he received a phone call from
headquarters informing him that NWM had uncovered an unexpected loss. Rushing back to London, he announced to an astonished City that the loss was 'very, very unlikely' to exceed £50
million. NatWest's value on the stock market immediately plunged
by £460 million. But it turned out that the bank had got it wrong.
A few weeks later NatWest had to reveal that the loss was nearly
double the original estimate, at £90 million.

Since the Barings disaster was supposed to have terrified every
bank in the world into tightening its controls, how could this have
happened? The main perpetrator was a former star trader, the
thirty-year-old Kyriacos Papouis, who dealt in OTC swaptions.
(These are options on swaps – effectively, bets or hedges on the
future movement of interest rates). In the regular revaluation of his
trading book, he had consistently overvalued his options positions
between 1994 and 1996. It was one reason he came to be regarded
as a star and it also, naturally, swelled the bonuses that NatWest
paid him and his immediate managers.

The most disturbing part of it, however, was that no one at
NWM had noticed the overvaluations for so long. It was only after
Papouis went to Bear Sterns that NatWest accountants discovered
the problem. The overvaluation of the options had disguised two
years' worth of trading losses.

Many in the options market were not particularly surprised.
NWM had been expanding rapidly in a bid to boost itself into the
'bulge bracket' of top global investment banks. Its exposure in the

swaps market, for instance, had mushroomed in 1996 from £379 billion to £550 billion which was nearly seven times the size of its entire £80 billion balance sheet. Additionally, it had £267 billion in interest rate options outstanding at the end of 1996 – more than three times its balance sheet size. Its methods of valuing options were regarded by competitors as crude, and its operations were growing too fast for its managers to keep up with. Five of them were eventually sacked for failing to supervise Papouis properly.

Who else might have blown the whistle on Papouis? The brokers who arranged many of the options he bought and sold would have known whether or not the rogue trader's valuations were reasonable. But they had a natural interest in not disputing his high estimates because it made them look good – they were selling him good deals. More worrying is that the losses were hidden in part by switching options between different accounts within NWM, which could not have been done without the knowledge of others in the bank apart from Papouis. NatWest has not explained how this happened or who was involved.

Clearly, NatWest suffered an impressive – though not particularly unusual – operational breakdown. But there is another problem built into the whole business of options. Valuing options, as noted in Chapter Two, is an art dressed up as a science. The Black–Scholes pricing formula depends among other things on an estimate of an option's volatility. But volatility is a slippery concept. In reality, the estimate is little better than a guess based on historical data. If the market departs from previous norms, the guess will be invalid. The more complex the option, the more difficult the process becomes. Since OTC swaptions are all slightly different, the estimate of one particular option's volatility is an inexact process usually based on a comparison with some other similar – but not identical – option. As with a second-hand car, you never really know what an OTC option is worth until you actually sell it or buy it. Placing a value on it in the interim is, in some ways, only a more sophisticated version of pinning the tail on the donkey.

So Papouis did not necessarily do anything illegal. There was no fraud and no concealment. When it came to putting a value on his options, he simply guessed very high. Of course, every bank has computer models that are supposed to inject some objective system into this process. But it seems that the models Papouis was using in his computer were more sophisticated than the models the 'middle office' clerks, who were supposed to check his results, were using in theirs. This is a widely recognized problem, known as model risk. As the mortgage-backed securities traders in Chapter Three found, model risk can be fatal. Besides, middle office managers are often lowly paid accountants with little in-depth knowledge of derivatives. In NatWest's case, the middle office may have assumed that Papouis's valuations were so high because his model was better than theirs.

A £90 million loss is not big enough, of course, to destroy a bank the size of NatWest, but it had wide ramifications. It caused the resignation of Martin Owen, NWM's chief executive, and placed a question mark over the future of Derek Wanless and Lord Alexander, NatWest's chairman. It also threw NWM's strategy of global growth into doubt and led to speculation that NatWest would have to merge or be taken over to save it from its reputation for lousy management.

And yet again it raised those nagging doubts: the problem was containable this time, but what if next time it is on a bigger scale in slightly different conditions? If leading international banks like NatWest still have not got their derivatives act together in a case as simple as this one, can there be any hope they ever will?

For another damaging example of how derivatives dealing is a major management problem, consider the options losses suffered by a leading US commerical bank. Its options department had been so hugely profitable for two years that the bank's senior executives seemed convinced they were in possession of a secret formula that enabled them to beat the market in all circumstances. None of the senior managers, however, knew the first thing about options trading. In another section of the dealing room a star trader – or so they had thought of him – lost tens of millions of dollars during the year and no longer seemed such a star. To keep him from causing any further damage he was moved sideways to take control of the options desk. He, too, knew precious little about options trading.

After several months in his new role, the trader discovered that the foreign exchange dealers were set to report a bigger profit for the year than the options operations, but bonus time was creeping up and he had his reputation to recover. Deciding that the options operation should be the star turn for a third year in a row, he took a big punt in the market by writing options that left the bank with a huge open exposure. The bank's options strategist, a kind of intellectual adviser to the dealers, warned against the move but was overruled. Normally, options trading is one of the most complex forms of dealing there is. Keeping an options book properly hedged is a tricky business akin to juggling five chain saws on the pitching deck of a ship in mid-ocean. It is called 'dynamic hedging', a matter of constant daily adjustment as the volatility of the markets changes and more options, or the underlying assets, have to be bought or sold to keep the risk in balance. The dealer did not bother with any of this. He wanted to make a killing which meant cranking up the risk. In any case, it is questionable whether he knew how to maintain a hedge on an options book.

The market duly went against him and he lost a fortune. Realizing the gravity of the situation, the dealer moved fast to lay the blame on the options strategist. Because he was better known to the bank's senior executives than the strategist, and because they did not really understand what had gone wrong, they bought his version of the story. The strategist was fired and the loss covered up. It was only when the strategist threatened to report the loss to the central bank that the executives changed their minds – in any case, the dealer was manifestly failing to rectify the loss as he had promised he could. So the bank brought back the strategist and sacked the dealer. In the end, the loss was limited to about $40 million which the bank reported before firing its entire options team and withdrawing from the business in disgust.

The barely contained chaos of bank derivatives operations is worrying because of the pivotal role banks play in the market. As they fastened on derivatives as an important new source of profit during the 1980s and 90s, they did not simply sell the stuff to clients as Bankers Trust did to the likes of P&G and Gibson Greetings. They became the biggest users in the world, transforming themselves from mere lenders into gamblers. Instead of advancing their capital for other people to use, they began using it themselves to place bets in the financial markets. This has produced a fundamental change in the character of banking which the industry's managers are still struggling to comprehend. The big banks still look like the traditional bastions of conservatism, respectability and caution; in reality they behave more like high rollers at a casino, stacking their chips in front of them at the roulette and poker tables. Some understand what they are doing better than others, but all of them are taking risks they would not have contemplated twenty years ago. While heightening the danger of individual bank failures, this has also increased the fragility of the banking system, undermining its resistance to unexpected shocks – indeed, raising the likelihood that such shocks will occur.

It has also changed the nature of the financial markets. Take swaps, for example. The market has grown to some $29 trillion in fifteen years. Common sense might suggest that the speed of this growth would have created unusual dangers. Publicly, bankers argue that this is not so. The figure of $29 trillion is misleading because it is only the 'notional' amount of capital outstanding in swaps. The actual amount at risk (the money that would be lost if something went wrong) is far less. If a bank undertakes a $100 million interest rate swap, the $100 million is the notional amount. But the bank has not actually handed over that amount of money to anyone, as it would have done with a loan. All it has done is agree with someone else to exchange interest payments on the $100 million. So if the counterparty goes bust, the bank does not stand to lose the capital but only the future interest payments it was due to receive. The actual amount at risk in the swaps market as a whole, therefore, is only a fraction of $29 trillion. No reason to worry, say the bankers.

Although it is true that the amount at risk is smaller, this argument ignores the sheer size of the numbers. In its most recent survey of the market the Bank for International Settlements concluded that it would have cost $2.2 trillion to replace all swaps at current market rates on 31 March 1995. As so often with derivatives, however, this figure is little better than a guess. If market conditions had been worse, the replacement cost (the amount at risk) would have been higher. If conditions were catastrophic it might become actually impossible for banks to replace defaulted swaps, in which case the potential losses don't bear thinking about. Even by today's standards $2.2 trillion is a lot of money in comparison to the share capital of the most aggressive banks in the swaps market. Few of the largest US investment banks have capital backing of more than about $16 billion, and most are considerably less than that. The share capital of Chase Manhattan, the largest US commercial bank, is less than $50 billion – a mere pimple compared to the outstanding risk in the swaps market.

The risk represented by $2.2 trillion is even greater when you consider that the swaps market is one of the most highly concentrated in the world. More than half of all currency and interest rate swaps are concentrated on a mere eight American banks. The same banks control more than 90 per cent of all derivatives business in the US. They include Chase Manhattan, Citibank, Morgan Stanley, J. P. Morgan, Salomon Brothers, Bankers Trust and NationsBank. Most of the rest of the world's swaps business is in the hands of a small number of British and European banks such as Barclays, National Westminster, Deutsche Bank and several French banks. A few Japanese institutions, such as Sumitomo Bank, are also players.

The swaps club is so small that a large proportion of the total traffic in swaps is between these institutions. When a big bank needs to hedge a swap with a client by doing a balancing deal with another bank, it is almost certain to use a member of the club. This has tied the big international banks together in a web of obligations that never existed before. It has increased their mutual dependency. The big banks are like a group of mountain climbers roped together by their swaps activity: if one of them falls into a crevasse there is a danger that it will drag the rest of them in with it.

Swaps, however, are only one element in the banking industry's obsessive love affair with derivatives. In selling a complex derivative deal to a client, a bank takes on risk just as the customer does. The question a bank always has to face when doing one of these deals is whether to hedge the risk it has taken on. If it decides not to hedge, it automatically becomes a speculator. It is impossible to tell how much of its risk any given bank has hedged but there is, in any case, an inherent problem with hedging. Unless two offsetting positions match each other exactly down to the precise amounts of money and day of maturity – which is a difficult feat to achieve – they are not a perfect hedge. As the saying goes, the only perfect hedge is in a Japanese garden. As soon as you cease to have a perfect hedge you become, to some extent, a speculator. You are betting on the market.

When recession hit the developed world in 1989 and dragged on into the early 1990s, the temptation to speculate became irresistible. Big banks followed the lead of institutions like Bankers Trust and Salomon Brothers. With few of their corporate customers wanting to borrow money, they began to gamble their own capital in the financial markets – proprietary trading, as it is called – to keep up their profits. The abolition of exchange controls in many countries during the 1980s had given many banks practice in the cut and thrust of the foreign exchange markets. But now they extended their dealing activities and committed more capital than ever before to proprietary trading. The larger banks, in short, became the biggest speculators in the world.

The effect this has had on the way banks earn their profits has been impressive, although it is not always easy to pick out from their published results. Twenty years ago, the proportion of their total profit made by the British clearing banks from market dealing was tiny; these days it fluctuates between about 17 per cent and 40 per cent. The same has happened in the US where proprietary trading has been the fastest growing source of profits for the seven largest commercial banks over the last seven years. Since the early 1980s, their *quarterly* income from dealing has soared from around $500 million to more than $2.5 billion.

Speculation, of course, is a very risky game so it is not surprising that the earnings of banks which indulge heavily in proprietary trading have become increasingly volatile. Some years they are spectacularly large, other years they shrink by half or more, depending on how favourable the markets have been and how cleverly each bank has placed its bets. Midland Bank (now part of Hong Kong and Shanghai Bank) has played harder than most and lost £500 million in the early 1990s largely because of a wrong bet on the direction of interest rates. US investment banks like Goldman Sachs and Salomon have always had fairly volatile earnings but Goldman's hit an unprecedented pothole in 1994 when the collapse in the bond market sent its profits into a nose dive. During the same period Bankers Trust's dealing losses were so large that there were rumours it was insolvent.

Since derivatives are the quintessential tools of speculation, they play a leading role in the banks's proprietary dealing activities. Which is how the banks, in a very few years, have taken up instruments originally designed for limiting risk and converted them into a method of taking on more risk.

By becoming speculators banks are playing a more dangerous game than before. Like any market participants, they have the problem of assessing and controlling market risk and credit risk. Some banks have become quite sophisticated in their risk analysis, a process of assessing what would happen to their derivatives positions in different market conditons, which they call 'stress testing'. Some test themselves more rigorously than others, although bank supervisors tend to believe that none of them are rigorous enough. (The failure of computer models to predict the CMO crashes in the early 1990s is an example of inadequate stress testing.) The supervisors worry that banks do not project sufficiently bad market conditions when testing their positions. Banks have a short term reason not to be too tough on themselves, since the tougher they are the more risk they have to admit they have. That ought to mean cutting back their derivatives dealing to reduce their risk, but less dealing might lead to lower profits at the end of the year and no banker wants that.

There is a further risk which, for many banks, has proved to be the most difficult of all to control. This is operational risk: the danger that a bank doesn't really know what it is doing. Few financial activities have ever presented such huge operational risks as derivatives trading. It turns out that derivatives, in all their complexity and novelty, are a massive management problem – a problem most banks are still a long way from completely solving. Dealers rewarded for the size of their deals, salesmen paid to sell the wrong products to the wrong customers, managers who do not even understand their own products or the activities of their dealers and salesmen – these are failings endemic to the derivatives markets. The chances of operational breakdwon are legion, and none holds more terror for banks than the ultimate operational risk: the rogue trader. There have been no more dramatic cases of this than when the patricians at Baring Brothers, the Queen's bankers, hired a fresh-faced twenty-six-year-old called Nick Leeson.

From the start, it was the blind leading the blind. None of the top men at Barings had any dealing experience or first-hand understanding of derivatives markets. Nick Leeson also had no dealing experience and his understanding of the markets was deeply flawed. It was a disaster that had to happen.

Leeson was born in Watford, Hertfordshire, the son of a plasterer, and enjoyed a modest lower-middle class upbringing. He went to school at Parminters which had close associations with the City of London and regularly sent alumni to work as clerks in the big clearing banks. Leeson was the oldest child of whom, according to his own account, a lot had always been expected, particularly by his mother. He worked conscientiously though not brilliantly at school, passing his maths O-level at the second attempt. His particular gift, however, was in making friends. People liked his big open face and easy manner, and seemed to trust him. The general verdict among neighbours was that he was a 'nice bright boy'.

What they did not seem to have noticed was his burning ambition and a distinct yobbishness – or perhaps they simply took that for granted. After watching a football match on one occasion, he and his friends crowded into a discothèque, took off their clothes and stood around naked on the dance floor. Shortly thereafter he was beaten up by some strangers who were upset that one of Leeson's friends had slipped his penis into the hand of an unsuspecting girl at the club. His friends, even his wife, regularly addressed him as 'Dickhead'.

But while Leeson seemed at home in such situations, he seemed equally at ease in the rather starched atmosphere of the City where he started working after he left school. He himself noticed this ability to fit effortlessly into two such different worlds and appears to have regarded it as the origin of his ability to lead a double life.

When his mother died he evidently felt a heavy responsibility to look after his younger siblings, which merged with a fierce drive to better himself. By the time he joined Morgan Stanley, his second employer, he was already showing signs of learning how to get ahead in the securities industry. Although only a junior back-office clerk helping to settle the trades done by the dealers, he asked his managers for a 100 per cent salary increase on the grounds that he thought he deserved it. Since he was requesting well above the amount someone in his job would normally get paid, Morgan Stanley refused but still agreed to give him a sizeable increase. The lesson he seems to have learnt is that it can't hurt to try it on a bit.

Now skilled in settlements, he joined Barings. One of the first things he did for his new employer was to help sort out a colossal administrative mess in its operation in Jakarta. A mountain of share certificates worth about £100 million was quietly mouldering in a bank vault in Indonesia. They could not be sold or passed on to the customers who had bought them because no one at Barings could sort out who owned what. Putting his back-office knowledge to use, Leeson worked for months to clear up the backlog and sort out the trades. The lesson he seems to have taken away from this experience was a profound contempt for Barings, its management and its understanding of its own business. It was on this assignment that he met and married his wife, Lisa.

Then came Singapore. Barings needed a back-office clerk to process its burgeoning arbitrage operation between the Tokyo, Singapore and Osaka markets. It also needed a floor manager for its dealings on the Singapore International Monetary Exchange, so in 1992 they gave both jobs to Leeson. This, he realized, was the big break he had been waiting for.

Leeson yearned to be on a trading floor, where the money and the glamour was, rather than in the back office. More than that, he wanted to be a star, a market legend whose mere presence in the trading pit could make prices move. He could not have found a more conducive environment in which to live out his fantasy than Barings.

It was totally unequipped to protect itself against a phenomenon like Nick Leeson. Its problem was that it did not know this. As Britain's oldest bank, founded on Christmas Day 1762, Barings had deep traditions but they were not traditions that had much to do with modern banking. It was profoundly conservative, risk averse and patrician. The Barings were not only rich but at the heart of the British Establishment and removed from the life of ordinary people as only Britain's class system enables wealthy folk to be. Peter Baring, Andrew Tuckey (the chairman designate) and Peter Norris (who ran the investment banking side which included Leeson's trading activities) all came from a world that knew little of people like Leeson and his exploits in discothèques.

Barings had been forced to change its ways when much of Britain's financial markets were deregulated in 1986. Big Bang, as it was called, changed the face of the City. American banks in particular poured in to buy up stockbroking houses and set up dealing rooms as if this was the new Klondike. Barings felt the wind of change but had no clear idea of what to do about it. With too little money to compete with the big banks, it bought Henderson Crossthwaite, a small broking firm which happened to bring with it a man named Christopher Heath.

He was among the first foreigners to spot the potential of the Japanese warrants market. Warrants were simply an option attached to bonds issued by Japanese companies. They gave the buyer of the bonds the right to buy the company's shares at a point in the future for a particular price. When the Japanese stock market took off in the 1980s, the value of the warrants shot up because they offered an incredibly cheap way to buy shares that were soaring in value by the day. Heath developed a strong business selling the warrants to foreign investors, and by 1989 became Britain's highest paid man with a salary of £2.5 million. He was also making a fortune for Barings. That same year his operation contributed around £50 million of the firm's total $74 million profit.

Heath's operation was, in essence, a highly specialized dealing machine. It not only put Barings into the Far East in a big way but placed it at the leading edge of financial developments because Barings now earned a higher proportion of its profit from trading in the new field of derivatives than almost any bank on the planet except, perhaps, Bankers Trust. Delighted as they were with the massive extra profits, however, the old-style bankers at Barings never really understood the aggressive, freewheeling opportunism of Heath and his men, and they never liked it either. When the Japanese warrants market went sour and Heath's profits dropped he was swiftly ejected from the company.

But his legacy lingered on, leaving Barings with a split personality, a divided culture. The dealers kept on dealing and the bankers kept on hating them. The dealers were also soaking up a huge proportion of the bank's capital which was causing administrative headaches and problems with the supervisors, and so Barings set about integrating the dealing business (Barings Securities) into the banking business. The result was chaos.

Almost none of the top men who ended up in control of the dealing operation were from the securities business or had experience in the markets. Leeson knew they were not interested in the settlements side of the business and he knew just how bad their control systems were for checking what he did. He was also acutely aware of how little they knew about derivatives. Ron Baker was the only one of Leeson's London bosses who had been a dealer, but his experience was in Eurobonds rather than futures and options. A former Bankers Trust employee, he was a gung-ho market animal who relished being responsible for the firm's star performer, although his occasionally uncouth behaviour seems to have shocked even Leeson himself. After the collapse of the bank, he admitted to Bank of England investigators his ignorance of the finer points of futures trading when he described a visit to Singapore in 1994 to watch Leeson in action: 'It was clear to me the minute I walked into the Simex pit that it was going to be very hard for anyone, let alone me, to make much of a value judgement about what was happening . . .'

This was the situation into which Leeson stepped and the reason why he came to be sent out to Singapore with no clear boss, no clear reporting lines and not even a clear job description. By default, he ended up being in charge of trading and back-office settlements which, from an organizational point of view, was a cardinal sin. It meant there was no one to check how he recorded his trading activity. This was the fundamental reason he was able to carry out his fraud. With profound but unintentional irony a management report on the Singapore operation said: 'The general manager [Leeson] likes to be involved in the back office, and does not regard it as an undue burden.' Well, no, in the circumstances, he wouldn't.

Even allowing Leeson to undertake proprietary dealing on its behalf shows how the top men of Barings were operating in late twentieth-century markets with a nineteenth-century mind-set. Leeson had not been to university, had no record of mathematical ability and almost no dealing experience. In choosing him they were acting like the old-fashioned London bankers they were: in the old days, the City's dealers had always been bright East End lads with a good head for figures. They bought things and they sold things just as they might have done in the street markets of Brick Lane or Portobello Road, and on the whole they knew their place which was well down the pecking order in a bank like Barings. It was a class and cultural phenomenon, and the patricians at the head of the bank were comfortable in a world organized that way. But although the bank had become a major derivatives player it had not noticed that the people who work in the business these days tend to have degrees and doctorates. An assessment of Leeson by Ron Baker in a report he wrote for Barings in 1994 shows just how unable they were to judge a qualified trader: 'Without him [i.e. Leeson] Barings Futures (Singapore) would lack a trader with the right combination of experience of trading sizeable lots, and a detailed appreciation of the trading strategies, familiarity with the local trader limits and practices, and contacts among traders and officials.' Baker couldn't have been more wrong.

A glance at the proprietary trading department of a US bank would have shown Barings' top brass how inadequate Leeson was for the job – indeed, how inadequate many of them were too. The top US bank dealing rooms are stuffed with university professors, dealers trained in higher mathematics, managers with long experience of derivatives. But they didn't look. The only thing they seemed to see was that the Americans made big money from proprietary trading and paid themselves unimaginably large bonuses. They wanted that too but did not bother to find out that the whole process required a degree of professionalism they did not possess.

Matters got even worse when Barings tried to integrate the

accounting systems of the banking and securities operations in 1994. This finally sealed the firm's fate. The ensuing confusion was what allowed Leeson's losses to go undetected and the bank's entire share capital to be remitted to him in Singapore in contravention of all common sense, not to mention the banking regulations. To Leeson's amazement, every threadbare, nonsensical explanation he gave to anyone who questioned his accounting sleights of hand was accepted. As he soon realized, everyone wanted to believe him; everyone's bonus depended on his dealing.

The whole Barings' approach to its proprietary trading, at least from its London headquarters, was seat-of-the-pants. One is tempted to call it amateurish, yet it was not only that. Barings was overtaken by developments in the financial markets with which it could not keep abreast. New products, new markets, new customers; it was all happening at such a pace that the bank could not run fast enough to keep up. And it was not alone. A legion of other banks over the last decade have faced the same problem and done much the same as Barings, although with less overtly disastrous consequences. The typical reaction of bankers to changes in their markets is to shoot first and ask questions later: if you don't do the business and make the profits now, you might miss the chance. Any mess this causes, the thinking usually runs, can be cleared up later. Leeson's bosses didn't really understand how he was making so much money but they fully expected his profits to decline when the other banks found out and copied him. This is what frequently happens in banking, and so they wanted him to make hay while the sun still shone. Which is why they gave him such a free rein.

His main tool was the now infamous 88888 error account, the secret repository in which he hid all his losses. All banks have error accounts to handle discrepancies created by out-trades until they are settled, but such accounts are never meant to hold large sums of money. Leeson's own rather self-serving account in his book *Rogue Trader* of how he came to set up the account presents it as a quixotic attempt to hide a relatively small sum lost by a female colleague on a mistaken trade. In fact, however, the 88888 account was opened more than two months before that incident. Even before he had been registered as a trader by Simex he began trading in Nikkei 225 futures contracts and instantly made a £40,000 loss,

which he stuffed into the secret account. By the end of the year he
had racked up losses of £2 million.

The following year Barings' Tokyo office began giving him
orders to buy or sell the Nikkei 225 on Simex as part of an arbitrage
strategy. To impress his bosses, Leeson would tell them that he
had bought lower than he had, and sold higher than he had. He
would hide the difference – invariably a loss – in the 88888 account.
The Tokyo office was, not surprisingly, astonished and deeply
impressed at his ability to deal at such good prices. They called
him the 'turbo arbitrageur'. They wanted to believe that he could
do what, even to them, seemed impossible.

By then, Leeson's brief reputation as a star trader – a Master of
the Universe as Tom Wolfe called them in *Bonfire of the Vanities*,
his novel about Wall Street – was growing. He was allowed to start
up as a proprietary trader using Barings' own capital and he quickly
established an expertise in the Nikkei 225 contracts. He even began
trading in options although no one at Barings had given him
permission to do so.

The fact that Barings, Simex and the Bank of England all
accepted his star status without serious question is a testimony to
the enduring gullibility of financial folk, and to the important role
fantasy plays in finance. Banks are in thrall to the myth of the
Master of the Universe, the champion trader, the Napoleon of the
markets who carries all before him and makes legendary profits.
They so badly want to believe it because it means easy money,
better pay and, in a way, that they are, after all, blessed by the gods.
Peter Baring, the chairman, seems to have felt this way when he
complacently told the Bank of England's supervision department
at the very moment Leeson was draining the life-blood from his
bank that 'the recovery in profitability had been amazing, leaving
Barings to conclude that it was not actually very difficult to make
money in the securities business'. It was as if his bank had been
given a secret elixir that was denied to the rest of the financial
industry. While Peter Baring's remark must qualify as one of the
stupidest things said by a banker in living memory, it reflected a
stubborn desire to believe what was most convenient. In that, he is
hardly unique among bankers.

Baring and his senior managers believed a trader who said he could always beat the market. It wasn't true; it hardly ever is. Almost no one is that smart. Naturally, some dealers are better than others but the plain, prosaic truth is that spectacular perform-ances year in, year out, are almost impossible to achieve. Traders who do staggeringly well do so for specific reasons: they may have genuinely better market analysis which gives them an edge until everyone else catches up; or they may deal in such massive amounts they can temporarily sway prices in their favour; or they may be committing fraud.

Leeson never had an edge. Indeed, for all his contempt for his bosses, he proved from the beginning to be as incompetent as they were. As a trader he was never better than pretty hopeless; his real profits, as opposed to the fake ones he reported to Barings, were chicken feed. What is striking about his own account of his antics, however, is that profits and losses appear to have meant little to him. The thing that really mattered in his eyes was the outward image of a successful trader: the stir he caused on the Simex trading floor, the adulation he received in Barings, the respect he got from Simex which loved him for all the business he brought to the market. The huge sums of money he gambled with evidently had little reality for him. He dealt as though spinning a roulette wheel with increasing abandon. For three years, everyone involved went along with his fantasy.

The business Barings thought he was doing was arbitraging the Nikkei 225 between Singapore and Osaka since the identical contract was traded in both places. When minute price differences opened up between the two markets, Leeson was supposed to exploit it by buying where the contract was cheaper and selling where it was more expensive. Since each trade involved a balancing purchase and sale, and because all outstanding positions were supposed to be closed out – reduced to zero – at the end of each day, this operation carried virtually no risk. The profits on each trade would be tiny, but if repeated often enough the process could deliver a useful return. This, however, did not apparently fit Leeson's view of what a Master of the Universe should be doing. He wanted to take big punts without a countervailing trade in the other market. And that is what he did, with disastrous consequences.

By the end of 1993 he had lost £25 million (all hidden in the secret account). To balance this out he sold options that brought in premiums of £30 million. This was extremely dangerous because if the options went against him he stood to lose a fortune. In the meantime, the fake figures made it look as though the profit from Singapore had soared from £1.18 million to £8.8 million in Leeson's first eighteen months on the job. He was, in effect, personally generating 20 per cent of Barings' entire profit for 1993. In 1994 he made £20 million – again, a fifth of the bank's total profit. Inevitably, he became the darling of the Barings management who, anxious not to lose their new star, jacked his pay up from £35,746 to £130,000.

As the dealing juggernaut gained momentum, Leeson – oblivious of his own incompetence as a trader – behaved more and more like a superstar who was above the rules. He changed his computer password to Superman. He was blackballed from the Singapore Cricket Club for hitting a fellow member at the snooker table. He dropped his trousers and exposed his backside to some girls in a bar – an extremely foolish thing to do in a state that flogs people for relatively slight misdemeanours like vandalism. When they threatened to call the police he sneeringly offered them his own mobile phone to use. He was duly arrested and Barings had to call in a lawyer who got him off with a small fine.

In 1994, James Baker, Barings' internal auditor, investigated the source of his massive profits – the only time anyone thought to do this. Caught up in the fiction of Leeson's stardom, he concluded that the young trader was so exceptionally talented that every effort should be made to prevent him being poached by a competitor. Baker failed to find the massive bets on the Nikkei 225 index that Leeson was hiding in the 88888 account, or the options he had sold.

As 1994 wore on, Leeson's dealing grew more frenetic. His strategy, such as it was, is called a short straddle: selling both put and call options on the Nikkei 225. This was theoretically a hedge since the puts and calls should cancel each other out, but it could only work if there was relatively little volatility in the market. As long as the market remained this way the options would expire 'out of the money' without being exercised and Leeson would keep the premium money. But if volatility increased there was a far higher probability that either the put or the call options would go 'into the money' and be exercised, in which case Leeson would lose hundreds of millions of dollars. It would not matter whether the market went up or down, he would still get scalped. The irony was that, through the mechanics of the market, the more options he sold the further he drove down the market's volatility. This depressed the price of the options (since option prices are determined, in large part, by volatility), which meant that Leeson had to sell even more of them to bring in enough premium income to balance his futures losses.

Other traders in Barings assumed that all this trading was on behalf of a genuine client, Philippe Bonnefoy, and other customers. In fact, Barings itself was the principal. By the end of 1994 Leeson had $270 million in futures losses, balanced by only $220 million in premium income from his options sales. To make up the difference and fool the auditors he forged a payment of $50 million purporting to come from a US broker called Spear, Leeds & Kellogg. Incredibly, not one at Coopers & Lybrand, the auditors, or Barings wondered why the fax on which the confirmation arrived said 'From Nick & Lisa' at the top. Leeson had sent it from his machine at home.

Blissfully unaware of the mayhem he was causing, Barings decided to give him a bonus of £450,000. By now, however, his losses were finally getting to him. He was drinking heavily, sleeping badly and gobbling sweets by the fistful on the Simex trading floor out of sheer nervousness.

On 17 January 1995 Nature delivered the knock-out blow. An earthquake measuring 7.2 on the Richter scale flattened the city of Kobe, throwing the Japanese markets into a panic. The Tokyo stock market fell slightly, wavered for a few days, then collapsed as if it had been poleaxed. This destroyed Leeson's 'straddle' strategy and his long futures position which lost more than £100 million in a few days. His reaction was to start buying the Nikkei 225 like a maniac to try to force the market back up. If he could do this, his futures would return to profit and his options straddle would also be safe again.

But if there was ever an exercise in futility, this was it. Leeson had as much chance of influencing the massive Tokyo stock market on his own as he would have done blowing storm clouds away with his own breath. He did not have the experience to understand that the world's financial markets were not just one big trading pit as he seems to have imagined them to be. In comparison to the total size of the Japanese capital markets which were moved by fundamental forces far beyond his control, his dealing was a pinprick.

Beyond help or redemption, he was making the fatal mistake of doubling up a bet rather than cutting his losses. 'He probably reckoned he had nothing more to lose and decided to go for broke. In his position, I'd probably have done the same,' said a London dealer later, echoing the sentiments of many others. In roulette, doubling up is a certain way to win – if you have enough cash. As long as you keep going, you will sooner or later come out ahead. The trouble is that you will probably run out of money before you reach that point. Leeson was about to find this out in the futures markets.

It is also clear from his own account that he never got over the feeling that the market was wrong and he was right. He continued to bludgeon it with his buying as if trying to punish the other traders for misbehaving. Yet Leeson's confidence in himself and contempt for his bosses never faltered. He continued to think the Japanese stock market would rise, making him perhaps the only dealer in the whole of Asia who held this view. He even began selling large amounts of futures contracts in Japanese government bonds, figuring that since the stock market was going to rise as a result of his dealing, the bond market would naturally fall. The exact opposite happened.

For every 100 points the Nikkei index dropped Leeson lost around £20 million, and the market was falling almost every day. To cover the variation margin calls piling up at Simex, Leeson demanded more and more money from Barings in London and, amazingly, he got it all. Despite growing suspicions, his superiors' fundamental belief in their star trader survived until the end. They sent him an amount that was twice the bank's own capital, believing that his dealing was on behalf of clients and that Barings did not stand to lose all this money itself.

He also got more cash by selling yet more options. By the time he controlled 80 per cent of the trading volume in the Nikkei contract and 50 per cent in government bonds, even he realized that he was out of control. His positions on Simex and in Osaka were the talk of the markets since they were about ten times bigger than the next largest players. He tried one subterfuge after another to delay detection but eventually realized it was ultimately hopeless. The auditors were closing in and he was running out of money. On his final day, 23 February, he lost £144 million. He finally gave up out of sheer exhaustion as much as anything.

Leeson left the Barings office that afternoon, avoiding the questions of the auditors, and got a friend to drive him and Lisa to the airport. The couple fled to Kuala Lumpur from where Leeson faxed an apology to the office but offered no explanation of what he had done. Later that evening Barings officials found a computer printout detailing the contents of the 88888 account. Then all hell broke loose.

The Leesons travelled on to Borneo as Nick chomped his way through mountains of Big Mac hamburgers to which he had become addicted. By then the hue and cry had been raised and the British media was combing South-East Asia in search of the perpetrator of one of the worst financial scandals in living memory. Finally, the Leesons tried flying home to Britain but were picked up by police in Frankfurt. After months in a German jail, Leeson was extradited to Singapore and sentenced to eight years in prison.

As a case study in the psychology of traders, his story has few equals. It is also a classic example of how a bank can let such a disaster happen to it, for the truth about rogue traders is as prosaic as it is about Masters of the Universe. The popular image is of a rogue male, alone, out of control and completely unstoppable, ignoring his bosses, thumbing his nose at the markets, defiantly rolling the dice – and losing on a heroic scale. Companies that suffer large losses tend to present their misfortune as the action of a rogue trader because they feel it somehow exonerates the management. 'It would have happened anyway; there was nothing we could have done to stop it,' has become a familiar boardroom mantra. But the record shows that it isn't really like this.

Dealers do indeed run amok at banks and companies alike. But their losses only become really huge when the incompetence or collusion of their managers allows them to. There is not a banker in the world who could put his hand on his heart and swear that he might not have a potential Leeson in his dealing room. There is not a banker who, in his heart of hearts, would swear that his management controls were so faultless that he could always stop a rogue dealer in time.

At least the business Leeson was doing was a relatively simple one to understand, even though his managers do not appear to have understood it at all well. But other banks have had to grapple with more insidious problems that in some ways should cause more concern. Derivatives trading requires sophisticated computer programmes, but on several occasions banks have found out too late that their programmes were not good enough. Chemical, for instance, lost $33 million in one year selling interest caps that were wrongly priced and hedged because the computer model was wrong. The bank only found this out when market volatility rose and its hedges came unstuck.

A more bizarre case happened at Kidder Peabody when a dealer named Joseph Jett was sacked in 1993, accused of having lost the bank $350 million. Here, on the face of it, was yet another rogue trader caught redhanded exploiting the system. That, at least, is what Kidder's senior management tried to claim. But unlike most dealers kicked out of their firm and vilified by their former managers, Jett sued. He claimed that far from being a rogue, he had behaved completely properly all along by following the orders of his bosses. At the centre of his case was a computer programme that was not everything it seemed to be.

Jett was highly educated – he went to the Massachusetts Institute of Technology and Harvard Business School. He was also a skilled mathematician and a computer expert (hence Kidder's unjustified later claim that he had somehow rigged the bank's computer). He made no secret of his ambition to use Wall Street to get seriously rich, although that hardly made him unusual. It was the intensity of his ambition that was out of the ordinary. After unremarkable dealing stints at CS First Boston and Morgan Stanley, he joined Kidder in 1991 with no experience of trading government bonds.

He soon gained a fearsome reputation in the bank for his desire to dominate the business.

The business was trading US Treasuries. When a dealer like Joseph Jett made a trade all he had to do was touch a finger to the dealing screen and the computer did the rest – booking the deal and calculating the profit or loss, which it would immediately flash back to the trader. Jett, of course, never had to handle physical bonds, the valuable bits of paper which underlay the market in which he was operating. Indeed, the instruments he was dealing in did not have any physical reality so the whole exercise was like a computer game. It was treated this way by everyone involved at Kidder. At one point, for instance, Jett had bought twice as much of a particular bond issue as actually existed in reality, yet neither he nor any of his superiors thought there was anything odd or untoward about this.

The subjects of this cyber-game were instruments known as US government 'strips' (an acronym for the Fed programme authorizing their issuance: Separate Trading of Registered Interest and Principal of Securities). It works like this: the investment bank asks the Fed to chop up an ordinary thirty year government bond into its constituent parts consisting of sixty half-yearly interest payments and a single principal payment. The constituent parts are the 'strips'. Later on you can put it all back together again to reconstitute the original bond – known as a 'recon'. It is somewhat like asking the bank to change a dollar bill into ten dimes or ten dimes into a dollar bill.

Each interest strip thus becomes a short term bond in its own right, but it does not behave like an ordinary bond. Although it begins by being very cheap to buy, its value constantly rises over time as the interest accrues day by day, until it reaches its full face value on the day of maturity. Suppose you bought a strip at $80 today; it will pay $100 at maturity. The $20 difference is the interest that accumulated on the bond between the time you bought it and time it matured. This price rise is inevitable and is not like the discount on an ordinary bond.

It is this price rise on strips that Jett exploited. He could do so because the computer told him he could. But the computer, unfortunately, had been wrongly programmed.

Simplifying somewhat for the sake of clarity, the fault was this: Jett would buy some strips and then immediately do a forward trade in which he agreed to sell them back to the Fed at a certain price in, say, ninety days' time to be reconstituted into the original bonds. Naturally, the forward price would be higher than the cash price because it would represent the extra interest accrued on the strips during the ninety days. The difference between the two prices, therefore, was not a dealing profit but merely accrued interest, just as you get on a bank savings account. Kidder's computer, however, did not understand this. It kept telling Jett that he was making a profit every time he did one of these trades. John Liftin, Kidder's general counsel, later explained: 'When you sell a strip forward, the price will be higher than today's price. Our accounting system recognizes that difference initially and treats it as a profit.'

Jett and his superiors appear to have believed everything the computer was telling them. And why not? It was making heroes of them all. Jett's profits soared, as did the bonuses he and his colleagues were paid. In 1993 a grateful Kidder awarded him a $9 million bonus and made him the chairman's 'man of the year'. Melvyn Mullin, his immediate superior and the man most responsible for designing the faulty computer programme, is thought to have got about $8 million that year while Edward Cerullo, who was in over-all charge of the bond trading department, was paid in the region of $17 million. The computer, very definitely, was their friend.

But there was a problem. By the time the forward trade matures the 'profit' might in reality have vanished or have turned into a loss. This is because the cost to Kidder of borrowing money to buy the strips might be equal to or more than the interest Kidder was accruing on the strips themselves. Since the computer might eventually spot this and wipe out the profit it had originally assigned to the deal, Jett's solution was to prevent the forward trades maturing. He would roll them over again and again in increasing amounts so that the computer kept showing the 'profits' and never showed up the losses he was actually making.

He began doing this a few months after he arrived at Kidder in

1991. By 1993 Kidder was dealing in more than $70 billion bonds a day. Jett's own positions were often up to $30 billion at any given time. He was king of the government bond market, leveraged to the eyeballs, rolling in profits. He had accumulated real losses of around $100 million but this isn't what the computer showed. Relying on the Kidder computer's accounting system, General Electric reported profits of $350 million from Jett's activities. Except that the profits were an illusion.

While the computer was misleading everyone, Jett's own personality made things worse. He was enormously, even arrogantly, self-confident and frighteningly intense. He browbeat salesmen into handing over their client accounts to him, sometimes telling them they were not worthy to handle such important customers. Entries in his personal diary show that he was also contemptuous of some of his senior colleagues. Jett laid out his philosophy in a speech in January 1994 in Boca Raton, Florida, at Kidder's annual staff retreat where performance is reviewed and future goals are set. While lesser players might regard dealing as a game, he said, to him it was war, a fight to kill his rivals and keep the spoils. Nothing less than total victory was good enough. He expected his colleagues to treat it the same way. For good measure, he also declared that in the coming year he would produce bigger profits than Mike Vranos, Kidder's other big hitter, on the mortgage backed securities side. It was, remarked a colleague, more like a religious revivalist speech than the kind of thing they were used to hearing at these occasions. Jett's staring eyes and aggressive manner created a kind of buffer zone around him and the government bond desk. On one level, at least, people were simply too frightened to interfere with him or ask him what he was doing. That, together with the profits he was generating, meant he was left very much alone to do as he liked.

During 1993 Kidder's owner, General Electric, became uneasy at the size of Jett's positions. Even for a big bank $30 billion in government bonds was a lot to carry each day, and Kidder was not a big bank. Kidder's top executives respectfully started asking their star trader to lower his positions but this of course threatened to upset Jett's profit machine. He could not reduce his bond holdings without actually closing out some of his forward 'recon' trades, but to do that would mean losing the profits which the computer had told him he had made.

His dealing strategies became more complex as he looked for ways to keep the computer churning out profits. Then came the bond market crash of February 1994 and Wall Street banks, like all the other major players around the world, haemorrhaged money. No one was immune. No one, that is, except Jett. In the first quarter of the year he reported a staggering $50 million profit.

In the end, it was all too good to be true. Kidder was readying itself for a sale. Jack Kemp, the head of GE, wanted to get rid of the investment bank. As usual in such circumstances, accountants were called in to clean the place up and make the business look its best before prospective buyers were allowed to look at it. The auditors introduced a new accounting system which no longer accepted the accrued interest on the strips as profit. Suddenly, the money machine blew up.

On a Friday afternoon, Jett was called in by his bosses to explain why a recent audit had concluded that Kidder had $350 million of 'unrecognized losses' from his trading. Cerullo, Richard O'Donnell, the chief financial officer, and John Liftin were frankly confused and needed Jett's help to understand. After two hours of explanations by Jett, they were still confused. The meeting broke up for the weekend. On Sunday the senior executives sacked Jett and accused him of carrying out a hidden fraud. The Securities and Exchange Commission had duly charged him with this.

In fact, Jett later produced strong evidence to show that he had made no secret of what he was doing. As well as the computer records, his trades were all scrupulously entered by hand – usually by his subordinates – in red hard-backed ledgers kept on top of Cerullo's desk. He had been repeatedly audited and questioned over the previous two years. Mullin, Cerullo, even Michael Carpenter, Kidder's chairman, had no excuse for not knowing what Jett's strategy was. If the senior executives did not know what he was doing, as they now claimed, they were grossly negligent. If they did know, they must have been part of the alleged fraud. Fraud by Jett was an inherently foolish allegation.

Jett himself insisted that he had done nothing wrong. He

thought he was doing great things as a market gladiator. Kidder's computer had told him so and for two years no one had pointed out that the computer had, as it were, its head on backwards. Others agreed with him. In December 1996, before the judge had made up her mind about the SEC's case, an arbitration panel of the National Association of Securities Dealers effectively exonerated Jett by giving him access to the $5 million in his Kidder accounts. Meanwhile, Jett came to see his humiliation by Kidder as a manifestation of ingrained racism on Wall Street.

But even if Jett was not guilty as charged by the SEC, the disturbing aspect of his story is the willingness of highly educated, intelligent and well trained traders to believe unquestioningly in the computer's world of virtual profits. It seems that none of them ever applied some basic common sense to what the computer was saying. Was this fraud or simply a computer fault? Or a computer fault that people who should have known better were happy to connive at? At least part of the reason why they did not question the electronic figures is that traders these days rely utterly on computers. The screens are not only their window on to the market, but their auditor and back office too. Computers, as far as the trader is concerned, are the source of almost everything: market information, the financial instruments themselves, the financing, delivery, payment, profit and loss calculations. There is no real world of bonds and cash and payment slips any more. The dealing world is in the computer, it is all electronic, all unreal. This does not necessarily encourage common sense but it certainly encourages a deep dependence on computers. Dealers are not used to questioning them. To do so would be to question the underpinnings of their world.

At the same time, the fantastic complexity of derivatives markets means that they could not work any other way than by a reliance on computers. Kidder Peabody's treasury bond debacle is a fine example of how the resulting virtual reality of the dealing process can seem more real to traders than the contradictory evidence of objective reality.

It would be wrong to imagine that what happened at Barings and Kidder Peabody was so exceptional that it could never happen in any other bank. Banks constantly make mistakes they do not admit to and losses they never make public. Given the vast size and complexity of their speculative trading, disguising mistakes is not particularly difficult. A rule of thumb used by many seasoned traders is that a bank can relatively easily hide any loss of up to about $20 million by simple accounting tricks (making up for it out of reserves, revaluing the lossmaking positions so that the loss diminishes or disappears, or shifting the position into the longer term investment portfolio where losses are accounted for more leniently).

Above about $50 million losses tend to be reported to supervisors and, eventually perhaps, to the public because they cannot so easily be hidden. Even here, the flexibility in accounting rules, the willingness of accountants to help clients massage their figures, and the complexity of some of the instruments involved leaves a pretty wide margin for creativity.

Take, for example, the accounting sleight of hand at one leading US bank that allowed it to invent its own profit figures. This came about because the chairman, a particularly macho individual who liked to make grand statements, gave his main institutional share-holders a forecast of year-end profits several months before the year actually closed. Unfortunately, the markets went bad in the last few weeks of the year, which hammered the bank's proprietary trading profits and left it well behind the chairman's forecast. This only became apparent when the accounts were calculated at the year end, but the chairman was not a man to let the facts get in the way of a good profits report. The word came down to the dealing room that all the traders were to re-examine their end-of-year positions and if they could find anything that could be revalued upwards, they were to do it. The people most likely to be able to play with their numbers were the options traders. By revising their estimate of market volatility at the end of the year, the options boys were able to conjure millions of dollars of brand new profit out of thin air. The bank's profit for the year, therefore, was suddenly a great deal healthier than it had been a few hours earlier.

The dealers were angry at what they were being asked to do. It was, after all, probably illegal. If the Federal Reserve Bank of New York had found out, it would have come down on them like the angel of vengeance. Just as important, however, was that their bonuses had been calculated on the earlier lower profit figure and were not being raised in line with the new profit, which hit them in the wallet where it hurt most. Nevertheless, they felt they had little choice but to comply. According to one who was there, 'We had a gun to our heads. There was a recession, the job market was very tight and the management made it clear that if you didn't do what they asked you wouldn't be around in the bank for much longer.'

When the bank's profits were finally announced, they miraculously matched the forecast made by the chairman months before. The shareholders were none the wiser. Nor, for that matter, was the Fed which never did find out.

CHAPTER 7

THE MAKING OF A DERIVATIVES TRADER

I shall dream about a thousand pounds to-night. I know I shall.

Alice in Wonderland

Dirk Thrust (as we shall call him) stood in the driveway of his friend's big house in Essex and gazed enviously at the midnight blue Porsche 911 that stood sleekly in front of the mock-Tudor garage. At that moment he understood what life had meant him for. He was going to find a job in the City. This was the late 1980s and everyone he knew seemed to work there. The capital markets, whatever they were, had become the sexy place to be. Once he had established himself, he would get stinking rich like his friend and own a Porsche 911 too.

At the time, this was an absolutely normal ambition for a young man of Dirk's age and background. He was twenty-four, middle class, and of no fixed employment. He wanted money, status and the chance to impress his own successful parents. The only unusual feature of his rise through the City of London's low life to security as a respected futures broker is that he made it to the top. Helped by quick wits and good luck, he earned enough to retire in his early thirties. His story mirrors those of countless young men and women who joined the ferocious competition to get into the derivatives markets with greater or lesser success during the 1980s and 90s.

But it is also the story of countless ordinary gullible men and women who were persuaded to entrust their savings to the futures markets and thereby lost a vast but unquantifiable amount of money. What most of them didn't know about futures was that private investors stand a frighteningly high chance of getting burned: about 95 per cent of them lose money. It seems in retrospect astonishing that so many people could lose so much with so little complaint, and that the authorities took so long to do anything about it. For Dirk Thrust, however, it was no big deal: the process of getting hold of that money was just a job and a stepping stone to better things in the City.

Dirk had been drifting for a couple of years when he saw the Porsche. He'd studied finance at university and then accountancy at a large firm of auditors. He'd hated it, and the trainee pay was lousy. After six months, he left. Several casual jobs later he was on the train home one evening from working as a barman in a London pub when he met an old university friend. They got talking. The friend worked in the City, said he had a house of his own and a car. He invited Dirk to take a look. Dirk couldn't resist, which is how his friend's driveway came to be his equivalent of the Road to Damascus. 'YES!' he thought excitedly. 'This is *it!*'

In those days the *Evening Standard* was full of box adverts saying things like 'Young trader wanted for international commodities dealing – £££ MASSIVE'. The one Dirk answered was placed by AMA Recruitment Consultants, an outfit which was retained to do the hiring for a firm of retail derivatives brokers called Empire Futures. At AMA's West End offices, Dirk found himself being interviewed alongside a group of about forty young men (there were no women), mostly from public school, dressed in sharp new suits and all eager to shoulder their way into the City. The woman in charge of the proceedings whittled down the original group and sent those on the remaining shortlist to be interviewed at Empire Futures. Dirk was among them. He did not know that the AMA woman would only receive a commission from Empire Futures if candidates hired from her shortlist stayed at the firm for longer than six months. He also did not know that it was a characteristic of employment at Empire Futures that just before their first six months were up, most employees were sacked. There was a lot Dirk didn't yet know about Empire Futures.

The company had a pedigree, if that's the word for it, which is worth describing because it set the pattern for many of the retail futures operations that came after. Empire had been set up by men who had learnt their trade from earlier retail futures broking firms that had attracted hostile publicity for their high pressure selling. The first and most notorious of these had been LHW, founded in 1981 by Colonel John Lockwood, and two much younger men in their twenties – John Hughes and Jeremy Walsh. Colonel Lockwood, Hughes's father in-law, had put up some capital to help start the firm but probably had little idea what futures were. Hughes and Walsh were the driving force behind the venture. They had the invaluable asset of having public school accents: when they opened their mouths they sounded like everyone's idea of investment bankers. They had boundless self-confidence, an insatiable urge to get rich and were not apparently overly troubled by their consciences or by any detailed knowledge of the futures markets. With an unerring instinct for human weakness, however, they saw the potential of those markets to make them wealthy.

Their scheme was to sell futures to the general public, which was not as crazy at it sounds. If people are willing to buy life insurance products which they don't understand from a salesman they have never met before, why not buy futures from some anonymous broker on the telephone? Hughes and Walsh reckoned there must be thousands prepared to gamble their money on the promise of vast profits. They were depressingly correct.

The *Zeitgeist* was on their side. To the average Briton, the 1980s were the years when money changed from being a rather embarrassing necessity to a desirable commodity. It became okay to talk about money, cool to make a profit, positively philanthropic to get rich. For much of the decade house prices surged, leaving many people feeling wealthy even if their immediate cash resources had not increased. Galvanized by Margaret Thatcher's crusade to foster entrepreneurialism, Britons were looking for ways to make money fast. Thanks partly to the privatization programme, private share ownership rose sharply and the City no longer seemed as mysterious and frightening to the average investor as it used to. Shares in this or that state monopoly were sold through user-friendly TV adverts: it was all rather amusing. Shares, futures, options – they all seemed the same to the average punter who was unaware that each product had vastly different risk levels. And because the government deliberately undervalued companies to ensure that investors saw a quick gain on their shares, people had a warm feeling towards this whole new activity: playing the financial markets was fun, easy and, above all, seemed to provide a risk-free profit. What could be better than that?

At the same time, the retail futures markets were virtually unregulated. There were so few rules and resources devoted to keeping them under control that it is reasonable to presume the regulators were hardly aware that a retail futures market existed. Until the Financial Services Act of 1986, nobody was responsible for overseeing or policing the sector at all. Even for professionals in the City of the early 1980s, futures still occupied much the same intellectual space as medieval alchemy. The London Financial Futures Exchange opened in 1981, and that was only a few years after the Bank of England had told representatives from Chicago that futures would never ever take off in Britain.

To give Hughes and Walsh their due, they showed considerable imagination in spotting the money making possibilities of these circumstances. The methods used by LHW and the companies that succeeded it varied relatively little over the next few years. The main technique was cold-calling – simply selecting names from the telephone directory, calling them up and persuading them to entrust thousands of pounds of savings to a complete stranger. They became experts at playing on the greed, naïvety and instinct for gambling that are more common among the population at large than most of us like to admit. They would take a person's money with the promise of investing it in futures at their own discretion and making it into a great deal more money. At first they dealt mainly in gold futures because it was easier for them and for their clients to understand, it sounded sexy and glamorous and somehow rather safe as well. As time went on they diversified into all kinds of commodity and financial futures, too.

Clients were told that the magic of futures was that if they invested, say £10,000 with LHW, the broker could buy 'on margin' investments worth £100,000. It was the siren song of leverage. That, the clients were blithely informed, would multiply their profits tenfold – way beyond anything they could hope to get with an ordinary share. No one mentioned what it did to any losses, and astonishingly few clients ever asked at the beginning. They were lured by LHW's promise of a special stop-loss policy that prevented investors losing money even if the market went against them. If by some misfortune they did lose money, they were told that all they had to do was invest more and adjust their stop-loss policy to ensure a loss did not happen again.

LHW's profit came mainly from the broking commission which could eat up more in a year than a client's original deposit. If LHW charged its clients, say, 1 per cent to buy futures on their behalf, it paid only a tenth of that amount to the professional broker through whom it executed the deal, thus pocketing a profit of 0.9 per cent for itself. Clients were also told that LHW's commission applied to the whole value of a trade and not merely to the money they put up as margin. Most clients assumed that if they entrusted £10,000 to LHW and LHW invested it for them, they would be liable to a £100 commission charge (1.0 per cent of £10,000), which seemed reasonable. In fact, if LHW used the £10,000 to buy £100,000 worth of futures the client paid £1,000 in commission (1.0 per cent of £100,000) – one-tenth of his original investment gone in one fell swoop.

LHW was merciless. Its procedure with customer accounts was to 'churn 'em and burn 'em', selling the original position, buying a new one, selling that and so on, charging a commission on each trade. Naturally, it was in LHW's interest to make a profit for the customer so that there remained money in the account to continue churning, but the predations of hefty commissions often quickly took their toll. Assuming no market losses or gains, it might take only ten or fifteen trades before the whole of the original investment had been used up in commission payments to the broker. One Edinburgh woman who was persuaded to put up £2,800 to buy platinum futures found that £1,037.75 had gone in commissions before the money was even invested.

Hard as it is to believe in retrospect, this was something that appears to have taken LHW's 6,500 retail investors a very long time to notice. Many probably never understood what was going on. Hughes defended the commission charges on the grounds that the special stop-loss policies were expensive and the company's unique research and selling facilities were costly to run. In any case, as he pointed out with no hint of irony, servicing small customers was an expensive business.

Whatever the rights and wrongs, their commission system made the founders of LHW rich. By the mid-1980s, both appear to have been millionaires although still in their early thirties. They became two of Britain's highest earners, reputedly pulling in £19 million between them in 1986 and 1987, years in which the company made profits of £19.4 million and £10.6 million. Within three years they had become the largest retail futures brokers in Britain.

They had struck a seam so rich it appeared almost limitless. To countless private investors, the nice young men with the educated accents at the other end of the phone sounded sincere, responsible and so enthusiastic. They were also careful to sound completely English. Salesmen with foreign sounding names were often advised to adopt an English pseudonym on the theory that English people do not trust foreigners.

In droves people fell for the glib promises of fast profits. Most handed over five, ten or twenty thousand pounds although some put up hundreds of thousands with only the sketchiest knowledge of what futures were. It is not clear how many millions of pounds of savings were siphoned into LHW, but it is tempting to draw the conclusion from the firm's success that there is indeed a fool born every minute.

By about 1985, the press had caught on to what was happening as more and more outraged investors who had been burned wrote in to the personal finance pages to tell their story. LHW became infamous. In 1986 it was refused membership of the London International Financial Futures Exchange. The newly formed regulatory body, the Association of Futures Brokers and Dealers (AFBD), also declined to recognize the firm. Hughes and Walsh resigned as directors (but still owned 85 per cent of the company) in the hope of making the firm acceptable to the AFBD. But LHW was rejected again the following year, then became the subject of a Serious Fraud Office investigation in 1988, before finally closing down in 1989.

By then two things had already happened. Some of those involved had simply set up under new company names in the safety of places like the Netherlands, beyond the reach of UK regulators, from where they continued to cold-call British customers. Others started copy-cat operations in London and carried on as before, untroubled by the authorities.

Empire Futures was one such firm. Among the founders, Peter Ellis had cut his teeth at LHW. Ellis was tall, with a large round face, brown hair and expensive suits, a man of massive self-confidence and charm. The way he walked, talked and even handled a telephone exuded self-assurance. He never stuttered or corrected himself, never seemed in doubt and could always cover up in conversation what he didn't know. He inspired awe among the youthful 'traders' because of the way he could seemingly charm money out of people with a single phone call. As sales director, he would give demonstrations to groups of goggling twenty-year-olds, dialling a prospective customer and then taking him through to the hit, when the investor would entrust him with some of his life savings. Using an old LHW technique, he always made his sales calls standing up because, he maintained, standing put the salesman in a position of power which communicated itself to the client subliminally through the salesman's own mental attitude. Only later did it occur to Dirk Thrust that these demonstrations might have been a set-up. At the time he prayed along with the other mesmerized trainees that one day he too would attain the same level of grace in salesmanship.

It was to Ellis that Dirk was sent for his interview, in a glass office at the back of the 'dealing' room. Their encounter was a caricature of the 1980s cult of salesmanship. In a previous job as a temporary advertising salesman, Dirk had once read a book on how to close a sale and he now clumsily attempted to apply its precepts step by step. He pressed Ellis relentlessly until Ellis agreed to hire him.

'YES!' thought Dirk in his innocence. 'I'm there!'

The dealing room of Empire Futures was a sixty-foot-long

hangar in the World Trade Centre, a building of prefab concrete blocks nestling into the flank of Tower Bridge. It was bare except for several long rows of tables. Each salesman was equipped with a telephone and a chair. They shared a few moth-eaten phone directories and lists supplied by the company containing the names of well-off people such as doctors and lawyers. Anywhere between twenty and sixty salesmen would work in this room twelve hours a day from 8 a.m. to 8 p.m. dialling endlessly, talking to total strangers, trying to sell them an idea in which they had no interest, before being told to go to hell. To make it sound like an authentic City dealing room instead of the retail sweatshop that it was, a tape recording of the real thing would often be played over loudspeakers. Clients were supposed to be reassured by the hum of City business in the background as the salesmen made their pitch. It seemed to work.

Dirk was given a salary of £5,000 a year plus commission of 4 per cent of whatever money he managed to pull in. To earn a liveable wage, therefore, he had to bring in a lot of money which meant relentless, back-breaking, demoralizing work, but he and the other sales boys stuck at it for the glory of being able to tell their friends at home that they were dealers in the City. They did not mention, of course, the real extent of their degradation. Most of the traders were too inexperienced to comprehend the moral muddiness of what they were doing, but everyone hoped that this hell would eventually lead to something grander. They dreamed of one day finding a place in one of the wholesale broking houses – a serious job in a serious firm earning very serious money. For such a prize, this temporary humiliation seemed a price worth paying.

Dirk and the other trainees received a five-day training course during which they learned fractionally more about futures than the people they were about to go and sell futures to. They also learned to fear Peter Ellis who maintained a reign of terror in the sales room.

During the training week he came into the classroom and announced that anyone who could not answer any question he put to them the following day would be sacked. The trainees hooted with laughter. They had been given a pile of papers to read which no one could hope to absorb in its entirety overnight. The following day, Ellis came in, picked a victim and started asking him questions. Inevitably, the moment came when the trainee ran dry.

'Do you not know the answer?' Ellis asked quietly.

'I haven't had time to read through the notes,' the trainee explained.

'I'd like you to put your jacket on and leave,' Ellis said after a pause. After a moment's bewildered silence the trainee picked up his jacket and departed without a word while the others sat stunned and frightened.

As a disciplinary technique, it needed no improvement. Ellis knew his audience and understood their desperation to get a job in the City. He knew that the threat of sacking was better than any whip to make them work.

The sentence of death was to be put on a 'terminal'. This meant that unless the trader pulled in a specified sum of money by the end of the month, he would be sacked. A large board hung from a wall at one end of the dealing room on which every dealer's score of client money collected was recorded on a bar chart against his name. Those on a terminal had a green line drawn somewhere in the chart to show how much they had to attain to remain employed – typically £20,000 – and how close they were getting as the month rolled on. The levels were set arbitrarily by Ellis and the other senior executives – the less they liked someone, the higher the level rose. Some, inevitably, were set so high up on the board they were completely unachievable, but the sweating employees would still try to reach them in the hope of a reprieve.

Rule by fear had become increasingly necessary as the 1980s wore on because firms like Empire Futures were finding it harder and harder to attract money. The regulators were becoming marginally more interested in their activities which did not help, but more important was the press publicity from cases like LHW. The public was getting to know about them and the general level of understanding about futures may even have been rising, making it harder to suck in the gullible. Since the LHW debacle, 1 per cent commissions were out of the question – charges were now a snip compared with the old method. What it all meant was that the mother-lode was becoming mined out. By 1989 the most an Empire salesman could hope to wheedle out of a new investor was

£10,000 to £20,000. Most of the time it was even less. The dealers had to work twice as hard for less profit.

For the same reason, their sales tactics became more desperate. The job required each salesman to make several hundred phone calls per week using lists of potentially wealthy people which the company could buy easily enough from magazines, insurance companies, marketing firms and anyone else who kept such data. When those ran out, dealers were expected to pick names from the phone directory more or less at random, or try to warm up old contacts. A customer who gave a categorical NO at the first call and remained unmoved in subsequent calls would quickly be forgotten. Anyone else who showed the slightest curiosity or hesitation became phone fodder. They would be plagued by phone calls for weeks or months; some unfortunates would still be receiving calls more than a year later. Those replying to an Empire Futures advert – the company had no trouble buying space in papers, including *The Financial Times* – were reckoned to be a particularly good target. In short, the slightest flicker of interest (a term that varied in meaning depending on the desperation of the salesman) from a prospect would send the brokers into a frenzy of telephoning.

Early in a salesman's career, the process tended to be excruciatingly painful for all concerned. He would be given a sheet of written questions and responses, a kind of salesman's litany, to help him in his conversations with customers. But it requires great skill to read something without sounding as if you are doing so, and the sound of someone reading to them no doubt put many customers off at the outset. For thin-skinned salesmen, it was agony but this was a job that demanded impregnable, armour-plated insensitivity. For three months Dirk sat opposite a young university graduate, the son of a barrister, whose doggedness and insensitivity became legendary in the dealing room. His technique was to read his script through to the end, irrespective of what customers said and his occasional successes came through wars of attrition. A typical conversation might go:

Salesman: Hello, sir, may I introduce you to financial futures?
Prospect: Not really.
Salesman: Let me tell you, sir, that futures are instruments that

enable you to bet whether the price of a commodity like gold, or shares or almost anything in fact, will go up or down. We can manage your money in these markets, sir, and almost guarantee to double your money in a month.

Prospect: Look, I don't mean to be rude, Mr . . .

Salesman: Stokes, sir. Now, if you open an account with us for as little as £50,000—

Prospect: How much!?

Salesman: £15,000, sir.

Prospect: I thought you said £50,000.

Salesman: No, that would be unreasonable to start with. I recommend £15,000 in the beginning, if that's okay with you, sir . . . (silence).

Prospect: Well look, I haven't got any details on you people. You'd better send me a brochure in the post and I'll decide when I've—

Salesman: But £5,000 will do to start an account, sir, just so that we can get you on board now before we miss the opportunity in the New York cocoa market.

Prospect: No, really—

Salesman: £2,000 is our minimum, sir . . .

And so on, fruitlessly. Having finished his patter, the salesman would hang up, wink knowingly at his colleagues and say, 'I think we have some interest there.' Sometimes, after another dozen or so calls, the customer would end up opening an account.

Dirk's own selling abilities improved rapidly. His first 'close' – when the customer actually handed over some money – was with a Yorkshire miner. Miners were reckoned to be fertile ground for futures salesmen because they were being given large sums in redundancy as the mining industry was closed down. They often had little idea what they wanted to do with their new affluence and, even better from the broker's point of view, had no knowledge of futures markets. Dirk's miner had £20,000 in tax free redundo burning a hole in his pocket. It took one initial call to explain the supposed attractions of futures and establish that he was interested. In a follow-up call Dirk brought up the subject of cocoa futures, warning the client that cocoa was an extremely risky market and perhaps inappropriate for ordinary members of the public. This was the negative sell. If Dirk had judged his customer right it would spark his curiosity, stimulate his gambling juices and challenge his manhood while simultaneously implying that Dirk himself must be a very honest man to have jeopardized his sale by giving such warnings.

The miner took the bait and it required only a minimal amount of pestering to get a cheque for £5,000 out of him. At this point, a senior salesman would always take over. Once the money was safely in the company's grasp, Ellis or one of the other senior executives would call the customer and read to him a document of caveats that was now required by the Association of Futures Brokers and Dealers, the main regulating body. However, this usually reinforced the negative sell and rarely caused a customer to change his mind.

Then it was time to invest the funds. The people who ran Empire Futures had little understanding of the markets and tended to lose money with staggering rapidity when they invested it themselves. It was clear to Dirk that much of the time they did not know whether to buy or sell – not that it mattered as long as they got the commission. Mostly they farmed the investment activity out to other fund managers. Since the managers were paid a fee for every transaction, they had a built-in incentive to churn every account – which they diligently did. The high dealing costs made it extremely hard for customers to make a profit for long. And while the wonders of leverage meant that profits could be huge, it also ensured that the losses were equally impressive. Even when customers did make a profit, the psychology of gambling is such that they would almost always reinvest it until it had all finally been lost.

It took only a few days to lose the miner's £5,000 – a quarter of his redundancy pay up in smoke. When his initial investment was gone, normal procedure was to ask the customer for more funds and he would frequently oblige. But there would always come a point when the money simply ran out.

As a rookie, Dirk was frequently given the task of ringing up clients who were only suitable for a 'blowout'. A blowout was a desperation measure in which the salesman would try to get more money knowing that he risked destroying any future potential business with a client. Depressingly, it sometimes worked. According to one story, a young salesman working for one of the retail futures firms had rung up a blowout victim who had once owned a string of chemist shops. Months before, he had been persuaded to try his luck in the futures markets and had discovered within himself a fearful gambling addiction. With the futures firm's expert help he lost thousands, selling one shop after another to feed his growing obsession. Eventually the day came when he stopped: all of his shops were gone. He had nothing left but £20,000 in a National Savings account and was renting back his last shop to stay in business. It was at this point that a junior salesman found his contact card and rang him up. The punter told him in hysterical terms to go away. The salesman persisted. The punter weakened. The salesman pressed on. By the end of the conversation the punter had parted company with more of his hard earned cash.

Telling a pensioner that his or her life savings have just been blown to smithereens cannot be an easy task, even for someone who has just profited handsomely as a result. It is not surprising that the senior salesmen whose job this usually was tended to be a battle-hardened and heartless crew.

For these people, selling futures was a way of life. One of the most successful was a tall, fair-haired, handsome individual with ice-blue eyes, a quietly hypnotic voice and a serious drug habit. The inside of his arm was pockmarked with needle jabs and he was often seen talking on the phone with a Vicks nasal spray up one nostril that did not contain nasal spray. He had a strangely powerful but detached way of talking, and what he said the clients usually did. One new client, a farmer, was so overcome by his magic that he turned up at the firm's office with a briefcase full of Krugerrands and the request that the salesman should take charge of all of it. Cannily, the salesman refused, which impressed the farmer even more. He played the client along and three months later took him for every penny he could lay his hands on.

As Dirk got to know his colleagues better, his disgust with the whole business deepened. In any case, he was only pulling in £2,000 to £4,000 a week for the firm which, at a commission of 4 per cent meant £80 to £160 – not enough, he felt, to live on. He grew rebellious. The final straw was the treatment Empire Futures meted out to one particular trainee who had not only been put on a terminal but had been told to stand all day long while he did his telephoning. Everyone else was allowed to sit. That day, inspectors from the Association of Futures Brokers and Dealers showed up as part of their spot checks on market participants. They spent several hours closeted with the senior executives, presumably being shown the company in its best possible light. After hearing the party line, however, they decided to talk to one of the ordinary salesmen to see if he told them a different story. Naturally, they selected the most visible person on the floor, the soon-to-be-sacked, standing-up trainee. There was tension in the dealing room as he chatted to the inspectors in one of the side offices. He had no reason, after all, not to tell them the truth: he was on a terminal, his job was as good as gone, he should have had no loyalty to the firm. But at the end of the interview the inspectors left smiling. Far from giving the game away, the salesman had defended the company to the hilt in the hope that his terminal would be lifted as a reward. It wasn't. At the end of the month he was gone.

Dirk lasted three months of this madness and then told Ellis he was leaving because the money wasn't good enough. It was a wise move. Empire Futures was eventually refused authorization to continue operating by the AFBD but that wasn't the end of Ellis's career as a financial salesman. He worked next for David Coakley Limited which was eventually thrown out of the investment industry and fined £100,000 for a string of offences including churning, relentless high-pressure sales calls, ignoring clients' instructions and failing to explain high-risk deals. Ellis admitted failing to act with skill, care and diligence, or ensuring that deals were suitable for clients, or were even necessary. He was fined £10,000 with £1,000 in costs, and agreed to pay £7,000 in compensation. Not that this stopped his career. By 1995 he owned a company called the London Currency Exchange with an office on Argyle Street, just off Oxford Street, which used cold-calling to sell spot currency deals to members of the public. Unlike futures, spot dealing is unregulated and has no compensation scheme for investors if things go wrong.

Through friends, Dirk ended up contacting another firm which I'll call Blaise & Co. Its offices were on a narrow echoing street opposite Hays Galleria on the south bank of the Thames. Dirk met the owner of the company in the marble foyer and was taken up to the second floor where he was ushered into a real dealing room: banks of screens everywhere, lights flashing on the trading desks, bustle, controlled chaos – everything he'd dreamed of. And of course he thought, 'YES! This is it!'

When he met the owner in the foyer the following Monday to start work, he was surprised to find that he was being taken to the fourth floor instead of the second. Stepping out of the lift he was led through some double doors and into a different world from the one he had seen a few days earlier. The carpets were worn and deeply coffee stained, the walls were shabby and a musty smell hung in the air. He was led through another set of doors with chipped paint on which was sticky-taped a sheet of paper bearing a photocopy of the company name. There were no dealing screens or flashing lights, only a few bare desks, some telephone directories and four people dismally working the phones. It was horribly familiar. When he asked about the glistening dealing room of his first visit, he was told that Blaise were occasionally allowed to 'use' it by the serious broking firm two floors below.

But Dirk needed money and he still hoped this might be the route into a real job in the City, so he started to work. He quickly found that Blaise was even more chaotic than Empire Futures. At first he could not even read the ragged computer printouts of client accounts and caused delight among their customers when he assured them that their money had increased. He only later discovered that what he thought were amounts in sterling were in fact in dollars and that, once converted into pounds, most accounts had lost money.

Indeed, Blaise's talent for busting its clients appears to have surpassed even that of Empire Futures. On one memorable occasion during the summer of 1988, a drought in the American Mid-West sent soy bean futures soaring on expectations of a lousy harvest. As prices hit the top the investment geniuses at Blaise decided it was time to invest, following the well-worn principle that 'the trend is your friend'. They bought heavily into soy bean futures. Within days, however, the Mid-West was hit by an almighty thunderstorm which cured the water shortage at a stroke:

unfortunately, conditions had never been better for growing soy beans. In the ensuing fenzy in the futures market, Blaise was unable to sell out of its position before the price fell drastically. Its customers probably never knew what hit them.

Dirk's embarrassment at his involvement in this world increased. One day a client who had invested several thousands of pounds with Blaise insisted on coming in to talk to him about his fund's alarming investment performance. Ashamed to be seen in his own dingy offices, Dirk met him at the door and led him away to a more salubrious part of the building. Since it was lunchtime, the place was relatively empty. As they passed one well appointed office a phone began to ring. Without breaking stride, Dirk went in, picked it up as if it were his own, plunged into a discussion of an imaginary deal with the astonished caller, jotted a few meaningless notes on a pad, slammed down the receiver, rearranged some papers on the desk and strode out again to lead his impressed client to the lift. In a nearby café, Dirk advised him to take his money away and find a reputable firm of dealers or, even better, stick it in a building society.

What boiler-room operations like Empire Futures did was to bring a whole lot of small investors into the market who would otherwise never have heard of futures. Their willingness to lose their own money is truly heroic and proves that the temptation to double up a bet in the face of big losses is not unique to rogue traders. No one has a monopoly on greed.

The regulatory authorities only got the problem under control in the mid-1990s when most of the boiler-room futures firms were stamped out on the British mainland. Some still operate from overseas, though, where they are even safer from the danger of legal action by angry customers than they were in Britain. In America, a similar phenomenon had worried the SEC for years, and it was still chasing recalcitrant firms well into the 1990s. For the average punter, however, the lure of leverage will never go away. As long as there is someone out there who can find a way of selling it, there are certain to be people willing to hand over good money to buy it.

Dirk, meanwhile, was desperate to get out of the whole sordid business. After a couple of months at Blaise, luck smiled and he finally got his big break. Wandering disconsolately on the second floor one lunchtime, he passed a room in which a furious argument seemed to be in progress. Since the door was ajar, he poked his head round it to see what the fuss was about. Inside was a group of young men seated round a polished lunch table groaning with food and wine bottles. A trolley stacked with more food stood at one side. The air was thick with cigar smoke and the noise was merely that of alcohol-induced bonhomie. Had he been more experienced, Dirk would have recognized this as a gathering of money brokers, the hardest-drinking, hardest-swearing contingent in the markets. Money brokers are made of different material to most people. They can come into work with a killer hangover and two hours' sleep, trade for four hours, consume a three-bottle lunch and continue dealing profitably in the afternoon before taking clients out for some late night carousing – five days a week. At the weekends they just drink and carouse. The world's largest money broking firms are all British.

Seeing Dirk at the door, the man at the head of the table waved him in with an invitation to 'have a pint of brandy, mate'. Dirk was hustled to a seat and a brimming glass of liquor was thrust into his hand. 'Who are you?' his host demanded.

'Dirk,' said Dirk.

'Okay, Dirk. Speak. Say something. Talk to me.'

Dirk talked. Afterwards, he couldn't remember what he said but whatever it was it must have come over well because by the end of lunch his host had offered him a job. They took him down the hall to their dealing room – banks of screens, lights flashing on trading desks . . . And Dirk, ever the optimist, thought 'YES!'

He was at last a member of a reputable wholesale broking firm, on a liveable salary of £15,000 a year. As a money broker the firm acted as an intermediary between banks trading in the short term money markets. Rather than risking its own capital on deals, its job was to match up buy and sell orders from different clients and take a commission on each trade.

Precisely what they did, though, was less important to Dirk than the fact that he didn't have to ring up complete strangers and ask them for their life savings any more. He finally had a desk in a real dealing room, he had his own flashing lights and dealing screens and telephones. Pretty soon, he reckoned, he'd have his own Porsche, too. All he had to do in the meantime was learn how to be a broker.

In a remarkably short time, he got his fancy car but he also discovered that the retail futures business had a lot in common with the wholesale end of the industry. The techniques and the attitude to getting business were similar. Only the customers were different and, of course, the sums of money were immeasurably larger.

CHAPTER 8

EVERYTHING BIGGER THAN IT SHOULD BE

I can do Addition, she said, if you give me time – but I
can't do Subtraction, under any circumstances.

Through the Looking Glass

Framed on his desk in Shell International's offices on Millbank,
by the Thames, the group's deputy corporate treasurer, Rupert
Cox, keeps a salutary reminder of caution. It is a cartoon taken
from a financial magazine showing a banker with a gleeful grin on
his face. He is standing on the chest of a prostrate corporate
treasurer, savagely stuffing derivatives contracts down his throat.
The caption reads: 'Is This How Bankers Sell Derivatives?'

'That was pretty much the way it was until quite recently,' Cox
says. But corporate treasurers were often far from being unwilling
victims. The problem is that modern businesses are troubled by an
irritatingly difficult question: can a company afford not to hedge
its risk? Is it being irresponsible if it does not take precautions
against, say, its foreign exchange exposure or the cost of its raw
materials? And if hedging is the only responsible way to go, then
should a company not swallow all the derivatives that bankers can
push down their throats?

There is no agreement among companies on the answers to
these questions. Some corporate treasurers believe that hedging
the risks related to a company's core businesses is essential. The
successful hedging of risk should make companies more efficient

and therefore more profitable. It should prevent unnecessary losses, of course. And because capital doesn't have to be tied up in areas where it might be needed to cover a potential loss, it can be applied more efficiently elsewhere. The money saved by using derivatives to cut foreign exchange costs or borrow money more cheaply may even turn an otherwise unprofitable project, such as building a new factory overseas, into a profitable one. Expansion becomes possible where, without derivatives, it seemed out of the question.

A different school of thought contends that companies should never hedge their risks under any circumstances. It is precisely those risks which investors wish to take on when they buy the company's shares. If the shareholders are worried about the risks a company is running they can buy the shares of another company instead, or diversify their holdings across a number of companies so that their risk is spread. The companies themselves have a duty not to muddy the clarity of their business with hedging.

Faced with such extreme philosophical differences, a corporation such as Shell, which has hugely diversified, multinational risks, is likely to tread a cautiously pragmatic path. Unlike companies which run their treasury departments as distinct 'profit centres', Shell does not try to make money from its use of derivatives. Its aim is to cut its costs and reduce risk. It is therefore a big user of interest rate swaps, borrowing fixed rate money relatively cheaply in the bond market and swapping it into floating rate funds when that suits its funding plans. It uses forward exchange rate contracts with banks to reduce its exposure to currency movements and it occasionally uses interest rate options to cap its exposure to rising rates, although the expense of buying options means the company uses them sparingly. It almost never sells options because the risks are simply too great.

The same is true of its physical oil operation. At any given time, Shell has millions of barrels of oil afloat in tankers on the high seas, and refineries around the world to keep supplied with its own or other companies' crude. In the time it takes to extract oil and deliver it by tanker the price may have moved so much that Shell's profit margin could be under threat. To hedge this risk it buys or sells futures on London's International Petroleum Exchange where North Sea Brent crude is the most popular contract. It is not always a perfect match with what Shell has to deliver since the quality of oil varies – hedging Nigerian crude with Brent contracts is not ideal – but it is better than nothing. Here again, Shell rarely uses options because of their higher risk.

That, at least, was and still is the theory at Shell, but not even the best run companies are immune to trouble. It would be hard to exaggerate the trauma inside the company caused by a $1 billion loss discovered in its Japanese subsidiary at the end of 1992. The losses resulted from unauthorized speculative futures dealing that had, unknown to Shell's senior management, gone on for several years. 'It was a hell of a shock to find this had been going on without being detected by group management or audits,' said Cox.

Showa Shell Sekiyu KK in Japan bought its oil in dollars but sold its refined products in yen, giving it a currency exposure that it hedged in the currency futures market. Under cover of its large futures dealing, the finance department began speculating – there is no other word for it – on a vast scale. From 1989 onwards it ran up $6.4 billion in dollar futures betting that the currency would rise (the amount it needed to buy its oil was less than $1 billion).

For three years neither Showa Shell's senior management nor Shell Group itself seem to have been remotely aware of what was going on. Shell's defence is that this was a conspiracy: 'If you have a group of people in collusion, they can get away with it for some time,' said a senior official. Which is true, as long as the conspirators have the luck to be operating in an organization lax enough to let them get away with it.

What made the situation more bizarre was that many of the futures deals were with Japanese banks who knew more or less how much Shell stood to lose but did not feel it was any of their business to tell anyone at the company. Under Japanese accounting rules, there was no loss until a futures contract actually matured. Anyone wanting to avoid taking a hit therefore simply had to roll over a loss making position for another few months rather than let it expire. The Japanese banks were, it seems, willing to roll over Showa Shell's contracts indefinitely. It was only when a banker, worried about the growing size of the paper losses, finally squealed that people inside Shell began to wonder if something was wrong. But by then it was too late.

Shell's managers struggled to come to terms with what had happened. For the first time, the company now actually wrote down its policy for derivatives dealing. Although it seems surprising, it had never before formally tried to define what it was trying to do with derivatives. Inevitably – because in such excercises there is always an element of closing the stable door after the horse has bolted – it decided on a very conservative strategy and has not wavered from it since.

Companies, particularly large ones, have certainly become more sophisticated in their understanding of derivatives in recent years and a rapidly growing number of companies actively use them to manage their foreign exchange or interest rate risks. But the last ten years have shown graphically that the directors running companies all too often know little or nothing about derivatives or how they should be used – or how they are actually being used by their employees.

Shell was only one of a string of big companies and municipalities that have lost heavily from the mid-1980s onwards. Sometimes it was rogue traders, sometimes bad luck, sometimes poor judgement. But in virtually every major case, it was also because the people ultimately in charge did not understand derivatives or the risks they implied.

In the early days, British companies led the field in derivative related blunders, although that is partly why they are now among the most conservative in the world in their use of futures and options. They were perhaps unfortunate in being so close to the City of London and its derivatives factories, and therefore close to temptation; but they also suffered from cavalier management and spectacularly inadequate financial controls. In most of these cases it did not even require the high pressure selling of a Bankers Trust to bring disaster. And in the end it was taxpayers, employees or shareholders who ended up paying the bill.

Allied Lyons, the drinks and foods company, was among the first to suffer an unexpected explosion deep in its hold when a $150 million loss turned up during 1991. The timing was no coincidence. Allied, like most other companies in the industrialized world, was suffering from the recession of the early 1990s. It had also recently made some large acquisitions which had depleted its store of cash and diluted its earnings. It needed, in short, to find a quick way of improving its financial performance. Just as the banks had done, companies all over the world turned to gambling on the money markets when the income from their traditional businesses flagged. And, like the banks, they turned to derivatives because of their peculiar accounting properties. Swaps, for example, remained off-balance sheet: since they were not an ordinary loan, they did not tie up large chunks of capital. Dealing on margin in futures and options also did not require much money. Companies could gamble without diverting financial resources away from their core businesses.

Corporations such as British Petroleum in Britain and General Electric in the US had led the way years earlier by turning their finance departments into independent profit centres. The department was supposed to use the cash generated by the company to turn a profit in the markets, like a captive bank inside the company. GE is the most striking example, having turned its financial division into one of the biggest derivatives players in the US. But GE and BP developed their treasury operations professionally by thinking through their strategy, hiring the right talent and educating their senior executives in what to expect. A great many more companies – Allied Lyons among them – did not. Many corporate treasurers saw a way to boost their profits without needing to consult the board or notify the shareholders since, if derivative trading did not show up on the balance sheet, no one need know about it. With impressive insouciance, they strolled into the casino, tossed their chips on the table, and lost their shirts.

The head of Allied's finance department was a forty-nine-year-old Canadian called Clifford Hatch, a scion of the family that had owned Hiram Walker, the drinks company, before Allied bought it. Under his command was a four-strong team of treasury dealers, including an aggressive former Eurobond salesman from CSFB named Michael Bartlett. Quite how well these people understood the markets they were dealing in is a moot point, but it is certain that the senior executives of Allied understood very little indeed.

In a letter to shareholders after the event Sir Derek Holden-Brown, the chairman, explained what had gone wrong. In 1989 the finance department had started producing some healthy profits by writing highly leveraged options contracts. The board liked the profits. The finance department expanded its operations which meant taking bigger risks. Sir Derek admitted he had no clear idea what these risks were.

The popular bet to make in Britain at the time was that the pound would rise against the dollar, and so Allied began selling call options on the dollar. But the dollar rose which meant the options lost Allied some money. The finance department wrote more of the same options, hoping the market would turn, and then more options, and more again. Normally such dealing should be controlled by careful hedging but Allied had none. Its exposure soared to $1.5 billion, past the finance department's unwritten exposure limits, and its losses grew as the dollar continued to rise. Finally, amid swirling market gossip about the company's heavy dealing and Bank of England warnings to take action, the board called a halt. Holden-Brown confessed that the company lacked the requisite trading skills, that Allied did not know how to measure or monitor its risk, or have the management controls to oversee its dealing. Both he and Hatch resigned.

Allied really had little excuse for its blunder. It was by no means the first corporation to have lost money on derivatives and it could have learnt useful lessons from its predecessors. Among the most spectacular earlier losers were Britain's local authorities, many of whom plunged blindly into an orgy of risk-taking which effectively bankrupted them and almost led to a massive hike in local taxes. Remarkably, the star performer in this drama, which looked as if it might undermine the fabric of British local government, was one of the smallest boroughs in the land.

Even on a sunny day the Hammersmith town hall on King Street looks grim. A forbidding Victorian brick pile constructed to impress, it makes no concessions to comfort or convenience, let alone modern essentials such as computer technology. Inside, its high-ceilinged rooms and endless echoing corridors seem impossible to heat. Apart from the telephones and an occasional coffee machine, the state of the offices in the late 1980s had apparently changed little from when the building was first put up. This was not, to say the least, state-of-the-art local government.

Rooms 301 and 302 on the third floor were the heart of the council's treasury operations. They had once been separated by a flimsy partition but they had been knocked together in the mid-80s. A central block of tables occupied the middle of the floor, stocked with computers and telephones. More work stations were positioned around the walls. An impression of high technological readiness, however, would have been misleading. Not all of the phones worked. The computers were so weak that e-mail messages could not be stored on them. In 1987, the division acquired a fax machine; the following year it got a single portable telephone. A reference library on the finer points of local authority finance and money markets consisted of a few well-thumbed volumes kept in a cupboard behind the door. Presiding over all of this, the head of the division sat at the end of the table nearest the exit with his deputy on his left. The two most senior officers of the finance department, however, worked in offices on the first floor, a long walk away down the chilly corridors.

It was from these unpromising headquarters that Hammersmith and Fulham council undertook an astonishing financial Odyssey. Almost single handedly this tiny local authority – the third smallest in Britain, and home to 150,000 people and three football teams – kick-started the sterling interest rate swap market by becoming one of the most aggressive swaps dealers in the world. By the end of the 1980s its swaps were worth a nominal £5 billion, around three-quarters of the entire sterling market and a significant blip on the radar of the global swaps market. It attained these commanding financial heights, moreover, by having no idea of what it was doing.

It all began, appropriately, in confusion. Councillor Howe, the Labour leader of the authority, read an article in 1983 on Liffe and grew interested. He told the finance director Clive Holtham to look into the possibility of hedging the council's investments with financial futures. Holtham, a diligent and competent official, went off to the City to find out what financial futures were and reported back that a little dabbling in these instrument might give the council some valuable financial experience. He had brought a more proactive style to the running of the normally stodgy treasury department and no doubt felt that this was an opportunity to do something a bit clever.

But Howe, who appears to have had only a hazy grasp of the difference between futures and options, replied that he had asked Holtham to look into options, not futures. 'I am most hopeful you will be able to clear your mind as to the difference,' he scolded the finance director. What he now suggested was that Hammersmith should sell options against shareholdings in its pension fund (giving the buyers the right to purchase the shares at some specified price in the future) as a way of making money.

This single confused exchange triggered the chain reaction that led to the Hammersmith swaps disaster.

Howe was interested in finding new sources of income for the council because, like half the local authorities in Britain, Hammersmith was suffering under new rules brought in by Margaret Thatcher, the prime minister, to limit its spending. Broadly, the rules said that the more the councils spent, the less financial support they would get from central government. Inevitably, councils reluctant to cut their spending searched frantically for new sources of income that fell outside the rules and would therefore not result in a cut in their government grant. Swaps, because no one drafting the rules had ever heard of them, did just that.

At the other end of town the bankers and brokers in the City were looking for ways to create a British swaps market in sterling. They had the product but no customers. The problem was that too few companies wanted to play this new game, and too many that did were of such poor credit quality that you wouldn't have wanted to swap your stamp collection with them, let alone your corporate debt. In any case, interest rates were jumping up and down so fast that taking any kind of view on their future, as a swap agreement would require, seemed too risky for most companies to contemplate.

So when Holtham started calling with innocent enquiries about financial futures, the financiers saw the answer to their prayers. Apart from the central government itself, local authorities were the best credit risk in the country: they were guaranteed by the central government through a body called the Public Works Loan Board. And now, it seemed, they might have an appetite for derivatives; if they wanted futures, could they not also be sold swaps, and options, and then perhaps swaptions, floptions, caps, floors ... The bankers and brokers could hardly contain their excitement. From Hammer-smith's forbidding offices you could almost hear the City's carni-vores five miles away licking their chops in anticipation.

A stream of City brokers flowed through Hammersmith's treas-ury department towards the end of 1983, all trying to persuade Holtham of the same thing. They told him to forget about selling options on shares in the pension fund (they were not particularly interested in this business). Far more important, they said, was for the council to find a way to reduce the cost of its debt. And it so happened they had just the solution. Swaps.

Holtham had a healthy suspicion of City folk because the council had recently been defrauded by a crooked broker who had sold it some bonds at the wrong prices. Yet he was sufficiently convinced by the men in pinstripes to sign his first swap agreement in December 1983 – a modest deal of £5 million for five years. The bank on the other side of the deal was Hambros; the broker who arranged it was R. P. Martin. Hammersmith switched a fixed rate loan into floating rate, betting that interest rates would fall.

Under the cautious eyes of Holtham and his deputy, Greville Norman, Hammersmith undertook only seven swaps between 1983 and 1987 to reduce the cost of the council's debt. Even so, there were already problems. The council's auditors, Deloitte Haskins and Sells reported in 1985 that the treasury department's records were unreliable. The council responded furiously by accusing the firm of not understanding the nature of local government and suggesting that unless the auditors wished to learn fast, the council would replace them. Miraculously, Deloitte's objections abruptly ceased.

But when Holtham and Norman both left the council, all sense of caution evaporated. Holtham was replaced by Robb, a man so little versed in derivatives that a colleague had to explain to him what swaps were. Norman was replaced by Terry Price, who had joined the council in 1984 as an accountant in the housing department. With no formal training he moved up to become head of investments and then took over Norman's job at the head of the block of tables in room 301. This put him in charge of the council's dealing operations, yet he had no market experience at all and only a hazy grasp of swaps and options dealing. He was young and, according to brokers who dealt with him, fancied himself as a sharp operator, a bit of a lad.

Between May and November 1987, he sold twenty-eight swap options. These gave the buyer the right to exchange his floating rate debt payments for Hammersmith's fixed rate debt payments at an agreed rate. This time the council was betting that interest rates would not rise. As long as interest rates stayed below 8 per cent the option would not be exercised. And the council got the option premium.

Anyone embarking on selling options needs a sophisticated system of risk management – powerful computers with a fancy programme, trained analysts and so forth. Hammersmith had none of this: Price and Robb did not understand the need for it. There were no fancy computer programmes for calculating risk or prices – indeed, there were virtually no computers at all. What happened in the distinctly low-tech atmosphere of room 301 was that whenever Price did a deal it was noted down by hand (sometimes by a teenage undergraduate on holiday assignment at the Council) in a black school exercise book known inevitably as 'The Black Book'. The dates when interest payments were due from swap counter parties were noted in a desk diary – blue for 1988, red for 1989. As a dealing control system it had a sort of Victorian quaintness. It was also totally inadequate.

Price's first twenty-eight deals brought in a useful sum of money from the option premiums. Indeed, none of the early options had actually been exercised which made the premium income look like money for old rope. As far as Price was concerned, he was adding to the council's wealth, which meant he was doing his job.

But by now he was bitten by the dealing bug and couldn't stop. From November 1987 until July 1988 he went into overdrive, agreeing 390 new transactions, including swaps and reversed swaps, swap options, caps, floors, floating rate agreements, cash options, gilt options and strangles. He was an eager customer for any new scheme the bankers and brokers put before him. By the end of this orgy of dealing, which stunned even seasoned City dealers, Hammersmith had taken on a notional principal risk of around £3.5 billion.

The original aim of reducing the council's borrowing costs had long been forgotten. Price and Robb were gunning for premium income and had, in the process, turned Hammersmith into the Bankers Trust of the local authority sector, but with a financial control system that Ebeneezer Scrooge might have found a little primitive. They probably did not actually know just how big their exposure was since they weren't keeping close score. They certainly did not impose any particular limits on themselves. All they cared about were the option premiums which Price calculated would be £700,000 in 1988 and more than £2 million for each of the next three years.

They were also hopelessly muddled on strategy and had no concept of how to hedge options. Price seems to have thought that he could use the premiums from lapsed options to cover losses on exercised options. The implication was that if the losses from exercised options grew – as they eventually did – he could simply sell more and more options and use the premium income to cover the losses. He appears to have been totally unaware that this would simply increase his over-all risk and probably ruin him in the end. He and Robb could not bring themselves to hedge their positions by *buying* swap options because that would have involved paying someone else a premium.

Moreover, with their eyes firmly on the amount of money they could make from selling options, Price and Robb would often only deal when option premiums rose. They failed to understand that premiums rise when the risk of interest movements is greatest: it rises because more people are competing to hedge their interest rate risk. So by selling options when the premium was at its highest, Price and Robb were in fact taking on the maximum amount of risk.

Most of their deals were based on the assumption that interest rates would not rise. Unfortunately, rates turned against them at the end of 1987. By mid-1988 they had gone up 2 per cent to 11 per cent. Price and Robb had given no thought to this possibility. Now they were about to get wiped out.

The gathering storm should have, but failed to, become apparent to the council one cold January night in 1988. While the heroes of the treasury department were doing battle in the swaps market, Hammersmith's councillors had remained blissfully ignorant of what was being done in their name. However, Councillor Kabir, the head of the finance committee, one day asked Robb to explain to him what swaps were. Conscientiously, Robb organized a meeting on a Friday evening at which Price, with the aid of flip charts, tried to explain to the hapless Kabir how swaps worked and what his strategy was. Kabir left the meeting completely confused. Even Robb seems to have been somewhat bamboozled by Price's explanations. After that, no councillor dared ask the treasury department about its dealing strategy for fear they might be subjected to another lecture from Price.

But by the middle of 1988, people in the City were beginning to worry. They would probably have realized sooner that something was wrong if Hammersmith had not dealt with so many banks and brokers that it was impossible for any one of them to see the big picture. Price had spread his trades among at least fifteen banks, including Barclays, Barings, Hambros, S. G. Warburg, Allied Irish Bank, Banco de Bilbao, Morgan Guarantee, Salomon Brothers, Citicorp and Sumitomo. In addition, he had used ten different brokers – virtually the entire complement that London had to offer. It took a while for the market to discover just how many people Hammersmith was dealing with – and, anyway, the brokers were prohibited by the Bank of England from discussing their clients' dealings with each other.

There was also an element of sheer disbelief. Dealers are always prone to exaggeration and bragging when talking to each other about their market exploits – it's part of the culture. So when they talked about the huge size and massive profits of their Hammersmith deals, other dealers naturally assumed these stories included a large element of fantasy. It took a while for people to realize that for once the stories were true.

The brokers began to get really scared when Terry Price's dealing parted company with common sense and market realities. One trader realized there was trouble when he saw Hammersmith selling someone an option to buy gilt-edged stock more cheaply than they could buy it that day in the cash market, leaving the council with an instant loss.

Price's dealing method was indeed clueless. The normal market procedure should have been to call a broker and ask 'What can you show me?' – what deals does the broker have and at what price? That way, like a poker player, the caller does not reveal his hand: is he a buyer or a seller, what kind of deal does he have in mind and at what price? The broker can't tell. Price, however, would lay all his cards on the table like the rookie that he was. He would say he wanted to do a deal that would bring in X amount of premium income and did the broker have anything that fitted this? Any broker worth his salt could then simply widen his spreads on whatever deals he had to sell or make up some deal that made no financial sense as long as it fitted Prices's request. In one case, a broker sold Hammersmith a swap option that gave the council a few thousand pounds in premium income but left it with an instant £2 million loss. Yet even when it began to look as though Hammersmith couldn't carry on much longer, the City thought its profits were safe. 'At the end Price was doubling up his bets like a maniac to prevent the collapse,' said one broker who dealt frequently with the council. 'But even then we felt that the council was guaranteed by the government. It couldn't go bust. The deals had to be honoured however stupid they were.' The City, in other words, was happy to humour Price because it believed that governments (i.e. taxpayers) always pay up.

It turned out to be a bad bet. Hammersmith was not the only council punting in the swaps market, although none of the others touched it for scale. The situation was starting to worry the authorities and in the middle of 1988 Howard Davies, controller of the Audit Commission (the government body responsible for overseeing local authority finances) declared that all of these swaps might be illegal. Local authorities, he said, might not have the authority to carry out such deals, in which case all outstanding swaps were null and void. Suddenly the bankers and brokers could see the gravy train running into the buffers.

It is probably no coincidence that shortly after this, someone in the City finally raised the alarm about Hammersmith. After all, if the party was over you may as well turn on the lights to see just how much mess there was. Around 27 July an anonymous caller rang one of Davies's assistants with the message that 'everything was bigger than it should be' about the council's dealings. Davies promptly insisted on an end to the council's swaps and options dealing but Hammersmith almost immediately broke the moratorium and sailed serenely on into 1989, striking new deals. It was only when the Audit Commission stepped firmly in to see what was going on that the extent of the damage emerged. The losses were clearly going to be huge but no one could be sure just how huge since it depended on how interest rates moved. Estimates put it at around £400 million – enough to bankrupt the council and require a vast increase in local taxes as well as a central government bailout. Ultimately, as always, it seemed that taxpayers would have to foot the bill.

At this point Robb seems to have decided that he and Price had been duped by the City all along, and he turned mean. He declared that since the Audit Commission thought local government swaps were illegal, he would not honour any deals unless ordered to by the courts. If the bankers and brokers wanted their money, they'd have to sue for it.

Many did. But the courts decided that swaps and options were indeed beyond the remit of local authorities, so Hammersmith and the other fifty or so councils which had done such deals were off the hook. It was a miraculous escape which cost the banks millions. They had, of course, hedged their deals with Hammersmith and other councils by doing offsetting deals elsewhere in the market. But while the Hammersmith swaps were now cancelled, the offsetting deals still had to be honoured which cost the banks a lot of money. 'The whole house of cards came tumbling down and the City took a real pasting,' says one of Hammersmith's former brokers. 'It set London back as a derivatives centre by twenty years.'

Poetic justice, perhaps, although most of the protagonists in this tale merely come out of it looking like knaves or fools.

The taxpayers of California's Orange County, a district so wealthy it ranks as the world's twenty-eighth richest economy, were not so lucky when in 1994 they were left with the largest unpaid bill in US municipal history. They, as well as 187 other cities, schools and other districts, are still paying for the $2 billion hole their treasurer blew in their pooled investment fund. The losses equalled at least $1,000 for every man, woman and child in the county, as well as the axing of 2,000 county jobs and chaos in the county's finances for years to come.

The money was lost by a silver-haired sixty-nine-year-old named Robert Citron who had run the fund for more than twenty years using, among other dealing aids, ten office telephones and the advice of a mail-order psychic to help him get the best returns. Cultivating what might be described as a kind of Californian money market chic, Citron liked to wear green silk shirts, white belts, plaid trousers and clashing sports jackets to work. In later years he resorted to more sober business suits but always accompanied by Amerindian turquoise jewellery. He drove around the neighbourhood in a large white Cadillac. The car horn played the theme tune of the University of Southern California and his bathroom was decorated in cardinal and gold, the USC colours. A bronze lump of horse manure took pride of place on his office desk.

Such signs of an outsize ego, however, were balanced by a low-key lifestyle. He lived in a modest house in Santa Ana, the capital of Orange County, had been married to the same woman for thirty-nine years and ate lunch with friends most days in the Santa Ana Elks Club (where he would carefully divvy up the bill on his wristwatch calculator). He was a hard worker, did not drink, smoke or gamble and was so conservative with his own money that he never even owned shares. His salary was an unremarkable £100,000 and there was no suggestion that he tried to enrich himself from Orange County's problems.

He became the local tax collector and treasurer in the 1970s under the novel slogan 'your friendly tax collector', and he learnt the job as he went along. As a young man he had studied medicine (his father was the doctor who cured W. C. Fields, the comedian, of alcoholism), but gave that up to study business. He soon dropped that too and left college without a degree. As county treasurer, however, he was a huge success which was why he kept the job for seven consecutive tenures. The fact was that over the years his returns were well above those of most other municipal funds and most market averages. It was why so many other bodies entrusted him with their funds, and why Orange County's executives happily left him alone. It was also why he survived as a Democrat in an area that was staunchly Republican. 'This is a person who has gotten us all millions of dollars,' explained Thomas Riley, one of Citron's supervisors, before the crisis. 'I don't know how the hell he does it, but it makes us all look good.'

How the hell Citron did it was by taking some highly risky punts in the markets which usually paid off, convincing him of the correctness of his own instincts. When he said interest rates were going down – which he did with almost religious fervour in 1994 – no one could convince him otherwise. Once asked why he was so sure interest rates would not rise, he replied: 'I am one of the largest investors in America. I know these things.' No one seriously questioned his investment decisions – he was master of his own little universe at the Orange County treasury department.

By 1994 he was under huge pressure to perform, just as the treasury department of Hammersmith and Fulham had been, as Orange County's inhabitants regularly voted to cut their own taxes. They had come to rely on his high returns to make up the difference: more than a third of the county's budget came from income provided by Citron's investments. To keep this up meant taking big risks.

There seems little doubt that Citron loved his role as saviour of the county's finances, and that it was ego rather than pecuniary gain that drove his investment strategy. He fended off the county's occasional half-hearted attempts to supervise what he did and took criticism of his market judgement as a personal affront. It also made it almost impossible for him to admit that his judgement might be wrong.

As with many similar financial disasters, ample warning signs started to appear well before the losses actually occurred and were ignored by everyone who could have done anything about them. In September 1993, Citron himself declared that he achieved such high yields by using reverse repurchase agreements and complex derivatives based on the premise that interest rates would decline over the next three years. By using these instruments, he added, the fund was leveraged by a factor of two to one – it had effectively borrowed twice its original capital.

During an election campaign in spring 1994, John Moorlach, an accountant who ran against Citron for the treasurer's job, claimed that the fund was dangerously highly leveraged. The electorate either did not understand him or did not care, but Moorlach was right. In the normally cautious world of municipal fund investment, Orange County's strategy was about as aggressive as it was possible to be.

Citron was a favourite on Wall Street for all the business he put the way of Merrill Lynch, Credit Suisse First Boston, J. P. Morgan and Goldman Sachs. Merrill did particularly well. Michael Stamenson, an aggressive salesman (who had already been involved in a $60 million loss sustained by the municipality of San Jose on some risky bonds), was a friend of Citron and did a great deal of business with him. In 1993 and 1994 the bank made $100 million on commissions and underwriting fees from Orange County. It also had $2.7 billion in loans to its best customer.

But early in 1994 Merrill grew seriously worried. The Federal Reserve Board, to almost everyone's surprise, started to raise interest rates rather than lower them. Merrill had worried on and off since 1992 about Citron's highly leveraged, high risk portfolio. Now press articles suggesting that this might cause problems for Orange County, together with an investigation by the SEC and the Treasury Department into the exploding derivatives market, caused an attack of collective hysteria among the bigwigs at Merrill. They tracked down Stamenson, who was on holiday in Europe, and ordered him on to a red-eye to New York. During a five-hour meeting they told him to explain what was going on at Orange County. Three days later they tracked him down in London again and whisked him back to headquarters aboard Concord for yet another debriefing. Merrill put together a 'SWAT' team of senior executives to design a new strategy for Orange County. Merrill sensed that things were getting shaky in Citron's operation; they also, perhaps, sensed the possibility of lawsuits.

Citron, meanwhile, had been taping his conversations with Merrill. The tapes show that while the broking firm made efforts to protect its reputation by sorting out the mess at Orange County before matters got any worse, Citron would not co-operate and began to accuse Merrill of having misled him about the financial instruments it had sold him.

The problem was this: to start with, Orange County had bought about $8 billion of highly volatile inverse floaters. These are derivatives ideal for gambling. For reasons too tedious to go into, their value falls as interest rates rise, and vice versa. They have two particular characteristics: they are extremely difficult to price (making them very profitable for banks to sell), and they are far more sensitive to interest rate movements than ordinary bonds. A small shift in rates can turn inverse floaters into a gold mine or disaster area. Since Citron's whole strategy was a bet that interest rates were heading downwards, his inverse floaters fell into the disaster category when rates rose. He had also bought some instruments called range floaters which only pay interest as long as general interest rates remain within a specified range. By mid 1994 interest rates had broken out of the range and the floaters were worth virtually nothing.

The rest of his portfolio was not strictly in derivatives but in reverse repos. Citron would lend bonds to a bank in return for a loan; with the loan he would buy more bonds which he would lend to the same or another bank for another loan with which he could buy more bonds, and so on. As long as interest rates fell, the bonds he bought would rise in value and Orange County would cash in. The risk, of course, was that if interest rates fell such a highly leveraged position would be under water. Which is exactly what happened.

When interest rates rose instead of following the downward path that he and the mail-order psychic had predicted, financial melt-down was inevitable. The more his investments lost money, the more Citron doubled up until his fund's total exposure was about $20 billion. The end came, as it always seems to, as a shock to almost everyone not directly involved with the investments. Only Citron and Merrill Lynch knew what was coming.

As Orange County's bonds fell in value, the banks would only renew the repos on the condition that he put up margin to cover the losses. The amounts finally grew so large that Orange County ran out of money. It put itself into bankruptcy which it thought would protect it from the predators on Wall Street who were showing every sign of panicking. Finding a loophole in the law, however, the banks liquidated Citron's positions, thus converting mere paper losses into real, tangible cash losses of $1.7 billion.

Despite some intense competition from other unfortunate institutions over the following two years it remains the single biggest
money market disaster on record.

Once the horrible truth was revealed on 2 December, Citron
was arrested. Two days later a deputation of county executives
brought him a resignation letter to sign and a couple of them
stayed behind afterwards to keep the shell-shocked former treasurer
company until the psychiatric social worker arrived to look after
him. Facing a possible fourteen years in jail, Citron protested in
court that he was just an ignorant country hick who had been
duped by the slick money men from Wall Street. 'In retrospect I
was not the sophisticated treasurer I said I was,' he declared. The
worrying thing is that this may well be true. In retrospect, all
Citron's years of investment success may simply have been luck
rather than – as he and everyone else had assumed – good
judgement.

Merrill, meanwhile, said it was not at fault, and has so far been
believed. The electors of Orange County insisted they were not to
blame either, even though it was their determination to cut taxes
that had been at least partly responsible for encouraging Citron to
play the markets the way he did. But no one came to bail the
electorate out or say that Citron's deals were unlawful: Orange
County's inhabitants, unlike Hammersmith's, had to pay. The only
saving grace was that, on the whole, they could afford to.

The fate of these local government authorities was unambiguous:
they were blown out of the water when markets turned against
them. But it is not always so simple: when, for example, is a loss
really a loss? When do you take a loss rather than hang on and
hope the market bails you out? Whose fault is it if your boss panics
over your dealing position and forces you to sell out at the wrong
time? What do you do if you're the boss and don't understand
what your dealers are doing?

These issues were raised by the murky story of the DM 3.3
billion ($1.9 billion) derivatives loss at Metallgesellschaft, one of
Germany's foremost commodities groups, which brought it to the
edge of collapse and triggered the largest rescue operation in
European corporate history. The company was run by Heinz

Schimmelbusch, a flamboyant forty-nine-year-old who had been hailed in Germany as Businessman of the Year in 1991 (curiously, awards of this sort often turn out to be the prelude to disaster for the recipient). Charismatic and engaging, he was brilliant at schmoozing the media and his bankers. He got a good press when he declared that 'We are the most foolproof company in all of Germany', as he tried to turn the doddering metal refining group into a high-tech conglomerate. He expanded the company like a balloon, took on DM 9 billion of debt and tried to get things going, but nothing worked. MG continued to languish and Schimmelbusch came under increasing pressure from MG's most powerful shareholder, Deutsche Bank.

He needed a miracle to save his job. For a while it looked as if that was what he was getting from MG Refining and Marketing, the US operation, until the end of 1993 when his strategy went horribly wrong and the subsidiary blew itself into tiny pieces in the oil market.

The first that Ronaldo Schmitz heard about the disaster was when a journalist rang him up to ask if the rumour of huge losses was true. As a director of Deutsche Bank, Schmitz was chairman of Metallgesellschaft's supervisory board and should have known what was happening. Refusing to comment to the journalist, he immediately rang Schimmelbusch, who said that nothing was wrong. Schimmelbusch, of course, should also have known otherwise but he later claimed that he had had no idea his company was up to its eyeballs in risk in the oil market.

In fact, it seems that hardly anyone but Arthur Benson, the trader responsible for MGRM's oil hedging strategy in the US, understood what had happened. Art Benson was a diminutive 5 foot 5 inches tall, had been around the business for years and liked to keep it in the family: he employed his wife, brother, son and daughter in his trading operation which was based in a village in Baltimore next to a Pizza Hut and a funeral parlour. He was a market animal. In a mid-1980s law suit accusing him of reneging on margin payments, his own lawyers had described him as a speculator 'caught up in an addiction to the market'. His decisions, they said, 'became, with regard to the market, irrational'. Although not exactly a sterling recommendation for the job of head trader at

MGRM, irrationality hardly made him exceptional as a derivatives dealer.

He had worked for Metallgesellschaft once before in the 1980s but had left after he reportedly lost the company $50 million in the markets. He joined Louis Dreyfus Energy, where his daredevil dealing was saved by the start of the Gulf War which pushed up the value of a massive long futures position in jet fuel he held and made him $500 million overnight. Impressed, Metallgesellschaft invited him back. It may seem peculiar for a company to rehire an employee it had previously sacked but it is actually typical of the game of musical chairs played with jobs in the dealing world. Memories are short – his previous losses would have been forgotten and Benson would have been surrounded by an aura of invincibility after his Gulf War success. It just goes to show that old dealers never die, they simply move to a new dealing desk.

MGRM had embarked on an aggressive policy of making fixed price contracts to supply US customers with oil and gasoline for up to ten years. To hedge this long term commitment, Benson came up with an unorthodox scheme to buy three month futures on the New York Mercantile Exchange, sell them near the end of each period and buy new futures at the start of the next three month period. The rationale for this strategy was that the market at the time was in *backwardation*, meaning that the spot price of oil was higher than the futures price. The value of the futures would therefore rise as they came closer to maturity. Benson could sell them for more than he had originally paid for them at the start of the period, realizing a nifty profit each time.

Because the scheme enabled MGRM to sell its oil and gasoline very cheaply the company did a lot of business which no doubt pleased its parent's management: by the end November 1993 it had contracts to supply the equivalent of 160 million barrels of oil, a staggering amount equal to nearly three months' total production in Kuwait. Benson hedged the entire amount through his short dated futures contracts. When his dealing exceeded the amount Nymex would allow to a single trader, he did the same deals in the OTC market.

The problem was that backwardations never last for ever. First, when the market noticed what Benson was doing, it naturally played against him. It sold him his futures more expensively and bought them more cheaply which reduced his profit. Then worries that OPEC would fail to agree on production quotas caused oil prices to drop towards the end of 1993 so that short term prices became cheaper than long term ones (known in the market as *contango*). At this point, the oil hit the fan with shattering abruptness and the mess was spectacular. Suddenly the logic of Benson's strategy was turned on its head. The value of his massive futures portfolio plummeted to earth like an airliner whose engines have failed in mid-air, because the contracts were now worth less instead of more as they approached maturity. MGRM calculated that it was losing $20 million to $30 million a month in November 1993. Adding to the pain, Nymex demanded variation margin on the loss making contracts and this, in turn, given the vast size of MG's market position, caused a liquidity crisis in the company. Panicked by these events and under pressure from its bewildered shareholders, Metallgesellschaft summarily closed out the futures positions, taking a staggering loss in the process.

According to Deutsche Bank the whole bloody episode was the fault of a rogue trader and a company management that wasn't in control. It would not even allow Schimmelbusch to rush to New York on a fire-fighting mission, arguing that to do so would only have 'thrown gasoline on the flames'. Instead, it sacked him and Benson. In retaliation, Benson accused his employers of having urged him to rig the US oil market by putting an illegal squeeze on Nymex. Purchase 'all the heating oil in New York harbour', he claims they told him.

And Benson and his supporters (who include Merton Miller the Nobel prizewinning US economist) have another, more disturbing, explanation of what happened. In their version, the losses on the futures contracts caused by the fall in oil prices were *not a problem*. The money lost on the hedging position would have been more than made up over the longer term by the advantage of buying cheaper oil on the cash market to fill the oil and gasoline supply contracts which had been fixed at a higher price. Metallgesellschaft and Deutsche Bank failed to understand that hedging is like a seesaw: if the hedge position loses money it is because the underlying business is gaining, and vice versa. All the bankers at

Deutsche saw was the short term loss on the futures position; they failed to grasp that the very same market forces (the oil price fall) would result in a longer term gain on their oil supply contracts.

But it was worse than that. The company suffered twice because early in 1994 – weeks after all MGRM's futures had been closed at a massive loss – the oil price rose again, making the oil supply business less profitable. By then, however, there were no longer any countervailing futures contracts hedging this business. Metallgesellschaft therefore lost all over again.

The disquieting implication is that Metallgesellschaft and Deutsche Bank committed hara-kiri without comprehending what they were doing. They panicked and sold out too soon. By failing to understand the nature of hedging they destroyed Benson's strategy and caused themselves quite unnecessary pain. The blunder was particularly embarrassing to Deutsche which was in the process of trying to establish itself as a derivatives player in other markets. It was, in a sense, Allied Lyons writ large. Yet again, top management had failed to understand what the experts at the coal face were doing. The only difference was that at Allied Lyons the managers never knew what hit them until it was too late, while at Metallgesellschaft their intervention made matters infinitely worse. In both cases the shareholders were badly served.

You can argue – as many do – that the derivatives disasters which have shaken the corporate world over the last few years were simply part of a learning process. In the early days, derivatives were poorly understood and control mechanisms inside companies for bridling the dealing passions for their treasury staff were inadequate. But, goes the argument, the lessons have been learnt and everything is now safe and sound.

There is no particular reason to assume that this is true. A recent confidential survey by Touche Ross, the multinational accountancy firm, found that about a third of the British corporate clients it questioned who regularly used foreign exchange and interest rate derivatives had no policy towards them. The rest, presumably, dealt in derivatives without any clear idea of what they were trying to achieve. Of those that said they did have a policy, only 65 per cent had actually written it down, barely half had set limits on how

derivatives could be used and the amounts in which they could be
dealt, and less than half had reviewed their policy within the last
twelve months. This hardly represents a corporate sector getting
to grips with derivatives culture. Companies are guiltily aware of
this. Try asking a corporate treasurer about his derivatives dealings
and the reply, if you get one at all, is likely to be shifty and evasive.

How can you, as a shareholder, tell if the company you've
invested in has put itself at unreasonable risk? It is a question that
nags a great deal at the biggest investors on the stock market, such
as insurance companies and pension funds. 'To play with derivatives, you need adequate risk and management controls,' said the
worried derivatives expert at a leading insurer. 'If you do whizzy
things, you need whizzy controls. The danger is that many
companies don't actually know what controls they need so they
don't put them in. The other danger is that even if they do know
what they need they still don't put them in because the controls
are too expensive.'

The rules for accounting for derivatives in company results only
began to catch up with market developments by the mid-1990s.
Before then, different derivatives could be accounted for in different ways, which left companies almost limitless opportunities to
obfuscate. The Financial Accounting Standards Board, which overseas US accounting rules, proposed in 1997 that companies should
bring their derivatives on to the balance sheet and report a fair
market value for them at the time the accounts were stuck. This
provoked fury among big companies such as Citicorp, Coca-Cola
and McDonald's who realized that it could play havoc with their
financial results. In any case, they argued, it is more or less
impossible to value exotic derivatives that way. Against this kind of
heavy hitting opposition, it remains to be seen if the new rule will
stick. But even if derivatives are given their fair market value in a
company's accounts, that still doesn't tell you much. What if a
company had a massive futures position on 29 December, got rid
of it at the year end so that it did not show up in its accounts and
then plunged into the market again on 2 January? You'll probably
never know. 'It would be great if you could reduce all the
information about a company's derivatives dealing into one reliable
number on the bottom line,' said Steve Wallman, the US Securities

and Exchange Commissioner in charge of derivatives issues. 'That's what investors want. Unfortunately, it's impossible.'

To attempt to get round this problem the authorities in Europe and America now want companies to write an essay in their report and accounts explaining what their derivatives strategy is, why they have it and how they use it. In at least one case this has resulted in an eighteen-page note at the back of a company's accounts – the kind of thing that makes even professional investors despair. No doubt someone will read these passages, but it is unclear how helpful they will be. It may indeed be more use in focusing the minds of company board directors on what they are doing than in enlightening shareholders. It is a salutary thought that there probably never will be an adequate way of warning you, the shareholder, whether the company in which you have invested is about to do an Allied Lyons.

One early warning mechanism that has proved about as effective as a valium-drugged guard-dog are the credit rating agencies such as Standard & Poor's and Moody's. Their job is to alert the markets to companies that are bad credit risks. They do this by knowing the companies in greater detail than any shareholder ever can from its accounts, interviewing the management, understanding the way it works. Unfortunately, in almost every major derivatives disaster the rating agencies were the dog that never barked. They failed to spot what was happening at Barings, at Orange County, at Metallgesellschaft, at Allied Lyons, at Shell . . .

Experience teaches that when disaster strikes it tends to be swift, brutal and unexpected. The big investment institutions who own more than three-quarters of the British stock market are resigned to this. 'As investors,' said Simon Kerr, head of derivatives at Clerical & Medical, one of the larger insurance companies, 'we can't be sure that companies know what they are doing with derivatives. Corporates have a responsibility to use derivatives to hedge their business risks. But do they really know what they're doing? Ultimately, we can't check. In these markets they can take on enormous market exposure very very quickly compared to the cash markets, and we'd never know. They might make a huge amount of money or they might lose a huge amount of money. That is the joy and terror of derivatives.'

CHAPTER 9

THE GOLDEN HORDE

Just as I'm five times as rich as you are, and five times as clever.

Through the Looking Glass

A senior British director of a well-known investment bank first understood the potentially lethal power of derivatives on a tour of the bank's Chicago subsidiary. The head trader of this operation insisted on showing him something he said was important, so one afternoon the two of them piled into a limo and headed off into the dead flat, freezing winter countryside. After driving for an hour, the mystified director asked the head trader where they were going.

'To see a dead guy,' said the trader. 'He's a client – no, he *was* a client. Now he isn't because, career-wise, he's dead.'

The corpse in question was a fund manager employed by a well-known investment management company. His troubles had started about a year earlier when his investment performance had fallen below the targets set him by his bosses. Investment targets are increasingly common in the investment industry. Naturally, investors want their funds to do well but the real pressure comes from within the investment management companies which insist that their fund managers must achieve certain specified levels of return each year. The intensifying competition between companies is largely responsible for this, and the targets tend to be set at the high end of what is reasonably achievable. A fund manager's bonus is closely tied to how successfully he reaches his target. If he fails to meet it consistently – say, in three quarters out of four – he may lose his job. What had happened to the corpse outside Chicago was what happens to most fund managers sooner or later: he had failed to meet his target return.

This had happened in the first quarter of the year. His response was all too predictable: he decided to gamble with derivatives as a quick way to recoup his position. Gearing up his fund with the use of futures and options, he hoped to guess the market right and regain his investment target by the end of the second quarter. Unfortunately, he guessed wrong and the fund plunged under-water. Facing the classic dealer's choice of doubling up or quitting, he doubled and got it wrong again. By the end of the third quarter his fund was a bombed out wasteland, with about half its money lost. Throughout this little tragedy, the main supplier of derivatives to the unfortunate fund manager was the investment bank whose representatives were now going to view the devastation for their own edification.

'For a few months, this fund manager was our best customer,' said the head dealer. 'We made a fortune out of him. His dealing volume grew and grew as his position became more desperate. We could see what was happening to him, how much he was losing. Eventually I had to cut off all business contact because his financial situation was too precarious. I had to tell my dealers: "Never ever do a deal with this guy. I don't care if he begs on his knees, don't do anything with him. Forget him. Treat him like he's dead."'

After an hour and a half the two bankers reached the investment company's offices and met the fund manager. 'I have never,' the bank director reported later, 'seen a man look so sick. It was terrible. He had a green tinge to his skin, he can't have slept for a month, even his eyes looked sick. He knew it was just a matter of time before he lost his job, and he knew he had wiped out the retirement money of his investors.' He also knew there was no longer anything he could do about his plight. Once word had got around that the investment bank had stopped doing business with him he became a pariah in the markets. He could neither double up again nor unwind his positions. He could do little but wait for the axe to fall at accounting time at the end of the month. 'He looked . . . well . . . like he was half dead,' the director said.

It is a tale that could be repeated about fund managers all over the industrialized world during the last few years. Investment funds of all kinds – pension funds, mutual funds, insurance funds – have become big users of derivatives. Like corporations and municipal authorities, however, many have turned out to be the stupid customers to whom bank salesmen are always hoping to sell derivatives. After the excesses of the early 1990s, hundreds of funds are left tending a menagerie of bizarre and dangerous instruments which have an unnerving propensity to self-destruct on the least expected moves in the markets. Many investment managers would be hard put to explain why they own instruments that may, for example, depend on the Deutsch mark/yen swap rate and pay a coupon of 13 per cent in the first year and then nothing thereafter – except that it seemed like a good idea at the time. Many fund managers do not have the expertise to hedge their derivatives properly or even understand what they own.

The danger of unexpected explosions is somewhat smaller among British funds, since they tend to be more conservative in their use of derivatives than Americans. But in Japan the suffering has been intense although, thanks to the poor levels of disclosure there, it has largely been in silence. In the late 1980s Japanese insurance companies and investment funds found a new way to invest in the Tokyo stock market, other than simply buying the shares. Convinced that the bull market would continue indefinitely, they started purchasing bonds that paid an abnormally high rate of interest. The payoff was that they would only get their principal back if the Nikkei stock index had risen by the time the bond matured. It was an out-and-out bet that the market would keep going up. The bonds were sold by US and European banks which were convinced the Tokyo market was too high and had to fall. They turned out to be right when, in 1990, the market suffered a mini-crash. A formula kicked in which meant that, in many cases, the bonds became worthless and investment funds which owned them got none of their money back at all. Their response was to sell put options, betting that the market would recover. Unfortunately for them, it kept dropping for another two years and they lost again.

What makes an investment manager buy risky derivatives? The reasons are no doubt legion, but among the most common is good salesmanship by banks. 'You have to remember that a lot of these fund managers are from out of town,' explained a London based derivatives salesman. 'Many of them are there because they failed to get into the City or Wall Street. They are in awe of the big banks and brokers. You wine them and dine them. Everyone's on an expense account. They want to be your friend because it makes them feel part of the big picture, part of the scene. It's how they get their kicks. And how can they be most friendly? They can buy things from you, especially the things you want to sell them. Sooner or later, they buy. Obviously the funds and the banks have a common interest in this, but it isn't the client's.'

And all too often investors want to deal for the sake of dealing. There is a story told of a Bankers Trust salesman – a former bodyguard of president Ronald Reagan, as it happens – who became one of the bank's biggest producers. The quants had just come up with a new deal structure that linked the US government bond rate to, of all things, the Greek drachma. The point of this deal, if there was one, does not matter. What matters is that the salesman had to find investors to sell it to. And he did. Ringing up one of his best clients he talked up the merits of an instrument linked to the drachma exchange rate as if he had discovered gold. Interested but wary, the investor said, 'Okay, tell me something about Greece.' Unable to think of anything about Greece on the spur of the moment, the salesman went home that evening and saw his young daughter's school atlas lying on the living-room floor. Tearing out the page that showed Greece, he hurried into work the next morning and faxed it through to his client. Satisfied, the client bought the derivatives.

Even funds that have used derivatives purely as a hedging tool have had cause to wonder just how useful they are. When a California pension fund lost $70 million on its hedging positions it began to question whether there was any point in hedging at all. It concluded that since pension funds are, by their nature, long term

investors to whom short term market movements are irrelevant
there was no need to protect against short term currency or stock
market fluctuations. Therefore, no hedging. It is not a view,
however, that has achieved anything like unanimous support among
investment funds.

How can you, an investor in a fund, know whether the managers
are using your money to dabble in derivatives? The simple answer
is that it's almost impossible. The amount of information funds
have to supply about their derivatives holdings is fairly scanty. Even
if they were required to give a full inventory of every derivatives
they had bought or sold, it would still be extremely hard in many
cases to determine whether they were being used for genuine
hedging of the underlying portfolio or whether they were outright
gambles.

But while ordinary investment fund managers grapple with the
complexities of hedging with varying degrees of success, there is
another kind of fund manager to whom they are the stuff of life
itself. These are the so-called hedge funds, the new financial
buccaneers whose activities have next to nothing to do with hedging
and whose investment funds float on a boundless sea of derivatives.

While it is true that George Soros, one of the world's best-known
financial adventurers, thought he was God when he was a boy, this
is not a necessary characteristic of all speculators. The most
successful generally have a healthy streak of humility that enables
them to cut out of bad investments before they lose heavily. 'Where
I think that I excel,' Soros himself once observed, 'is in recognizing
my mistakes, you see. And that is the secret of my success.'
However, an exalted confidence in their own intelligence and
certainty in their own judgement is also typical of most hedge fund
managers. Even if they don't believe they are divine, they do
believe they can achieve the nearly impossible feat of consistently
beating the market year after year. Remarkably, many of them do.

They are the professional speculators, *par excellence*. Unlike the
proprietary traders at the banks, hedge fund managers usually risk
their own millions along with those of their clients. To call them
investors is misleading, since the term usually implies some medium
to long term commitment to the assets held. Hedge fund managers

have no commitment to anything that does not look likely to produce a higher than average profit over the reasonably short term – which could mean the next ten minutes. Their sole aim is to produce as much profit as possible at the end of the year. They regularly rack up returns of 20, 30, 50 per cent which common sense and simple maths suggests should be well-nigh impossible. These are the hot money specialists, the ultimate short-termists. They are, within the confines of the financial markets, the quintessence of greed.

They are also among the world's leading users of derivatives. They have to be. A characteristic of most hedge funds is an extremely high degree of leverage which is one reason they can produce abnormally high returns. This is partly achieved through large bank loans and partly through the use of futures and options. A fund like Soros's Quantum fund borrows and then leverages the loan through derivatives to increase its bet – leverage on top of leverage. Another reason for the heavy reliance of hedge funds on derivatives is the need for mobility. The funds don't linger in markets where the returns do not look unusually good, and since investment conditions are constantly changing around the world, their money is on a perpetual migration from market to market, country to country. They are the Golden Horde of the financial world. To make their migrations possible, they stick to the most liquid markets – and none are more liquid than futures and options. For example, instead of selling fifty different Mexican shareholdings and buying fifty German ones – a cumbersome and expensive process – a fund would simply sell Mexican stock index futures and buy German index futures at a fraction of the cost and twice the speed.

Hedge funds were invented in the US in 1949 by Alexander Winslow Jones, a former journalist. He was a stock picker who decided that if some stocks were good enough to buy long, others must be bad enough to sell short. Surprisingly, no one seems to have thought of this before. Holding long and short positions in the same portfolio was, in those unsophisticated times, regarded as a hedge – hence the name hedge fund. The early funds were concentrated in equities and during the 1960s the idea caught on. But it was not until the deregulation of financial markets in the

1980s, the scrapping of exchange controls and the growth of the derivatives markets that they really took off.

As the hedge funds grew larger the managers realized they could not remain in equities alone and still produce the same returns, so they branched out into other fields. At the same time, the pure speculators saw the opportunity to use hedge funds as vehicles to play in any market they wanted. The big attraction was that the funds are largely unregulated, unlike ordinary mutual funds and units trusts which are subjected to continuous official scrutiny. In the US a fund with under a hundred 'partners' (i.e. investors) does not have to file returns with the SEC. Even better from a speculator's point of view, if the fund is registered offshore – as Soros's multi-billion dollar Quantum fund is – no regulator or tax man anywhere can touch it. There are no restrictions on what, where or how the fund can invest; it is as free as it is possible to be to roam the world looking for treasure.

By the second half of 1996 the hedge fund industry had about $120 billion of funds under management. It is impossible to say with any precision how many times over this money was leveraged, since the funds are extremely secretive and their levels of leverage are, in any case, constantly changing with their investment strategies. About a third of all the assets in the industry is in the hands of the fifteen biggest US fund managers such as Soros, Paul Tudor Jones, Julian Robertson, Bruce Covenor and (before he retired in 1996) Michael Steinhard. The rest is divided between a huge variety of investment vehicles, some worth several hundred million dollars, some a mere one or two million. At the lower end it is a kind of cottage industry – one man and his dog investing the money of a few friends out of his living room using a personal computer and a couple of trading screens on the dining room table. There is precious little glamour in single handedly tracking a twenty-four-hour global market: it tends to lead to a cycle of sleep deprivation, investment losses and finally nervous breakdown that means the smallest funds often don't last long.

But then, the world of hedge funds is undeniably strange. Hedge fund managers are by nature solitary and often difficult people, the hermits of the financial markets. Some, like David Weil in London, are Buddhists; Soros himself has a personal philosophy of the markets that is so opaque hardly anyone apart, presumably, from Soros himself has been able to understand it. Many of the most successful hedge fund managers have never been to business school or even worked for a major Wall Street or City firm. Hedge fund managers are not, in general, modest people which is one reason why they tend not to operate easily in large organizations. They have a tendency to think that they are right while everyone else is wrong which, to more corporate minded folk, can be intensely irritating – particularly when it turns out to be true.

Success is the only thing that matters about a hedge fund. Managers are paid by performance, unlike an ordinary investment fund where they are paid on a percentage of asset value. In a hedge fund, exceptional profits provide exceptional pay. Most managers take 20 per cent of the profits on top of an annual management fee of anything between 1 and 5 per cent of assets before sharing out what's left to the investors. The clever part about this arrangement is that the managers do not have to pay anything back if the fund loses money the next year. For example, Crispin Odey, a hedge fund manager in London, set up his fund in the early 1990s, earned a performance fee of $25 million in 1993 when the fund did well but still kept the money when his fund slumped to a devastating loss the following year. This is also how Soros, in 1993, became the highest paid man in America with a salary of more than $1.1 billion, which was more than the GNP of forty-two member nations of the UN at the time.

Who are the investors willing to put their money in such funds and pay such astronomical fees? They are rich people, mainly, who can afford to take a higher level of risk for a higher rate of return – people, you might say, who can afford to speculate. Getting hold of their money, however, isn't easy. When hedge fund managers turn to professional money raisers for help they do it reluctantly and only because they have to. They hate it because the money raisers take a large cut of the booty, thus reducing the manager's own slice. But investment managers are often not the kind of people who like dealing with clients. Many would prefer not to have clients at all if they could find a way to do without them. In any case, they probably do not have the right contacts. So they turn to men like Marty Ho, who is now based in Connecticut, the world centre of the hedge fund industry. He has spent his career getting to know rich people and tapping them for billions to put into hedge funds.

'It's not an easy thing to get people, even rich people, to write big cheques,' says Ho. 'It's an art, not a science. After all, a hedge fund is not a commodity that people *need*. It's something you have to make them *want*.' He got started thanks to a remarkable memory for irrelevant facts. He joined Grosvenor, one of the early hedge funds based in Boston, and began making contacts. As his store of knowledge about the industry grew, he went freelance.

Since wealthy people tend to hang around with other wealthy people, knowing about the industry meant, in part, knowing where to find the rich investors. Every year, for example, Ho attends the gathering of the Gatekeepers – the individuals employed to look after the money of America's richest families – who meet annually in Chicago to swap notes and schmooze. The Gatekeepers, says Ho, don't necessarily know anything about money, but they are trusted by the families that employ them – often they are family friends – so they are an essential point of contact. Once you're in the charmed circle, it gets a little easier.

'When you meet wealthy people they talk about baseball. Then the serious conversation starts about money and you exchange information – like swapping baseball cards. I mention a few fund managers and I reel off their performance figures and all kinds of statistics. That makes great cocktail talk in wealthy circles. When they hear it they want to talk to you. You have to remember, these are not sophisticated investors, although that is how the SEC defines them because they have so much money. Usually, they don't know what they want, but they're greedy and their motivation in finding a top hedge fund is not only to outdo the market index. They want to outdo their neighbour as well. They all have big cars and big houses, so how else can they compete? They can say, "I was the first into Paul Tudor Jones's fund, or Michael Steinhardt's".

'So they listen to me and then say, "When you have the right manager, tell him to give me a call." So I put them in touch. A smart fund manager will listen to what the client wants and then tell him what he wants to hear. If the client wants a defensive fund, that's how the manager will sell himself.'

But knowing the client is only half of Ho's business. The other half is knowing the fund managers. He became like a rabbi to them, sitting and listening to what they said and trying to get inside their heads so that he could judge who was likely to make money and who was not. 'I got to know who had a drink problem, who had a girlfriend on the side, who was about to get married, who had debts. It all matters because it affects the way they trade. I knew a guy who was drunk nearly every day but this wasn't a problem because when he drank he traded like a god. *Like a god*. After a while his partner got fed up with seeing him rat-arsed each afternoon. When they took away his champagne, smashed all the bottles and wouldn't allow him to drink, I knew it was all over. The guy couldn't trade any more. Within a month or two, the fund folded.'

With his store of knowledge, Ho puts investors and managers together and reaps a rich reward. Money raisers get paid by both sides: they typically take a 2 per cent cut when the assets are put into the fund. Then they take 20 per cent each year of the fund manager's 20 per cent performance fee. One money raiser who procured $2 billion for Julian Robertson's Tiger fund got a $40 million flat fee, followed by performance fees between 1989 and 1993, before the fund started to make losses, totalling more than $100 million.

From beginning to end, an investor's money is constantly being whittled down by fees to middlemen and fund managers. To remove 2 per cent of the capital and more than a fifth of the profit and still end up with a pay-out above the run of ordinary investment funds is indeed a remarkable feat. To do so, an investment manager either needs to have some kind of edge over his competitors, or he needs to take bigger risks. Hedge funds, on the whole, do both, which is one reason the emerging hedge fund industry became so deeply entangled with the fledgling derivatives markets.

The scene: a couple of guys, a secretary, a lot of computer machinery, some Reuters and Bloomberg screens, a few telephones and £5 million – all of it squeezed into a two-room office in an unremarkable modern building in the picturesque Cotswolds village of Morton-on-Marsh. It is a world away from the glamour of George Soros's Quantum fund but Cambridge Financial Products, as this low-key outfit calls itself, is one of the same species: a hedge fund.

Peter Udale and Tosh Nagata, who run Cambridge Financial Products, set themselves up in 1994. The only trouble was that they had no one's money to invest. After an uncertain few months, the German subsidiary of a Canadian bank decided to give them a try and handed them £5 million to look after. Their aim is to take very small risks by looking for discrepancies in the values of similar assets. They might, for instance, spot that a bank's interest rate swap price was low compared with the price of seven year Japanese government bonds. By a process of buying and selling the bonds and carrying out an interest rate swap with the bank they might eventually winkle out a tiny profit of around 0.04 per cent.

Using derivatives is often the only way to make money out of this technique. The low transaction costs and high liquidity of futures contracts means that a quant fund could exploit a mere 1 per cent price discrepancy between two shares to make a profit. This would be impossible if it dealt in the cash market where the spread between the bid and offer price of an FTSE-100 stock, for instance, would more than wipe out any chance of making money.

The pace of this kind of activity is not hectic. They may do one or two deals a day, if that, and spend the rest of the time calculating the values of assets in ten or twelve different markets. Their return in the first year was solid if unspectacular but to get more clients they need to build up a track record. What they do is labour intensive, not particularly high tech and, so far at least, not particularly remunerative.

Udale and Nagata are part of the tribal diaspora that took place in the early 1990s when a large number of Bankers Trust employees left to join other banks or set up their own investment funds, spreading the techniques they had learned at Bankers across the financial universe. For Udale and Nagata, as for many hedge fund managers, it was a lifestyle choice as much as anything. They had young families and they wanted to get away from London. With the right computers and communications, you can run a hedge fund from anywhere.

There are about as many styles of investing as there are fund managers, but hedge funds tend to come in two main flavours. Cambridge Financial Products is a mild example of a quant or 'black box' fund, driven primarily by mathematics. The edge they have over ordinary investment funds is mathematical sophistication. Market fundamentals count for virtually nothing: what matters are the mathematical relationships between markets or between securities in the same market. A visit to a quant fund can be an eerie experience. There seems to be no activity except a couple of guys with their feet up on the desk sipping iced coffee through straws. They are the fund managers but most of the time they don't actually have to do anything. All the work went into designing the computer programme – the 'black box' – which is now sorting through the tens of thousands of prices fed into it from a variety of markets, grinding through hundreds of calculations per minute, calculating price discrepancies and even putting through the buy and sell orders automatically. The managers simply make sure the computer does not break down. The rest of the time they are refining the programme, adding new markets to its range, improving the calculations and, with any luck, their profits too. Since a fund like this may only hold a market position for five minutes or so and close out all its positions at the end of the day, the risk should be very low.

Profitable though this can be, it is not exactly glamorous. That reward goes to the other genus of hedge fund which might be collected under the heading of 'directional funds'. The managers can do the fancy sums, but in the end their method is to back hunches like most other investors. They just do it on a far larger scale and, in general, in a much more sophisticated way. These hedge funds long ago gave up the idea of hedging: when they think they have identified a good bet, they take massive positions. Often, like George Soros, they are betting on the direction of whole markets or economies – hence 'directional funds'.

Most of the biggest and best known hedge funds fall into this category. Rather than the steady, unspectacular accretion of little gains that many quant funds go for, the likes of Julian Robertson, Michael Steinhardt, Paul Tudor Jones and Bruce Coverner take huge gains or losses from even bigger bets. They prefer to go against the trend of the market since running with the herd is never likely to produce outsize profits. The trick is to spot opportunities the rest of the world has missed and then back those hunches to the hilt. The most successful hedge fund managers seem to have a better understanding of markets, a better analysis of situations, than most other players. But they are also freer to chase their profits because they are unfettered by rules dictating how their funds must be invested, as the managers of most ordinary funds are.

George Soros is by far the best known hedge fund manager not only because he is more willing than most of this secretive community to speak up in public but because his investment record is truly remarkable. If you had invested $100,000 when he set up his fund in 1973 and reinvested all the income you would have been worth $130 million by 1995 – a 35 per cent compound return per year.

Soros is stocky, his hair brushed carefully back in a thick wave, his clothes immaculate. He speaks carefully as if worried that someone might catch him out on some slip of fact or logic, in an accent tinged with Hungarian. When he talks about the markets, however, he sounds completely self-assured and totally dispassionate, as if betting a fortune of a couple of billion dollars every day was no more than an interesting intellectual experiment.

He is another successful financier who was forced as a child to flee from the Nazis and finally made his way to the US. Born in Hungary into an upper middle class family, he spent much of his childhood sheltering in the cellars of friends' houses until the war ended. Two years later he went to England where he studied at the London School of Economics and then worked at the small merchant bank, Singer & Friedlander. In 1956 he moved to New York where, having decided he was never going to make the grade as a philosopher, he joined a series of second line investment banks and broking houses, ending up at Arnold & S. Bleischroeder as a securities analyst – an unexceptional progress that characterizes the careers of many hedge fund managers before they branch out on their own.

Soros did so in 1969. He set up the Quantum fund with another ambitious Wall Street outsider, Jim Rogers, who had grown up in a Mid-Western town called Demopolis, whose population was so small that the Rogers family phone number was simply '4'. He, too, had no formal business school training but was a brilliant stock analyst: Quantum began as a classic old-fashioned stock-picking hedge fund. The partnership of Soros, the dealer, and Rogers, the stock analyst, did spectacularly well but when it grew larger than Rogers was comfortable with he bailed out. Soros teamed up with other temporary partners but his most successful catch was a young investment manager called Stanley Druckenmiller, who joined Quantum in the late 1980s and has handled the day-to-day running of the fund ever since, leaving Soros free to tour the world on philanthropic missions to spend his millions.

First, however, Druckenmiller had to learn the Soros investment style. According to Wall Street legend, one of his early bets with Quantum's money went remarkably well and the new manager was feeling pleased with himself. When Soros asked how big the winning position was, Druckenmiller said it was 'quite large'. 'How large?' asked Soros. 'A billion dollars,' said Druckenmiller. 'You call that a position?' said Soros. If you believe you have a winning hand, back it to the hilt, was his philosophy. Druckenmiller added another $1 billion to the position and doubled his profits.

No winning position is probably more famous in the recent history of investing, however, than the one Quantum took in 1992 against the British pound, the one that 'broke the Bank of England' when sterling was forced out of the European exchange rate mechanism and made Soros a profit of $1 billion overnight. It was typical of the Soros-Druckenmiller partnership but also of the way large hedge funds in general tend to operate.

In the early autumn of 1992 the managers at Quantum were becoming convinced that Britain could not hold its place in the ERM because the high interest rates forced on it by the Bundesbank were wrecking its recession-racked economy. Plenty of other speculators had come to the same conclusion and a series of attacks on the pound were forcing the Bank of England to spend huge amounts of foreign exchange reserves to keep the pound as strong as the ERM required it to be.

The question was how long would it be before the Bank's money ran out. It was Druckenmiller who got the timing right: by mid-September he believed the UK could not hang on much longer. It was Soros who supplied the confidence to throw all his chips on the table. Convinced that the Bundesbank would not lower rates to help the British out – that this was a 'one way bet' – Quantum began investing on 10 September. Within six days it had built up a $10 billion position and would have bet even more had it not run out of time. 'I told him [Druckenmiller] to go for the jugular,' Soros said later. 'It's like shooting fish in a barrel. As long as the barrel holds up you keep on shooting the fish.'

Quantum's strategy was quite complex because it was designed to mop up every bit of advantage from the financial mayhem that a British withdrawal from the ERM would cause. It relied heavily on futures and options because there was no other way to amass such huge holdings so quickly. Druckenmiller sold $7 billion worth of sterling short, anticipating a devaluation. He also expected a short term rise in the Deutschmark, so he bought $6 billion of them. For the same reason he also purchased some French francs. He also bought $500 million of British stocks on the assumption that British shares would rise after the devaluation. He sold German and French equities, expecting them to fall, and bought German and French bonds on the grounds that a rise in the mark would lead to a fall in German interest rates.

Even as Druckenmiller was feverishly pouring money into the market, the British government gave way. On 'Black Wednesday', 16 September, a haggard and rather angry looking Norman Lamont, Chancellor of the Exchequer, stood outside his house in Downing Street and told the TV cameras that sterling was coming out of the currency system. At 7.00 a.m. in New York, Soros was woken by a phone call from Druckenmiller informing him that he was richer by just short of $1 billion. When Quantum's holdings in other weak European currencies were added into the equation, the total windfall was about $2 billion.

To say that Soros was solely responsible for the Bank of

England's capitulation would be absurd. The foreign exchange markets are simply too big for any single speculator to have that kind of power. But it is fair to say that he played a recognizable role in pushing down the pound. To give an idea of the size of his bet, his combined sterling and mark positions were not far short of the $15 to $20 billion which the Bank spent in supporting the pound. Governments should indeed fear what big speculators can do.

How powerful are the hedge funds, collectively if not individually? How much damage can they really do and what threat do they pose to the financial system? In April 1994, George Soros told the House Banking Committee that they posed no threat at all. 'I reject any assertion or implication that our activities are destabilizing.' The defence of hedge funds is the classic defence offered by all speculators in all ages. By taking a different view of the market to the rest of the herd they actually provide a stabilizing influence. It is, claimed Soros, the insurance funds and mutual funds – the unimaginative lumpen investor class who all swing one way and then all swing the other – which actually poses the biggest threat to market stability.

Leaving aside the fact that he is talking his own book here, the World's Greatest Investor has a point. In normal times, speculators undoubtedly supply essential liquidity to markets. They are the grease on the axle, the oil in the cogwheels. In normal times.

When a crisis strikes a market, however, the story isn't so simple. Thanks to the use of derivatives which gives speculators such vast leverage and speed of movement from one market to the next, speculators are likely to rock the boat more violently than anyone else. They don't sit out big losses when a market falls; they cut and run. With enough hedge funds running in the same direction at the same time, there is every danger of the boat capsizing.

Soros admitted as much to the House Banking Committee, although he put the blame on the banks which issue derivatives rather than on the hedge funds. In reality, the blame should fall on both. Soros said that 'if the market moves against the issuer, the issuer is forced to move in the same direction as the market, and thereby amplify the initial price disturbance ... This raises the spectre of financial dislocation.'

He should know since he himself was fresh from a particularly nasty encounter with the spectre of financial dislocation. A few weeks before this statement Soros had been one of many hedge fund managers and banks whose speculating had been instrumental in creating one of the most threatening financial disturbances of recent years. During the bond market crash of early 1994, his Quantum funds lost $650 million in a couple of days – an event still known inside the Quantum fund as the St Valentine's Day Massacre. But he got off relatively lightly. Some funds lost over $1 billion, others went out of business and one large American bank was rumoured to have been bankrupted by the bond sell-off. The Fed itself thought for a while that it had precipitated the financial melt-down that it has feared for so long.

The sort of 'dislocation' Soros was talking about was this: suppose a dealer sells a put option on $100 million of 10 year bonds (giving the customer the right to buy the bonds at some point). To hedge the put option the dealer has to sell some of the bonds, but to remain properly hedged in all market conditions can be fiendishly difficult. The maths of hedging forces him to buy bonds as they rise and sell them as they fall which exacerbates the market movement. If enough dealers have taken the same bet at the same time, their combined efforts to hedge themselves will be self-defeating: the more they hedge by selling bonds, the more the bond price will fall, obliging them to sell some more bonds, and so on. Although Soros calls the resulting mess a financial dislocation, most people call it a market crash.

And a crash is what was set in motion when, on 4 February 1994, the Federal Reserve Open Market Committee, the body of central bank officials which sets US interest rates, decided to increase rates by a modest 0.25 per cent. Something unprecedented and totally unexpected happened in the world's bond markets: they collapsed with a suddenness and ferocity that scared the authorities and left everyone shell-schocked. In the middle of the mayhem a bewildered President Clinton asked his Treasury Secretary, Robert Rubin, to explain what on earth was going on. Rubin's answer was

that the market was not working the way it always had in the past.
The Treasury Secretary had spent years as a highly successful Wall
Street trader, worked his way up to become deputy chairman of
Goldman Sachs and made $100 million or so for himself on the
way. If anyone would know whether something had gone horribly
wrong with the markets, Rubin was probably the man.

He told the President that the markets had ceased to pay any
attention to economic fundamentals – factors such as inflation and
growth – which have traditionally always driven bond prices.
Instead the bond markets were marching – or rather, panicking –
to some rhythm of their own that outsiders could not immediately
discern. There was some new dynamic that was apparently beyond
anyone's ability to control or even predict.

What it boiled down to was that the Fed had figured without
the hedge funds and derivatives markets. The hot money was
heavily invested in bonds all over the world, but particularly in
Europe, confidently expecting interest rates to decline because of
the weakness of many leading economies. With supreme arrogance,
the hedge funds had decided this was a one-way bet. And when
hedge funds decide they have identified a sure thing, they don't
just add a little extra weighting in their portfolio, they bet the
ranch – or a large chunk of it, anyway. One way of doing so is to
borrow money from the banks, but that is only the beginning.
Using their own capital plus borrowed cash, they had leveraged
their bet many times over by buying bond futures and options.
This is the only way that a fund manager such as Michael
Steinhardt, for example, could give his $4.5 billion hedge fund a
bond market position of $30 billion. Ordinary investment funds
then came in behind the hedge funds when they saw bond prices
rising and bought more bonds.

The Fed had intended its interest rate rise as an uncontroversial
vote of confidence in the strength of the US economy. (It had
considered a larger increase but Alan Greenspan, the chairman,
had insisted that 0.25 per cent was sufficient.) Even that small
amount, however, was enough to spook the bond markets. The
funds took one look at the interest rate rise and gave a collective
shriek of pain and panic. The size of the move didn't matter, it was
the direction that counted. Investors reasoned – if that's the right

word for it – that if the Fed was raising interest rates it must be because inflation had started to rise. And if inflation and interest rates were going up in the US they would also rise in other countries, which meant bond prices would be heading down – which meant anyone caught holding bonds would get killed.

The first to move were the hedge funds, acting on reflex. They had no choice. They could not afford the luxury of thinking first because the time it took to do so could cost them millions. Leveraged to the hilt, they could not bear even a small downward shift in bond prices. For example, Michael Steinhardt, the rotund and ebullient manager of one of the New York's largest and most successful hedge funds, was losing $7 million for every 0.01 per cent move in European interest rates. Bonds cascaded on to the market in an avalanche as the funds tried to unload. A trader attempting to sell bond futures in the Chicago Board of Trade told the *Wall Street Journal* that the eerie sound coming over his intercom from the pit was a wail of pain something akin to childbirth.

Crispin Odey, among the largest English hedge fund managers, watched in horror as his investment strategy was blown to pieces like that of the other funds. Operating from an elegant Regency building in Mayfair, he was the blue-eyed boy of the British hedge fund scene. He exudes a schoolboyish enthusiasm and has a professorial tendency to spin elaborate theories about the markets. In a remarkably short time – four years – he had built his fund up from scratch to almost $1 billion and had had a fantastically successful year in 1993. The prospect of disaster seemed a very remote possibility in the winter of 1994. He'd been riding the bond bandwagon since 1990, had made a lot of money out of it and had leveraged the fund's capital about five times over.

Like many hedge fund managers, Odey just couldn't believe what was happening to him. 'I was in a great state of denial,' he admits, when bond prices started falling. 'I couldn't understand the reasoning of the market.' That lost him precious time as others sold bonds as if their lives depended on it and the market collapsed.

Michael Steinhardt was also having a torrid time, but for slightly different reasons. A trade dispute between the US and Japan, together with a rise in Japanese interest rates, set off an unexpected surge in the yen and a fall in the dollar. Several hedge funds including Soros's lost heavily on the currency move, but Steinhardt lost badly as Japanese bond prices fell. The size of hedge fund losses in Japan led to massive margin calls on future positions which many funds could only afford by selling other assets. Among the other assets they chose to sell were US and European bonds, and so the wider bond price collapse received a further push. As bond prices in Europe followed those of the US and Japan downwards Steinhardt decided that his only option was to bail out completely. Hardly leaving his office for four days, he sold bonds at whatever price he could get. In those ninety-six hours he lost $800 million.

And bond prices kept falling. Wall Street banks started off by obligingly buying back European bonds from panicking clients to whom they had sold them not long before, but soon the only way they could afford the purchases was to sell their holdings of US treasury bonds – so the market lurched downwards again. The banks also sold bonds for another reason: the rise in interest rates had sent the maturities on their holdings of mortgage backed bonds shooting outwards. Since longer term bonds are riskier to hold, the banks looked for a way to reduce the over-all maturity of their bond portfolios. Their solution was to sell long-dated Treasury bonds – probably around $20 billion of them suddenly hit the market. Yet again, the market dropped.

Then the rumours started. They said that Bankers Trust had lost $1 billion, that it had told its traders to stop taking positions, that it was bust. Like all the best rumours it had the merit of plausibility. With its large proprietary trading operation Bankers behaved more like a hedge fund in its market dealing than most other banks, and everyone knew it was up to its eyebrows in highly leveraged derivatives. It wasn't hard to believe that in the middle of the market's agony Bankers really had got toasted.

This was precisely what the Fed had always feared. William McDonough, president of the New York Fed, had been warning for years about 'the nightmare scenario' that could result from a disruption in the markets. The danger of the Bankers Trust rumour, whether it was true or not, was that it would shake confidence in the banks as reliable counterparties which would worsen the disruption. If people feared that banks were going bust, the stock market would start to suffer too. On 2 March, Bankers shares did not open on the New York Stock Exchange because of the rumours, and the Dow Jones index promptly plunged 50 points in half an hour.

At 11.00 a.m. under pressure from the Fed, Bankers issued a reassuring statement that it was still in profit for the year. What it didn't say was that its proprietary dealers had thought it was well hedged by spreading its bond holdings across many countries including Britain, France, Germany, several Latin American nations, Japan and the US. But when all of these markets fell simultaneously it turned out to be no hedge at all. Bankers told its dealers to slow down their trading – the move that had triggered the rumours. Bankers's losses were large but it wasn't bust.

What mattered, though, was to make sure the frightened markets *believed* that the bank was all right. McDonough started working the phones to the other banks, reassuring them that Bankers was still okay. It worked, but now he had another problem. He had discovered that central bankers in other countries were contemplating a move that could turn the crash into a total disaster. To punish the hedge funds for what they had already done some European central banks wanted to tell the commercial banks to cut off their credit to the funds. That would almost certainly have precipitated the collapse of many funds, with incalculable effects on the bond markets. McDonough got back on the phone and dissuaded them. For a couple of weeks it looked as if the markets were steadying.

Until Luis Donaldo Colosio, a Mexican presidential candidate, was shot dead on 23 March. No one could have predicted this event, and most Wall Street traders couldn't predict the effect either. Investors never like signs of instability in places that are already considered potentially unstable, so their instant reaction was to sell off Mexican bonds. More unexpectedly, however, they sold off bonds from every other emerging market too. It was as if investors couldn't distinguish a difference between Mexico, the Philippines, Korea, Malaysia and Argentina. No doubt the geopolitical knowledge of the average fund manager in Wyoming is fairly skimpy at times, but what frightened many well-informed investors was that they couldn't be sure exactly how ignorant the fund manager in Wyoming actually was. They decided to be the first to sell their emerging markets bonds, just to be on the safe side. Some large Wall Street firms only made matters worse by refusing to handle large deals. Quite rapidly, it became impossible to know what many emerging market bonds were worth.

Even less predictably, the emerging markets sell-off triggered another fall in the US treasury bond market and in Europe. Why? Derivatives. Many Western investors had linked their emerging market bonds to Treasury bonds as a hedge or as part of some more complex futures and options strategies. The idea that capital markets are distinct from each other was proved to be well and truly dead as the fall in emerging markets was transmitted to the US and Europe. Bond prices went into their now familiar downward lurch. As they tumbled, bond yields rose from 6.2 per cent at the start of the year to 7.6 per cent in early May. In a market where a move of one- or two-tenths of a percentage point is seen as a significant earth tremor, this was a seismic catastrophe.

As always after such a bruising event, people looked for a villain and quickly fixed the blame on the hedge funds for starting the panic and then leading the rout. They had been instrumental in building up the overhanging long position in bonds that had made the market nervous of any move in interest rates. They had, moreover, leveraged themselves so heavily that when the market began to fall they were obliged to dump huge quantities of their holdings – a case, as Soros put it, of amplifying the intitial price disturbance. Thus many of their fancy hedging tools and pricing models turned out to be useless when the time came. They were, in the end, nothing more than a big bet that bond prices would rise.

To make matters worse during the crash, a liquidity crisis developed. Although this can happen from time to time in the cash markets, no one thought it could happen in the futures markets where, in theory, there is always a speculator on the other side of the market to take your contracts off your hands. That was always supposed to be one of the beauties of the derivatives markets. But not this time. The trouble was that those same speculators were, to a large extent, the hedge funds. But the funds were now on the same side of the market as everyone else. They had started the selling and every other investor in the world, it seemed, had joined in until there was no one left to sell to. At times, you just couldn't get rid of bonds for love or money. Steinhardt remarked afterwards: 'I just remember losing money and staying up nights trying to peddle things, and being unable to sell anything at the market price.' He could only get out of his European bonds at well below the market level which, of course, drove prices down still further.

It was a frightening example of how the new market system can go badly wrong. Usually a benevolent force providing essential liquidity, the speculators drove the market down far faster than it would have gone without them. It was as if one of the teams in a game of tug-of-war had simply dropped their end of the rope and gone round to join the opposing team on the other end. With both teams pulling in the same direction, bond prices got dragged off the scale.

It was an event that could only have happened in the 1990s. Before the derivatives markets and before hedge funds, bond prices could not have moved so fast nor so unexpectedly. The rest of the market was absolutely right to blame them.

'The market always wants to blame the people who made money in periods of volatility,' grumbles Crispin Odey, but in this case it wasn't really true because, far from making money, the hedge fund industry got a third-degree burn. Odey's own fund shrank by three-quarters in value from about $1 billion at the end of 1993 to $250 million a year later, thanks to trading losses and clients withdrawing their money. Steinhardt ended up with a total loss of about $1.2 billion. Soros lost heavily, several funds in London and new York went out of business, and some fund managers were so traumatized by the whole experience that they retired. Money flooded out of the remaining funds for a time until investors – perennially short of memory – forgot the pain and started to return late in 1995. By the middle of 1996, the hedge funds were bigger than ever.

'There's nothing like losing money for testing your ideas,' says Odey philosophically. Or to test the strength of the markets. So far, none of the largest hedge funds have gone under but this does not mean they won't. No one is infallible, not even George Soros. Once the game against the Bank of England had been won in 1992,

Soros could safely call it a one-way bet. Hedge fund managers have a habit of talking about their successes as if they had been inevitable from the very beginning. But gargantuan gains do not come without taking gargantuan risks, whatever a speculator may tell you. And Soros, like all other hedge fund managers, has been on the losing end of some very large plays. The year after his success with sterling he lost about $1 billion betting that the yen would fall against the dollar. It didn't. He did relatively badly again in 1995 and lost still more money in the copper market in 1997, trying to drive the price down from what he regarded as unrealistic levels. The strategy was correct since the price was being propped up artificially by Sumitomo, the massive Japanese trading group, but Soros got the timing wrong and gave up too soon. If he had waited another three months, when Sumitomo finally cracked and the price plunged nearly 30 per cent, he would have made a hefty profit. His failure to do so is a good reminder that even the king of the hedge funds can screw up.

If a big hedge fund collapsed, the effects could be daunting. It would probably happen in the midst of some major market upheaval such as the bond market collapse of 1994. Its assets would probably be liquidated in a panic creating further market disruption. To make matters worse, the effects would almost certainly also feed through to the banking sector because hedge funds use huge amounts of bank credit as one of their major sources of leverage. The fact is that the two largest groups of speculators in the world – the hedge funds and the banks – are connected like Siamese twins. Lending to hedge funds is a large additional exposure to the financial markets for the banks, on top of their proprietary trading activities. Given the big-bet strategy of many large hedge funds, it has to be considered high risk lending. It was partly the fear that Bankers Trust had made massive loans to ailing hedge funds during the bond market collapse of 1994 which fuelled the rumours of the bank's imminent collapse.

There is, of course, no sign of the hedge fund industry shrinking or becoming less aggressive in its trading habits, or of using derivatives any less. Indeed, the industry has never looked healthier or more predatory, and the size of its assets seems to grow by the month. Nor is there much chance of the funds being more heavily regulated as long as they base themselves in offshore centres beyond the reach of the world's main financial authorities. After the bond market crash, members of Congress grew worried about hedge funds; many wanted them more closely controlled so that they could not continue disrupting markets. Soros himself contritely told Congress that he thought the funds should be more closely regulated. But this is not easy to do, even if the political will exists to do it. So far, at any rate, nothing has been done.

CHAPTER 10

WHO'S IN CHARGE?

'Off with her head!' the Queen shouted at the top of her
voice. Nobody moved.

Alice in Wonderland

The first that the senior executives of Morgan Stanley in London
knew of the Barings crisis was when one of them received a
telephone call on a Friday evening in the middle of a staff
party at a large West End hotel. Peter Baring was on the line,
begging for a meeting as soon as possible because he wanted to sell
his family bank. The startled executive agreed.

They met the following morning at Morgan Stanley's offices in
Canary Wharf with a spectacular view over the Thames. The
British contingent consisted of Peter Baring and his head of
investment banking, Peter Norris, who was among those most
responsible for allowing the crisis to happen.

'It was pathetic,' said one of the Morgan Stanley team afterwards.
'Peter Baring kept a stiff upper lip but looked as though he was
choking back the tears. He was obviously in a state of shock. He
said that three days earlier he had been preparing to announce
record profits for the bank in 1994; then, forty-eight hours ago, he
had learned that his bank was bust; and now he was offering to sell
it to us for one pound sterling. Norris, on the other hand, behaved
as though the whole meeting was a waste of time. He just sat there
sulking, not saying much, not being much help. It was the most

astonishing display of arrogance. He knew the bank was bust but seemed to think he could sort the whole thing out by himself.'

Barings had come to Morgan Stanley because it believed the US bank had substantial futures positions in the Far East that would offset Barings's own loss making positions. By taking over Barings, Morgan Stanley could in effect neutralize the British bank's losses. The Americans thought over the proposition for a few hours and reached the conclusion that they did not need to buy into this particular headache. They turned Peter Baring down.

This was stage one in the final death agonies of Britain's oldest merchant bank. At the same time, other senior Barings executives were meeting with other banks in London with the same request and met with an equal lack of success. Stage two was for the Bank of England, the banking supervisor, to see what it could do.

London's senior bankers gathered in the high-ceilinged first-floor committee room in the Bank of England on the morning of Sunday, 28 February 1995, with the aim of putting together a rescue package for Barings. They had been asked to do so by the Bank of England, which had been caught unaware by the Barings crisis but had to do something. Its duty is to protect bank depositors when possible, so its usual reaction is to find a way of propping up any institution in trouble. That rule had been broken a few years earlier when the Bank of Credit & Commerce International was allowed to fail but that was an institution hopelessly riddled with fraud. In any case, it was foreign so the likelihood of organizing a lifeboat with contributions from the UK banking community had been remote. Yet Barings, whose survival was at issue now, was not only British but at the heart of the Establishment, the Queen's bank, the oldest and most august merchant bank in the City. Peter Baring, the chairman, certainly had no doubts that his family institution would be saved.

Eddie George, the governor of the Bank of England, presided over the meeting, having been hauled back from a skiing holiday. He was becoming something of a veteran at this sort of crisis. It was he who had taken the decision to let BCCI go under, but he had also participated in organizing the lifeboat that had saved Johnson Matthey Bankers in the early 1980s. He knew, therefore, just how dodgy these rescue attempts could be. The British banking community had hated the Johnson Matthey lifeboat which they felt they had been forced into against their will. Some had threatened not to join it, saying they did not see why they should pay to bail out an incompetent competitor, and the whole thing had created bad blood in the City for years afterwards. Now the Bank was trying to set up another lifeboat. The question was, would the banking community toe the line again or would it refuse this time?

By the time a makeshift lunch of pizza ordered by the uniformed Bank of England doormen arrived, the idea of a lifeboat was stone dead and Barings looked doomed. The other British banks refused to rally round simply in order to keep Mr Baring and his staff in the style to which they were accustomed. Part of the problem was the arrogance of Barings's demands, such as that it should not have to pay any fees to its rescuers until all its loans had been repaid, that the Barings family majority shareholding in the bank should not be diluted, and that the staff should still get their $95 million in bonuses for 1994. On top of that, the bank said it needed $650 million – nearly twice what most of the other bankers had originally been led to believe – and that it could not be certain just how big the final loss on its Far Eastern futures positions would be. The other banks, in other words, were being asked to pour money into a potentially bottomless pit. Not surprisingly, they didn't like the idea.

As the meeting degenerated into a series of disconnected discussions between bankers during the afternoon, someone suggested approaching the Sultan of Brunei as the all-purpose rich uncle who might be relied on to throw his money away in a useless cause. Contact was duly made but the Sultan declined to help. After that it was all over. To the astonishment and despair of the Barings and their senior executives, the bank was put into administration (a form of bankruptcy).

The Bank of England tried to put a brave face on it. It too had refused to act as lender of last resort to Barings, citing the unknown size of the eventual losses as the reason. Once Barings had been left to collapse, the Bank pointed out that its job was not to prevent all bank failures because banks had to be aware that they would not always get bailed out whenever they made a mess of things. Yet it cannot be overemphasized what a profound embarrassment the whole Barings episode was to the Old Lady of Threadneedle Street. Almost everything that could go wrong with the process of supervising a bank had in fact gone wrong. ING, the Dutch Bank, was finally persuaded to take on the corpse of Barings so there was in the end a rescue, but that was a matter of luck, owing nothing to the ingenuity of the City or the Bank of England.

The natural reaction of everyone involved was to claim that the Barings debacle was a unique and, by implication, unrepeatable event caused by a freak combination of unlucky circumstances. This is a dangerous attitude to take. The shortcomings within Barings aside, what it brought into the light was a series of profound weaknesses in the regulatory system and the market's inability to deal with them. Most significant in many ways was the refusal of the other British banks to help Barings. This is important. It may mark the last time a bank can expect help from its peers and the last time the Bank of England attempts to rescue a British bank this way. The principle of supporting an ailing competitor for the greater good of the market is probably dead.

The fact that Barings ran into trouble in the first place was due to the incompetence of its management, but it also reflects very badly on the Bank of England as its regulator. While several City institutions got wind of Barings' problems before the collapse came, the Bank seems to have been taken completely by surprise. It does not appear to have known precisely what Barings was doing in the Far East or been aware of its management shortcomings in London. This ignorance was not the result of some accidental oversight: it is a direct result of its style as a supervisor. To be sure, it is no easy task to keep a close eye on every bank in the City. As the world's largest international banking centre, London has the largest collection of financial institutions from all parts of the globe. Understanding the business of banks from China to Chicago is a daunting task. But when all is said and done, the Bank of England's record as regulator of the banking industry is not impressive.

For all its protestations that its procedures have been tightened up over the last few years, its method of regulation might best be described as being of the fireside chat variety. A meeting is held in which the Bank's supervisory official and one or two members of the bank being supervised discuss in the most general terms how business is going and what the bank is doing. It is usually brief (often three or four hours at most), polite, and not particularly taxing for anyone.

There was nothing exceptional, for example, in the encounter between Peter Baring and Brian Quinn, the executive director for supervision at the Bank at the time, on 13 September 1993. Over a cup of tea in Quinn's office they chatted about developments at Barings bank. Peter Baring told the supervisor how well it seemed to be recovering from a crisis in its securities business and what substantial profits it was making. This was during a time when the entire bank was undergoing a profound reorganization which created the management chaos that enabled Nick Leeson to rack up $830 million in losses eighteen months later – but Baring and Quinn did not discuss that. Quinn apparently did not ask, and Baring did not volunteer the information. Instead, according to the Bank's records of the meeting, Baring said that 'the recovery in profitability had been amazing, leaving Barings to conclude it was not actually terribly difficult to make money in the securities business'. Quinn seems to have accepted without question this juvenile assessment of the bank's performance, which was unfortunate since the information was completely wrong. Unknown to Peter Baring at the time was that Nick Leeson's profits, the main element of this supposedly amazing recovery, were fictitious.

That was the last time before it went bust in February 1995 that Barings was bothered with the process of supervision, except to gain a special exemption from supervisory limits on its dealings with the Osaka futures and options exchange where Leeson was already building up his fatal positions. The limits are meant to prevent banks from accumulating a dangerously large exposure to any one customer. The exemption was granted informally and apparently without question by Christopher Thompson, the Bank of England executive in charge of supervising merchant banks. The exemption, moreover, had no time limit. It was only withdrawn in January 1995, a few weeks before Barings collapsed.

The Bank had never actually sent its officials out to visit Barings and see for themselves how it was run. It rarely does this with any bank which is hardly surprising since at the time of the Barings collapse it had only 322 people to supervise 518 banks. A proper bank inspection takes weeks if not months of work by many skilled supervisory officials but the Bank does not have the resources for this. Instead, it relies heavily for its supervisory information on what each bank's management tells it – and the dangers in that need hardly be spelled out.

It also relies on reports by the accountants who audit the banks. The problem here is that the accountants are employed by the banks they audit so their views can never be regarded as completely objective. If they become too critical they may not get the repeat business next year. And in a remarkable number of cases they seem to be unfortunately oblivious to the shortcomings of their clients, as Coopers & Lybrand were to Barings'. Their reports to supervisors, therefore, may sometimes be little better than the blind leading the blind.

Does this mean that the likes of Eddie George and Brian Quinn are fools or naves to operate such a fault-prone system? The answer is no: the British system works this way for a reason. Financial services are the country's biggest industry. They are also the biggest foreign currency earner for Britain – bigger than oil or tourism or pharmaceuticals – and banking is an important contributor. In short, banking and other kinds of financial business make a vast amount of money for Britain. This is largely because of London's position as one of the world's great financial centres. To ensure this status doesn't change, the hundreds of financial institutions, both British and foreign, which operate there must be kept happy and they are happiest when they do not have a regulator breathing down their necks every day. Bankers prefer to be left alone to do what they want. If the regulators get too heavy handed, a lot of banks may simply decamp to Paris or Frankfurt or Singapore or Liberia, or wherever will offer them good telephone connections, decent restaurants and, above all, relaxed regulation.

That, at any rate, is the Bank of England's fear. This is why, after the Barings collapse, it insisted that there was nothing wrong with its system of regulation but that the implementation of it had simply gone a little awry. In reality, however, the distinction

between system and implementation is an illusion. There are many
ways the bank could improve its implementation if it wanted to,
but that would mean altering the system. It could hire more
supervisory officers; it could carry out more rigorous inspections;
it could train its own staff better; it could really try to find out what
banks in the City are doing. It just doesn't want to in case the
natives get restless and leave. Instead, it pretends that its particular
brand of relaxed regulation is an inevitable fact of London life, like
drizzle and warm beer. (Responsibility for banking supervision is
being switched from the Bank to the Savings and Investments
Board but there is unlikely to be much change in the way regulation
is conducted.)

So there isn't much prospect of change. The Board of Banking
Supervision, a Bank of England controlled body which conducted
an enquiry into the Barings debacle in 1995, absolved the Bank
from any major blunder in its supervisory role. Eddie George
declared after the Board's report was published that he saw no need
for major change in the way the Bank operated. His view is that
accidents happen, and the occasional Barings-type disaster may
actually be good for the system because it keeps everyone on their
toes.

This is the kind of talk that makes people at the US Federal
Reserve hold their head in their hands and groan. Not to put too
fine a point on it, the Bank's supervisory system infuriates the Fed.
In public, senior Fed officials are diplomatically complimentary
about Britain's efforts at regulation, but get them in private and
they tend to be frankly contemptuous of the Bank's record and
procedures. They don't like to be named when they say things like:
'The Bank has its methods, the trouble is they don't really work.
No one over there goes into banks and really finds out what's going
on. Unless they change, there are going to be more collapses like
Barings in the future.'

The US regulatory system begins with the mountain of information which banks, like all companies in the US, must file with
the Securities and Exchange Commission. It far outstrips the
amount European companies are obliged to reveal about themselves and many US executives grumble that it is not worth the
effort and expense. After all, nobody reads most of what is filed at

the SEC. But any system of regulation has to start with information, the more of it the better. It is at least there to be seen if anyone cares to look.

The meat of the US system, though, is the inspection the Fed tries to carry out at least once a year on every major commercial bank in New York. Cups of tea don't come into it. The shape of bank examinations, particularly those of the larger banks, is planned like a military operation at the dowdy offices of the Federal Reserve Bank of New York's supervision department, located in an insurance company building near Wall Street. The inspectors are often quite young – either straight out of university or from business school – although they are led by more seasoned campaigners. Their strength, however, is as much in numbers as expertise. They arrive first in moderate strength, like a platoon of skirmishers, staking out which areas of the bank will receive special attention. They hold initial meetings with the bank's managers who grit their teeth but have little choice other than to co-operate. After about a month of this, the examination gains momentum. Suddenly the bank finds itself subject to an invasion, as seventy or eighty Fed stormtroopers arrive and take up full time residence on the premises for a month or more. The examination continues all day every day with the inspectors having the right to ask anything, see anything, demand anything of the bank under inspection until they decide they have seen enough. The shock troops then withdraw and a smaller occupation force remains to tidy up the details which may take another three or four weeks. At the same time, a similar exercise is being carried out by Fed inspectors at the bank's main overseas subsidiaries. The entire examination process takes three months, followed by another two months or so of analysis and report writing, until the results are digested and presented to the bank's board. If the Fed finds things it is not happy with, it tells the bank to mend its ways under pain of public admonition, fines or worse. And once the Fed has gone, the bank has a respite of only six or seven months until the whole process starts again.

This type of supervision is certainly more thorough than taking tea at the Bank of England, and more likely to catch burgeoning bank problems before they ripen and explode, but inevitably it requires far more manpower. The New York Fed employs about

650 inspectors to look after about 400 banks, but when you add in the inspectors employed by the other banking authorities – the Comptroller of the Currency, the New York State banking authority and the Federal deposit insurance scheme – the ratio of inspectors to banks is something like three to one.

It is probably fair to say that every US banker loathes being inspected. It is tiring, time consuming, distracting and irritating. Worse, it takes them away from the all-important business of making money. From a bank's point of view, the only good thing about it is that it reassures top management: if there is a rogue trader lurking somewhere in the bank, the Fed's ferreting may root him out.

But not necessarily. 'If anyone thinks we are the ultimate fraud detection system, they are wrong. We aren't. Someone involved in a fairly sophisticated, fairly complex fraud – especially if it is a conspiracy in which everyone is lying to us – will probably get away with it,' says one of the Fed's top supervisors. 'It's not that difficult. It's just that in the end the truth will come out when something goes wrong at the bank.' Which is fine if all it means is a few million dollars in losses, but less fine if it eventually ends in bankruptcy.

Because, of course, just like the Bank of England, the Fed has its upsets from time to time. In the early 1990s it was obliged to set up an emergency bond redemption office in its own gymnasium to accommodate hordes of panicking bondholders caught in the collapse of Drexel Burnham Lambert, an investment bank that choked on a surfeit of junk bonds. And even as the Fed was wringing its hands over the Bank of England's failure with Barings it was informed that a trader in Daiwa Bank's New York dealing room had run up losses of around $1.3 billion – the embarrassing part being that the process had taken him nine years and in all that time the Fed had never noticed. The regulators had even been duped into thinking that Daiwa had closed down a dealing room on Wall Street as the Fed had ordered it to, when in fact the room was still fully functional. Whenever the Japanese bank knew the bank inspectors were due to pay a visit, it moved its dealers to its mid-town trading floor for the day and filled the Wall Street office with boxes to look like a storeroom.

When it comes to regulating the investment banks, the US system becomes even more fragile and fragmented. There is no single lead regulator; different parts of investment banking are supervised by four or five main bodies, chief among which is the SEC in charge of securities trading. There are hardly any rules about how much risk an investment bank may take on – the likes of Salomon, Goldmans or Lehman generally leverage their capital between forty to eighty times in their market dealing but they could go much higher if the mood took them. The quality of training among the US regulators is often as poor as it is in Britain. And there is no obligation on the part of any regulator to support an investment bank in trouble. In the recent past, the Federal government has tended to come to the aid of ailing banks such as Drexel Burnham Lambert, a second line securities house, but there has never been a test of how the authorities would react if one of the leading investment banks hit the buffers.

Bank regulation, in short, is never easy. It is incredibly difficult to spot when a bank is lying, or incompetent, or simply overexposed in ways it shouldn't be. The accounts published by banks tend to be like a trick done with smoke and mirrors, only showing what the bank wants them to show. It is amazingly easy to hide from even the most expert scrutiny, those things which banks do not want supervisors or auditors to see. It is particularly easy to manipulate a bank's profits by using derivatives where normal accounting rules may not apply, and valuing a derivatives book is a subjective judgement.

When it comes to regulating derivatives markets themselves, the problems are just as great. George Soros told the House Banking Committee in 1994 that he thought the derivatives markets should be regulated more fully. Since then, no one has found an effective way to do so. In a market so fluid and inventive, where do you start drawing the rules limiting derivatives use? As soon as regulations could be thought of, they would be circumvented.

The completely international nature of derivatives markets also makes the conventional contacts between regulators of different countries look hopelessly inadequate. Even within countries regulatory systems are often confused. In Britain, the Securities and Investments Board oversees most of the market, but the Bank of

England is responsible for the banks which use them. In the US things are even more fragmented. The Fed and related bodies oversee the commercial banks, the SEC has responsibility for 'securities', and the CFTC looks after 'futures' and 'commodity options'. Sometimes their zones of responsibility overlap. Inevitably there are turf wars between them. Just as inevitably, unseen gaps in the regulatory net are likely to open up and absurd anomalies have tended to multiply over the years so that, for instance, different kinds of options are supervised by different bodies and there can be genuine confusion over who regulates them.

A fitful debate rages over whether to merge all the regulatory groups into one, change their spheres of responsibility or simply bang their heads together more often. Nothing Congress has done in the last few years has clarified the situation. The ugly truth about all this is that, in the end, there is no supervisory system in the world that adequately handles derivatives whose complex, slippery and ever-changing nature is always at least one step ahead of the latest regulations.

Which raises the question of how much the regulators themselves understand derivatives. Ten years ago, their grasp of the subject was poor to dismal; it has since improved to moderate. For the last few years in London, the SFA has probably had the greatest understanding although the Bank of England has recently been catching up. The trouble is that the markets change so fast and new products keep appearing with such speed that it is virtually impossible for anyone who is not right at the cutting edge to keep up. Regulators, by their nature as people outside the markets, are not at the cutting edge. In any case, you don't find the top rocket scientists at the Bank of England. Regulators are, in most essentials, well paid civil servants. But for that salary you cannot capture the services of any self-respecting derivatives genius who knows he can get several times the money working in a commercial bank.

No one has found a way round these problems, which is why the regulatory structure is metamorphosing into something completely new. The basic idea of the new system is: if you can't regulate them, why not let them regulate themselves.

The traditional method of supervising banks was to assess the size and riskiness of their loans and oblige the banks to set aside a given portion of their capital to cover the risk that some of the loans would not be repaid. This was relatively simple, straight-forward and it applied to everyone. Above all, the regulators knew where they were and what was going on.

That all changed when derivatives became big business. It took the regulators several years to realize that derivatives *were* indeed big business, but when they did they tried to squeeze them into the old regulatory structure. Like the feet of Cinderella's ugly sisters, derivatives didn't fit the glass slipper. It took the central bankers several more years to discover this, but when they did they expended much energy in telling banks not to indulge too heavily in these dangerous instruments. The Bank of England issued repeated warnings that some banks in the City probably did not understand the extent of the risk they were taking on in their swaps books and proprietary trading. It was undoubtedly true that many – perhaps most – did not, and what was equally true was that the Bank itself did not understand what the risks were either. Which was one of the things making it so nervous.

During this phase, which lasted from the mid-1980s into the early 1990s, the entire regulatory system as far as derivatives were concerned was pretty much flying by wire. There was no one in the cockpit who actually understood the controls or even knew if the aeroplane was safe. Many suspected it was heading straight for a mountainside but the regulators did not know enough about individual derivative instruments or the markets that spawned them to guide everyone into safer airspace. Still, everyone was having a fine time making money so they kept the throttle fully open just the same.

Amid the din of money making, however, the industry threw up its own prophets of doom. Among the most respected was Gerald Corrigan, a former President of the New York Fed now working at Goldman Sachs, who emerged in the 1990s like an Elijah warning of disasters to come if the people did not mend their ways. As a central banker with experience of handling the Shearson Lehman collapse, he knew more than most about the weaknesses of the financial system. He argued that most recent bank disasters were the result of a breakdown of internal controls, but such breakdowns were only likely to become more frequent: 'The increasing complexity of financial markets can over-ride the ability of even the most sophisticated efforts to monitor and manage risks,' he said. It is literally impossible to design a perfectly fail-safe system at the level of the individual firm, he told a Congressional subcommittee on telecommications and finance in 1994.

Meanwhile, on the macro scale the systemic risks were also increasing. 'The complexity of derivatives makes it hard for the top management of firms and regulatory authorities to design and implement appropriate safeguards,' he declared. In 1995 he told the International Monetary Conference: 'There is little doubt in my mind that a repeat performance of the 1987 stock market crash would be more difficult to contain today than it was in 1987.' Derivatives had brought about an unprecedented interlinking of markets which meant that disaster in one was likely to spread to others faster than anyone could move to prevent it.

Corrigan, and many other less prominent financiers who shared his opinions, had a point. It just took a while before anyone paid much attention.

They started doing so when things began to go horribly wrong in the markets – Hammersmith & Fulham, Allied Lyons, Bankers Trust, Shell, Orange County – spurring the banking industry into a frenzy of moral zeal. Proposals for improvements fell into two predictable groups: the bureaucrats and politicians favoured tinkering with the existing regulatory bodies which was a process they understood and would keep them busy and happy for a long time. The bankers, realizing that the prevailing confusion left them free to do much as they liked, preferred to leave the system in its existing shambles but suggested that banks should behave better.

In most respects, the bankers are winning the argument. The problem is that if you allow the rule-makers to make too many rules, banks will take their business away to less strictly regulated countries. Since no one in Britain or America wants that, the solution is to have more of what there already is: self-regulation. Even though self-regulation in the City of London has turned out to be a distinctly dubious way of policing the financial sector, the derivatives markets are pushing it further than it has ever gone before.

Banks, to be sure, have to prove to their regulators that they have the internal controls to prevent the kind of thing that brought down Barings. They are, moreover, supposed to promise not to stretch or break any of their internal rules at any time, not to rip off their customers, not to lie to their supervisors, not to regard their profit or their bonuses as the paramount consideration in all circumstances. A procession of authorities ranging from the Group of 30 (the 30 being the biggest and most active banks in the market) to the Bank for International Settlements (the central bankers' central bank in Switzerland) have published codes for what they term 'best market practice'. Some of these amount to handbooks on how banks and traders should conduct themselves. But they all have one thing in common: the belief that the only practical way to regulate derivatives is for bankers to promise to behave themselves.

They are probably right; there probably isn't any other way of doing it.

It may by now seem clear to the reader that over the last few years many bankers have found that this good behaviour has not come naturally to them. Integrity and honesty have been, and still are, greatly honoured in the breach. It may seem illogical, therefore, that proposals for the better running of the derivatives markets should hinge on these qualities, yet that is how the system works.

And the central banks are proposing to go further. They have decided that it is far too complicated to lay down a common system for calculating the risk inherent in derivatives. They are undoubtedly right since in the OTC market no two instruments are quite the same. In any case, there are as many ways of calculating and assessing risk as there are banks with derivatives pricing programmes on their computers. The solution, therefore, has been to let the banks themselves do their own risk assessments. They can then tell the regulators, and the regulators are supposed to believe them. This, of course, turns the traditional regulatory system on its head. The central banks are devolving – some might say abrogating – responsibility to the very people they are supposed to be regulating. In the upside-down, looking-glass world of derivatives this perhaps seems only appropriate.

This system of extreme self-regulation has not been tried before in modern banking. The supervisors naturally have to be sure the banks have good enough computer programmes to assess their own risk profile properly. And of course they have to trust all the banks to tell the truth all of the time. After that, institutions like the Bank of England, the Fed and SEC begin to look somewhat incidental to the whole process. This is scary. Sooner or later people are going to start asking who is in charge. The answer is no longer clear.

Except, possibly, in the event of disaster. Central bankers still retain their traditional role as lenders of last resort. Naturally, they take this very seriously. They may let small banks like Barings or Shearson Lehman go bust because the financial ramifications, they believe, can be contained. But if a big bank, a Barclays or a Citibank, were on the brink of bankruptcy the implications for the world financial system would be enormous. It would trigger a string of defaults, possibly bringing down several big banks simul-taneously, undermining the chain of credit and payments that keeps the financial system turning over smoothly. The mayhem caused by such a situation would be unthinkable. So the central banks would never let it happen – in which case, it is often argued, there is no real danger. No big bank would be allowed to go bust, so no disaster would happen.

This is a seductive argument but it misses the point. Banking, as everyone knows, depends on credibility. Banks work because people believe they are safe – when they no longer believe this they take their money away and banks start to collapse. Like levitation, faith in the system is what keeps it up. As soon as faith starts to erode the system begins to suffer as if it had a speeded up form of Aids. Once the process begins, it is hard to stop. This is not a hypothet-ical statement. It has happened several times in the past and happened in a subdued form after the Barings collapse when hundreds of millions of pounds in deposits flooded out of the City's other merchant banks. Several of the largest institutional investors stopped doing any business whatsoever with the merchant banks. For some banks, it reached near-crisis proportions and the Bank of England was obliged to lend money to them at cheap rates to prevent the problem worsening. It made no difference that Barings was finally rescued by ING – faith in the merchant banks had received a body blow.

Now consider if the same were to happen on a larger scale, with a leading international bank teetering on the edge of bankruptcy. There are at least four problems here. First, central bankers are only human. They may take time to put their rescue plan into action, they may have inaccurate information, they may make mistakes that worsen the situation.

The second problem is that any crisis of this sort is extremely unlikely to be limited to one country. These days the interconnections of the banking system are completely international, which means that central banks and other regulators in several different countries will have to co-operate in co-ordinated action. The precedents for this happening, even in relatively simple cases, are not good. When the Bank of England was trying to close out Barings futures and options positions to prevent the bank from collapsing, the Japanese authorities refused to persuade the Tokyo futures exchange to help. A few years earlier, when BCCI was imploding, the Bank of England refused to give crucial information to US regulators, thus delaying discovery of the fraud at the heart of the bank.

Turf battles between regulators aside, differences in laws and regulations between countries can delay or thwart attempts at co-ordination. Few countries, for example, even agree on a common definition of bankruptcy. This compounds the danger of mistakes and may make the whole rescue process slower and more confused.

The third problem is that if a bank has foundered largely on derivatives losses, the complication of sorting it out will almost certainly be gargantuan. If it is anything like Barings, it may even be impossible to assess precisely how big the bank's losses are, which impedes any rescue attempt right from the start.

But the fourth and biggest problem is that faith not only in the stricken bank but in other big banks will be badly damaged and possibly fatally undermined by even the *threat* of default. Fast as the central banks may react, the markets will be reacting faster. Lack of confidence, the disease fatal to all financial markets, would sweep through the system. While the central bank is concentrating on rescuing one institution the markets may be forcing others into

equally bad trouble. Suddenly the central bank is confronted with
the need to rescue not just one but several big financial institutions
– an infinitely more complex, not to say expensive, task that will
cause further delay. And as it delays, the disease continues to eat at
other parts of the system.

The promise to prop up ailing banks worked well in a relatively
slow moving, simple world – the world of fifteen years ago. It looks
far less convincing now. The fact is, no one knows how the markets
would behave if confronted with one or two major bank defaults.
What is known is that they can and do react instantaneously to any
news, good or bad, with the touch of a telephone button or
computer key. The financial world is no longer simple and it moves
at the speed of light.

The best hope for stopping a crisis probably lies in the markets
themselves. Would they have enough sense of responsibility and
even self-preservation to protect an ailing bank, maintain credit
lines, refuse to panic? Would other banks come to the aid of rival
institutions in trouble, even those from foreign countries? The way
the banking community refused to rescue Barings suggests that
they would not (until ING bought wreckage for £1).

There is certainly no particular reason for optimism given the
way the modern financial markets have come to operate. This
particular game of roulette is not about common survival but
individual success. It isn't a team game: each player stands alone,
jealously eyeing his competitors' chips. They are rivals first and
last. Who knows – for the trader behind his dealing screen the
sight of imminent financial meltdown may look like the ultimate
gamble, the most thrilling spin of the wheel he's seen in his young
life. The challenge would be to escape with as much of his profit
intact as possible, rather than rallying to some bankrupt adversary's
defence. Gambling is a habit, but is it one the financial markets can
break when the time comes?

CHAPTER 11

CONCLUSION

To soothe public concern, bankers often present derivatives as nothing more than a passing fad, something like junk bonds or property loans which will eventually become just another footnote in financial history. That is misleading. We live in a free market system. Derivatives are a creation of it, a necessary and fundamental part of it. They will not magically disappear with the next recession or lose popularity when the next financial wheeze comes along. There is no question of abolishing them, or expecting that they will somehow politely retire to the back of the hall so that no one need worry about them. They are built into the foundations of the financial system; to remove them now would risk bringing down the building.

This is why, despite all the disasters, the losses, the bad publicity and the complaints of regulators, derivatives keep on growing at a staggering rate. In 1995 the swaps market alone grew by more than 50 per cent, or about $6.5 trillion (roughly the size of the entire US economy).

But it is hard to avoid the conclusion that a great deal of the frantic activity in the derivatives markets is waste of effort. Much of the time, the effect is to chop up risks that people are familiar with and understand quite well, only to repackage them into new risks that are at best very poorly understood. From the banks' point of view this has been anything but pointless: over the last ten years they have made millions selling the repackaged stuff, often to investors who did not need it. From any other point of view, however, the benefits have been highly questionable. Apart from their value as hedging instruments, derivatives do not produce anything. They are a zero sum game: they merely redistribute money, they do not create it. Are the billions spent on dealing systems, risk management systems, back office systems, supervisory systems and trader's salaries – all to support the frenetic dealing in the derivatives markets – an efficient use of resources? The answer, I suspect, is 'probably not'.

There is some evidence that since the worst excesses of the early 1990s, progress has been made towards controlling derivatives. The Group of 30 and a host of other bodies have drawn up codes of practice and guidelines to help banks and other users of derivatives construct strong enough management controls to handle these explosive instruments. Computer programmes for managing the risk involved in derivatives have become more sophisticated. Regulators in many parts of the world have grown more experienced in dealing with derivatives. Accounting rules have become a little more subtle to accommodate them. The mechanisms that make capitalism such a flexible and accommodating system are working to absorb derivatives into the over-all financial structure.

But however efficient the checks and balances become, the financial system is inherently more fragile than it used to be. Derivatives, the freedom of the markets and the tyranny of the traders make it easier than ever before for excessive concentrations of risk to build up into pressure points which may prove more than the system can bear.

At the same time there is a moral hazard. The money culture of the 1980s did not disappear when the decade ended: it is alive and well and causing bigger problems than ever. The pressure on dealers to produce profits, and the incentives for them to push their trading to the limits and beyond, has caused bigger dealing disasters between 1992 and 1996 than ever occured in the 1980s. Ultimately, there is no foolproof way of preventing a rogue dealer getting out of hand.

The unavoidable fact about derivatives is that while helping to limit risk, they have also encouraged unprecedented speculation.

History suggests that speculation sooner or later leads to disruption. Derivatives have turned the financial markets into a high-tech, international, twenty-four-hour casino. The youthful players, some of the best-paid people in the world, have control of the game. How safely it is played depends on them.

GLOSSARY

arbitrage: trading strategy in which an asset is bought cheap in one market and immediately sold more expensively in another market. It becomes possible when the price of identical assets gets to diverge in two different markets. It is fondly supposed by many bankers to be riskless.

bond: a loan in the form of an interest paying security with a maturity date at which the full value of the loan is repaid.

book value: value at which a security such as a bond is recorded in the financial statements (the books) of its owner. This may be at the historical price paid when it was bought or at the current market value.

Bank of England: British central bank, sorely in need of modernization. Its primary functions are to control inflation and interest rates. Supervision of banks has recently been moved to the SIB. It also has a vague supervisory role over the whole of the City of London.

call option: an option giving the buyer the right, but not the obligation, to purchase the asset underlying the option at a specified price.

cap: a call option giving the buyer the right to limit his interest rate payments to a specified maximum level.

collar: a combination of a cap and a floor limiting the buyer's exposure within a specified upper and lower limit.

Commodity Futures Trading Commission (CFTC): US federal regulatory agency overseeing futures and commodities options trading.

derivatives: a financial contract whose value is related to – derived from – an underlying asset such as a bond, share, currency or commodity, giving the buyer control of the underlying asset. The purchase price of the derivative is usually a fraction of the value of the underlying asset. This gives the buyer leverage which may result in huge gains or losses relative to the downpayment on the derivative depending on whether the underlying asset rises or falls in price.

face value: the value of a bond which the borrower promises to repay at maturity. The face value (or par value) is usually different from the market value which fluctuates with interest rate movements.

Federal Reserve Board: The US central bank, comprised of 12 regional Federal Reserve Banks. The 'Fed' is responsible for setting the level of US interest rates as the main tool to achieve its mandate of low inflation and reasonable economic growth.

floor: a put option giving the buyer the right to prevent the interest he expects to receive from falling below a specified level.

forward contract: a contract to buy or sell an underlying asset at a specified future time and price (the forward rate). It is unlike a futures contract in that it is not negotiable – it can't be sold on to someone else. It is unlike an option in that the holder of the futures contract has to meet its conditions at maturity.

futures contract: a negotiable contract to buy or sell a standardized amount of the underlying asset at a specific time and price. Futures are bought and sold on exchanges such as the Chicago Merc, Liffe and the Osaka futures exchange.

hedge fund: investment fund using advanced investment techniques to try to produce abnormally high returns. Some funds take abnormally high risks in doing so while others – such as so-called 'market neutral' funds – claim to take abnormally low risks. Hedge funds are often big users of derivatives either to leverage their speculative positions or limit their risk by hedging.

hedging: the process of minimizing risk, usually by taking an opposite market position to the original risk. It is the reverse of speculation although, confusingly, the two are sometimes hard to tell apart.

inverse floater: a structured note whose interest payments fluctuate in the opposite direction to the movement of interest rates. Its value rises and interest rates fall, and vice versa.

leverage: buying a financial asset without having to pay the full purchase price. This is usually achieved by borrowing or by deferring payment as with buying futures contracts on margin. The leverage ratio is the total value of the assets purchased divided by the initial cash required to buy them.

liquidity: a measure of how quickly assets can be bought and sold. The more liquid a market the more easily deals can be transacted and, usually, the finer the prices become.

long position: the investor has bought an asset. (A seller of assets he does not own holds a short position.)

margin: a payment by the buyer of a futures contract guaranteeing payment if the contract incurs losses. A margin call is a demand by a broker or customer for additional funds if the contract loses money.

mark to market: valuing an asset to its actual price if it were sold then and there on the open market. In the case of futures contracts this may also involve the payment of profits or losses (variation margin) compared to the original purchase price.

maturity: the date at which a bond is fully repaid or any other financial contract expires.

mortgage backed securities: tradable securities created by bundling residential mortgages of similar size, maturity and credit rating into a pool paying interest and maturing at a particular date.

notional value: the face value of a contract (not to be confused with its market value).

option contract: a derivative giving the right – but not the obligation – to buy or sell an underlying asset at a specified price at or before a specified time.

option premium: the price of an option contract.

over-the-counter market (OTC): a market in customized contracts between financial professionals. Unlike the exchanges it has no particular location and is not regulated or governed by a single body.

put option: an option giving the owner the right to sell the underlying asset at a specified price at or before a specified time.

quant (see also rocket scientist):   a quantitative analyst conversant in higher mathematics and sophisticated statistical techniques. Sometimes also known as 'nerd'.

repurchase agreement (repo):   a contract between two parties in which one party agrees to sell a security to the other and buy it back again at as specific price and time. The seller receives cash which is, in effect, a loan. The difference in price between the sell and buy price – the repo rate – which is expressed as an interest rate, is the cost of the loan.

reverse repo: a repo agreement where a broker lends money to a client, using assets belonging to the client as collateral. If the securities fall in value during the period of the loan, the client suffers the loss.

risk management: the process of controlling financial risk, usually by using derivatives to increase or reduce risk according to market movements.

rocket scientist: colloquial term for financial operator with impressive mathematical and computer skills able to invent derivatives of frightening complexity, construct advanced computer pricing models and handle the other advanced techniques adopted by the financial markets since the early 1980s. Although often physicists and engineers by training, rocket scientists do not necessarily build rockets.

Securities and Exchange Commission (SEC):   US federal regulatory agency overseeing the securities markets such as the equity and bond markets. The CFTC oversees the futures and commodity options markets.

short position: the seller of assets he does not own has gone 'short'. A buyer of assets has gone long.

Savings and Investments Board (SIB):   UK regulatory body responsible for a wide range of City business. It has required almost constant reform since its creation in 1986 and is now taking over banking regulation from the Bank of England.

speculation: the process of trying to make a profit by taking deliberate risks. The opposite is hedging.

spread: the difference between buying and selling prices.

stock index (*plural – indexes*): a notional basket of equities assets used to express the value of a stock market as a whole. The FTSE-100 stock index, for instance, is the most widely used measure of UK stock market performance. Although it is an abstract concept it can trade in the form of a derivative instrument, as in the FTSE-100 futures contract, as a way of betting on the movement of the London stock market. Indexes also exist for other forms of assets such as bonds, currencies, and commodities.

straddle: trading strategy in which the trader bets that the market will not go above or below an upper and lower price limit.

strip: a part of a security, stripped away from the original instrument and traded separately. An interest rate strip, for example, is the interest cashflow element of a bond removed from the bond and sold as an asset in its own right.

structured notes: species of highly customized security, often of diabolical complexity with interest payments that vary over time according to an agreed formula. They often include collars, puts or calls, with payments indexed to equity prices, exchange rates or interest rates.

swap: an agreement between two parties to exchange a stream of cashflows in the future, usually relating to loans, according to a pre-arranged formula.

value at risk: the measure of the market risk of a portfolio. It shows the worst possible loss on a given probability.

volatility: a measure of risk. It is also a measure of the range by which the price of an asset may move around its expected value.

yield: a measure of the return on a security taking into account its price and interest rate.

yield curve: relationship between interest rates of different maturities. When short term interest rates are lower than longer term rates the yield curve is 'positive'. In the reverse situation it is 'negative'.

LIST OF ABBREVIATIONS

AFBD – Association of Future Brokers and Dealers
CEO – Chief Executive Officer
CFTC – Commodity Futures Trading Commission
Libor – London Interbank Offered Rate
LIFFE – London Financial Futures Exchange
OTC – Over-the-Counter
SEC – Securities Exchange Commission
SIB – Savings and Investments Board
SFA – Securities and Futures Association

INDEX